PORTFOLIO / PENGUIN

Extreme Trust

Don Peppers and **Martha Rogers, Ph.D.**, have coauthored nine books, including the global bestseller *The One to One Future*. Widely credited with igniting the customer strategy revolution in business, they founded Peppers & Rogers Group, a management consulting firm whose clients have included USAA, Nordstrom, Ford, Vodafone (UK), Momentum Energy (Australia), AkBank (Turkey), Etihad (UAE), Saudi Telecom, and Absa Bank (South Africa). World renowned keynote presenters and boardroom strategists, Peppers is a Top 100 LinkedIn "Influencer" with a quarter million followers and Rogers has served on the faculty at Duke University's Fuqua School of Business and is the founder of Trustability Metrix.

Visit www.extremetrustpaperback.com

D0057766

ADDITIONAL BOOKS BY
DON PEPPERS AND MARTHA ROGERS, Ph.D.

The One to One Future

Enterprise One to One

The One to One Fieldbook
(with Bob Dorf)

The One to One Manager

One to One B2B

Return on Customer

Rules to Break and Laws to Follow

Managing Customer Experiences and Relationships
(reference and textbook, 3rd edition)

Extreme
Trust

Turning Proactive Honesty
and Flawless Execution into
Long-Term Profits

Don Peppers and

Martha Rogers, Ph.D.

PORTFOLIO / PENGUIN

PORTFOLIO / PENGUIN

An imprint of Penguin Random House LLC
375 Hudson Street
New York, New York 10014
penguin.com

First published by Portfolio / Penguin, a member of Penguin Group (USA) Inc. 2012
This revised edition published 2016

LIBRARY OF CONGRESS CATALOGING-IN-PUBLICATION DATA

Names: Peppers, Don, author. | Rogers, Martha, 1952– author.
Title: Extreme trust : turning proactive honesty and flawless execution into
    long-term profits / Don Peppers and Martha Rogers, Ph.D.
Description: Revised edition. | New York : Portfolio/Penguin, [2016] |
    Includes bibliographical references and index.
Identifiers: LCCN 2016007808 | ISBN 9780143108559
Subjects: LCSH: Business ethics. | Customer relations—Management. | Trust. |
    Honesty.
Classification: LCC HF5387 .P434 2016 | DDC 174/.4—dc23

Printed in the United States of America
10 9 8 7 6 5 4 3 2

Set in Adobe Garamond Pro
Designed by Cassandro Garruzzo

Contents

Part 1

Trustability: Not Just a Good Idea. Inevitable. 1

Part 2

Why Your CFO Will Learn to Love Trustability 33

Part 3

Do the Right Thing 67

Part 4

Do Things Right: Honest Competence 105

Part 5

Be Proactive 131

Part 6

How to Build a Trustable Business   163

Part 7

Trustability Tests   217

Extreme
Trust

1

Trustability:

Not Just a Good Idea.

Inevitable.

Chapter 1

Yesterday, Trustworthy Was Good Enough. Today, Only Trustability Will Do.

Play fair. Immediately after the first Gulf War in 1991, USAA—the insurance and banking company based in San Antonio, Texas—sent out refund checks to several thousand customers, called "members" by USAA. The idea was that since the men and women who had been serving at the front couldn't drive their cars back in the United States during the several months they were posted in the Middle East, USAA suspended the charges for the premiums during the time soldiers were overseas and sent out unsolicited refunds once the military personnel got home. USAA consistently comes out as the most trusted financial services organization in the United States, and customers believe USAA will always do what's right for them, never oversell them, and always be there for them when a member needs the company. The company was originally established to serve current and former U.S. military officers, but today USAA serves everyone, although not everyone is eligible for every product offered. Once you become a member, however, your children can also become USAA members, and USAA's loyal customer base now runs into the third generation. The employee culture at USAA is based on a simple idea: Treat the customer the way you'd want to be treated if you were the customer.

And as for those refund checks? Nearly 2,500 of them were sent back to USAA by grateful customers who told USAA to keep the money and just be there "when we need you."[1]

Imagine for a moment that you run any other bank or insurance company in the United States.

How will you compete against a financial services institution that customers love so much they sometimes refuse to accept refunds and are loyal into the third generation and counting?

What's the difference between USAA and the other financial services companies we all know about? Many of those companies, with names familiar to customers around the world, are not bad companies. On the contrary: Their officers are ethical. Their legal departments make sure they don't break any laws. They issue privacy policies and policy statements of all kinds, and then for the most part they do exactly what they say they're going to do. And yet none of us—not even the executives of these well-run institutions—could imagine customers refusing to take refunds from those companies. The companies are lucky if a customer keeps doing business for several years, and they don't even think about multigenerational loyalty. *What is the difference?*

Most businesses today consider themselves to be trustworthy, and by yesterday's standards they are. They post their prices accurately, they try to maintain the quality and reliability of their products, and they generally do what they say they're going to do. But that's as far as most businesses go, and by tomorrow's standards it won't be nearly good enough. Not even close.

The fact is that far too many businesses still generate substantial profits by fooling customers, or by taking advantage of customer mistakes or lack of knowledge, or simply by not telling customers what they need to know to make informed decisions. They don't break any laws, and they don't do anything overtly dishonest. But think for a minute about the standard, generally accepted way some industries have made money for the past several decades:

- To credit card companies, a marginally sophisticated borrower who can never resist spending, rolls his balance from month to month, and often incurs late fees is considered a *most valuable customer*. The common industry term for a credit card user who dutifully pays his bill in full every month is "deadbeat."

- Mobile phone carriers profit from customers signing up for more expensive calling plans than their usage requires, and from roaming and data services accessed by accident.

- Retail banks make a substantial portion of their operating profit from overdraft charges and other fees assessed for what are usually just simple customer errors.[2] (Many standard bank processes are explicitly designed to *encourage* overdrafts.)[3]

- Some merchandise offered in pop-ups and on late-night TV is worth very little but hooks buyers into paying a little money to have their names and contact information loaded onto a mailing list, which is the truly profitable product sold by the direct marketing company.

- Even today the overwhelming majority of companies don't allow customers to post product or service reviews on their own websites.

- Companies can drive you crazy when they offer you a product and you refuse it, and then they offer it to you again. And pretty soon, *again*!

Despite the best intentions of good people running companies large and small around the world, is it any wonder that customers don't trust companies?

In this book we will show that a lot of traditional, widely accepted, and perfectly legal business practices just can't be trusted by customers, and will soon become extinct, driven to dust by rising levels of transparency, increasing consumer demand for fair treatment,[4] and competitive pressure. A business can continue to try to keep things out of its customers' sight, but technology now makes it more than likely that customers will still find out, one way or another. Some things that companies, governments, and other organizations never meant for people to know, they *will* know. Any business that fails to prepare for this new reality will soon be competed out of business by rivals who figure out how to do a better job of earning the trust of their customers.

Transparency will increase because of technological progress, and progress is inevitable. It cannot be avoided, averted, or slowed down. But what makes this particular aspect of technology so different is the degree to which it will heighten and magnify our connectedness, as people. We are all social by nature. We like being with others, telling stories, whispering rumors, playing games, laughing, entertaining, and being entertained. We like to share ideas, get feedback, discuss nuances, and sharpen our own thinking with other people's perspectives. We even look to others in order to know what our own true feelings should be. Being social is an essential ingredient of human nature. The term "antisocial" is an indictment, implying that someone is unfriendly, cold, or misanthropic. If you're antisocial, something's wrong with you.

As important as our social nature is, however, social media and other interactive technologies have injected it with steroids. Before our very eyes, we are being transformed into a dynamic and robust network of electronically interconnected people in a worldwide, 24/7 bazaar of creating and sharing, collaborating, publishing, critiquing, helping, learning, entertaining, competing, and having fun. The volume and speed of our interactions with others grow in lockstep with Moore's law,[5] which specifies that computers will get about a thousand times more powerful every fifteen to twenty years. But this also means that every fifteen to twenty years we will interact a thousand times as much with others—by voice, phone, text, e-mail, status update, and other means we don't even know about yet.[6] The steady march of technological progress brings us steadily better devices, better online tools and platforms, and better mechanisms for managing. What it adds up to is *more* interactions that are faster, cheaper, and more convenient. At this rate we are destined to interact everywhere, all the time, with anyone anywhere.[7,8]

You've probably observed this yourself. It's been hard to miss. If you're a baby boomer, just think about how your own interactions with friends, family, and business colleagues have increased over the years, as the tools to connect have been increasingly computerized. How often did you send out pictures of your friends or your kids or just interesting tidbits to friends or family members before Facebook? And how often did you keep up with your old high school buddies? Remember life before cell phones? How about before e-mail? If you are in your teens or twenties, you can't even remember what business communications were like before fax machines, when letters were often dictated to a secretary, who used shorthand, typed it out, and then sent it with stamps through snail mail (or to foreign countries via cable). Once upon a time, "phones" were just landline phones, without voice mail or answering machines or texting.[9]

We have all been living through this revolution in communication and interaction. But while we are often fascinated by the rapid innovations we encounter, it's easy to overlook the broader, more general implications of these new technologies. Technology has now changed the landscape of competition so much that a new, more extreme form of trustworthiness will be required in order to be successful. Simply doing what you say you're going to do and charging customers what you say you're going to charge them will no longer be sufficient. Instead, businesses will be expected to protect the interests of their customers *proactively*—to go out of their way, to commit resources, and to use their insights and expertise in such a way as to help customers avoid making mistakes or acting against their own interests simply through their own oversight.*

We've coined the term "trustability" to encapsulate this new form of Extreme Trust, and what we mean by trustability is very simple: "proactive trustworthiness."

---

* An important issue beyond the scope of this book is the idea of companies "doing right for the community." We believe a company that is proactively caring for customers will also treat its own associates well, will genuinely care about the environment (and not just slap on a "green" initiative), and will be a good citizen of the towns and countries where the company makes money. See C. B. Bhattacharya and Sankar Sen, "Doing Better at Doing Good: When, Why, and How Consumers Respond to Corporate Social Initiatives," *California Management Review* 47, no. 1 (Fall 2004), and John Mackey and Raj Sisodia's *Conscious Capitalism*, 2014. The point is this: A trustable company will work toward doing the right thing in all its decisions and will balance the needs of the company with the needs of constituents throughout its operation. The reverse, however, is not necessarily true; there are companies that have some good environmental or charitable initiatives originated in the public relations departments that don't necessarily play fair with customers as an intrinsic business strategy.

Chapter 2

Trustability: A Higher Form of Trustworthiness

Although most businesses and other organizations operating today *think* that they're already customer-centric and that they are basically trustworthy, their customers would disagree. How is the customer service at your organization? Seventy-five percent of CEOs think they "provide above-average customer service," but 59 percent of consumers say they are somewhat or extremely upset with these same companies' service. In one infamous study reported by Bill Price and David Jaffe, 80 percent of executives thought their companies provided superior customer service, but only 8 percent of the customers of those companies thought they received superior customer service.[1]

Being *trustworthy* is certainly better than being untrustworthy, but soon even *trustworthiness* won't be sufficient. Instead, companies will have to be *trustable*.

For instance, is your company careful to follow the rule of law? Do you train your people on your company's ethics policy in order to ensure compliance? That's admirable, of course, and it's exactly what any trustworthy company must do. But a *trustable* company would go further:

■ Rather than merely following the rule of law, a *trustable* company will follow the Golden Rule toward customers and build its corporate culture around that principle.

Does your company try to do what's best for the customer whenever possible, balanced against your company's costs and financial requirements? That's great, but a *trustable* company:

8

- Designs its business model purposely so as to ensure that whatever's best for the customer *is* financially better for the firm, overall.

In every aspect of a company's business practices, the difference between trust and *extreme* trust should be obvious, once we accept the fact that trustability means proactively watching out for customers' interests. While a trustworthy company fulfills all its promises to customers and does what it says it will do, a *trustable* company:

- Follows through on the *spirit* of what it promises by proactively looking out for its customers' interests.

While a trustworthy company manages and coordinates all brand messaging to ensure a compelling and consistent story, a *trustable* company:

- Recognizes that what customers and other people say about the brand is far more important than anything the company says about itself.

While a trustworthy company uses a loyalty program, churn reduction, and/or win-back initiative to retain its customers longer, a *trustable* company:

- Seeks to ensure that customers *want* to remain loyal because they know the firm watches out for them and acts in their interest.

While a trustworthy company focuses on quarterly profits as the most important, comprehensive, and measurable KPI,* a *trustable* company:

---

*   Key Performance Indicator.

- Uses customer analytics to balance its quarterly profits against changes in its customers' long-term value.

Trustability is a higher standard than mere trustworthiness.

Rather than simply working to maintain honest prices and reasonable service, in the near future companies will have to go out of their way to protect each customer's interest *proactively*, taking extra steps when necessary to ensure that a customer doesn't make a mistake, or overlook some benefit or service, or fail to do or not do something that would have been better for the customer.

Although most of today's successful companies are certainly trustworthy, the vast majority of companies today would certainly *not* be considered *trustable*.

Trust, yes, but *Extreme* Trust? No.

A company might be scrupulous in its ethics, completely honest in its brand messaging, and highly involved in tracking its customer satisfaction, but will it be *proactively* watching out for its customers' interests? If it wants to succeed in the Age of Transparency, yes. Because we will all be more and more interconnected—never less—we will live in an increasingly transparent world, and trustability is the only competitive response a company can have. Trustability is not a fad. It will outlive all of us and our children.

An affluent friend's wife realized one day that the credit card her husband had been using for three years carried no bonuses—no miles, no points, no cash back. (Scott Adams's Dilbert would have referred to him, despite his many talents, as a member of "the stupid rich" market segment.) Since he charged over $50,000 a year on this one card, the couple had forfeited significant benefits. The wife called the large, well-known issuing bank and complained, pointing out that since our friend was classified as a "private client" his relationship with the bank was supposed to get a regular review. The client manager who took her call explained that the card did carry a benefit—a very low

APR/interest rate. "So what?" the wife shot back. "Check your records. He pays off the entire balance every month. He doesn't even need a low APR." So they answered with what they thought was a surefire defense of their behavior: "Well, this is the card he picked out." The wife's reaction? "Not good enough!" Her point? He just grabbed any old card one day to get out of their office as fast as he could; if this bank couldn't be trusted to make sure he's carrying the right credit card, then they can't be trusted with any banking and investment oversight for him. The wife has since closed out all their accounts and moved everything to a bank where she believes the company would rather have a legitimate long-term customer than a little short-term cash. The couple has never heard from the old bank, where her husband had been a customer for over two decades.

Chapter 3

How Businesses Will Practice Proactivity

What would it really mean for a business to be "*proactively* trustworthy," rather than merely "trustworthy"?

Even though it might be highly disruptive as a competitive strategy, it isn't overly difficult to imagine how trustability would operate in any given business category. We only need to put ourselves in the customer's shoes. To drive it home for real, let's drill down to what it would mean for one specific business. We'll come back to explore other types of businesses in future chapters, but for now let's just explore what trustability would mean for a mobile telephone carrier.

How Mobile Phone Companies Operate Today. The typical mobile carrier today is not very proactive about protecting the interests of its customers. Verizon Wireless, for instance, used to sell many of its smartphones with buttons that could easily result in connecting to the Internet unintentionally, generating a per-usage data charge of as much as $2 at a time. After an FCC investigation, the company installed a "landing page" for users accessing the Internet—so if you do push a button by mistake you can cancel the transaction before incurring a fee. Even with this change, however, many users continued to find mysterious data charges on their phone bills. If someone "never" uses the Internet from their mobile phone because of the cost, for instance, then why would they have incurred these charges, except by mistake?

According to the *New York Times*, the company seemed to be charg-ing customers for their mistakes intentionally, in full knowledge that the charges were erroneous. This, at least, was the allegation leveled by one of Verizon's own customer service reps, in a communication with one of the newspaper's reporters. Verizon's phones had a feature that allowed us-ers to block accidental Internet access altogether, but according to this employee the company had instructed its reps *not* to inform customers about this feature unless they specifically asked about it! And the com-pany went to some effort to ensure that refunds were only grudgingly given, if at all, covering a maximum of a single month of erroneous charges.

Now think about this for a bit, because the truth of the matter is, even if all these allegations are 100 percent true, Verizon did nothing il-legal or even technically "untrustworthy." It isn't cheating a customer to charge them what you say you're going to charge them when they them-selves use their very own fingers to press a button that makes it happen. It isn't technically a violation of trust simply to refrain from telling a cus-tomer how to avoid making mistakes with your product. So why was this employee so upset? Because *even though the company wasn't proactively de-ceiving customers, it wasn't proactively protecting their interests either.* Veri-zon was trustworthy, in the old-fashioned sense, but not *trustable*, the way companies have to be in the Age of Transparency. No Extreme Trust here.[1] In many ways, we like what we've seen in Verizon's approach to building customer value. There are a lot of executives at Verizon working hard to exhibit goodwill and competence. So this story about making money on customer mistakes disappointed us.

Untrustable policies proliferate at today's mobile carriers in many other ways, some not so insidious. A few years ago we did a consult-ing project for a large wireless phone carrier, for instance. The company's executives wanted their firm to be more trustable with consumers, and a number of initiatives were identified to help achieve that objective. But just to be sure the company wasn't overlooking anything, an e-mail was circulated to all employees and frontline staff asking them to help identify any additional untrustable policies or practices to be addressed. To the great surprise of the company's executives as well as our own consultants, all of whom thought the firm was already operating with its customers' best interests at heart, several hundred employees replied to the e-mail, identifying dozens of additional issues, such as:

- Poor network quality sometimes caused dropped calls and lost data, and while the carrier was working hard to improve quality, it also needed a better system for helping customers get either compensation or at least sympathy for bad experiences.

- Very few people at the company paid attention to the refund and return policy, because refunds and returns on new phones are obviously not a high-priority marketing transaction. As a result, however, no one understood the policy well, it was too complicated for customers, and it often became a source of conflict, all but invisible to the company's executive team.

- Customers often incurred roaming or data charges without knowing how or why, and there was no proactive initiative to inform customers regarding how these charges had been incurred.

- Marketing offers often implied a "free" service or a very low price when in fact there seemed to be a roadblock to fulfillment, such as a complicated mail-in rebate or the low price applying only under very special conditions.

- Customers like interacting with the carrier's call center reps (high satisfaction scores), but the reps regretted that once they logged a complaint or an issue, they never found out what eventually happened to the problem or the customer, because there was little or no follow-up.

The large number of participants and their sheer enthusiasm for the company's trustability initiative indicated deep-seated support within the company's employee base for turning the already-good company into an even more trustable operator. Everyone is a customer, after all, and everyone wants to work for a company that doesn't take advantage of customers, just because they can, or because customer expense and inconvenience aren't important enough to them to worry about.

How a Trustable Mobile Phone Company Would Operate. Within an environment of smartphones and increasingly capable wireless services, the charges a mobile carrier assesses can be complex, and complexity presents a tempting opportunity to take advantage of customers. It might involve allowing customers to incur unintended data charges, or it might be failing to put a customer on the most beneficial or cost-efficient calling plan for their usage patterns. Or it could result from simple neglect (categorized as incompetence): If a customer is due to get a new phone at the end of his two-year contract, for instance, but doesn't notice when a period of two years elapses, a trustable mobile phone company would proactively remind him and invite him to come in to choose a new one. However, most mobile operators do not, preferring to "let sleeping dogs lie," and continue to collect on a fully paid-up contract while waiting for the customer to request an upgrade for some other reason.

A genuinely trustable telecom operator would proactively assign customers to the most economical calling plans automatically, based on their calling, texting, and data usage. Very few operators do this today, however, and those that do often use it as an excuse to extend a postpaid contract.

We confidently predict that this will soon be a widely accepted "best practice" in the mobile category, as carriers proactively assign the most economical calling plans to each of their customers, even crediting customers with refunds where appropriate. Already, mobile companies in crowded retail markets around the world are trying to position themselves as more trustable in order to gain a competitive advantage.

Immediately after the publication of *Extreme Trust* in hardcover, for instance, Vodafone Turkey launched a "Customer Bill of Rights" program designed to do exactly that. The company assures its customers that it will always act in their interest, whether that involves proactively assigning a customer to the right calling plan or counseling a customer on how to spend less for messaging and roaming.

Other mobile companies (and some other subscription-based businesses) have started sending e-mails or making outbound calls to customers at bill-paying time to remind them of the upcoming payment deadline. AT&T calls at least some of its customers before the due date by which a late fee would be assessed. A friend of ours reports having received one of these proactive service calls, and said: "Experiencing this was pretty nice. I personally feel that AT&T is looking out for me by doing this. They're building customer trust." So at least in this arena, AT&T is not one of those me-first companies, always trying to fool customers out of their money.

A trustable telecom operator would almost certainly have an unconditional money-back guarantee available to cover any and all customer complaints. In the same way today's best online merchants offer unconditional refunds, tomorrow's telecom operator will use such a policy to ensure that customers always receive the service they expect.

And since genuine trustability requires being completely transparent, if a customer is about to subscribe from a home or business address prone to poor network coverage or slow broadband connectivity, a trustable telecom company would advise him or her in advance of this weakness in its offering, perhaps providing a discount or other benefit until such time as service in the customer's home area is improved. After all, with today's online tools it won't take a new customer any time at all to have the flaws in a company's system pointed out by other customers, so the best strategy for a mobile carrier with a weakness in its offering is simply to communicate frankly about flaws and weaknesses in advance, as a way to inspire customers that they can have confidence in the company's suggestions and recommendations.

Mere trustworthiness, fine until now, will no longer be enough to compete with companies that have figured out how to be genuinely trustable. Our goal is to help you build a solid plan for succeeding in the Age of Transparency. The question we'll be examining shortly is this: *How much more would a customer be willing to pay to do business with a mobile carrier he considers to be trustable?*

Chapter 4

Why This Book Is Different from Others You've Read on "Trust"

Everybody's talking about "trust" these days, and many use the term as a synonym for what we might call "reputation," or "regard," or "popularity," or "familiarity." Brand equity like this is valuable and worth pursuing, but it's not the same as "trustworthiness," any more than fresh paint and a freshly mown lawn reveal whether or not a house has a solid foundation.

Some of the best books on business and personal relationships have been written on the broader subject of trust. These books—even just the really good ones—are too numerous to mention here, but we do want to acknowledge the works of Stephen M. R. Covey, Charles H. Green, and a host of others, and we suspect you've read at least some of them. We also appreciate the work done by the Edelman Trust Barometer[1] and Bruce Temkin, who keep the discussion bubbling and centered. In *this* book we will focus on why simple trustworthiness is no longer sufficient, and why a more extreme form of trust—trustability—will soon be the new standard by which consumers measure the businesses and brands they buy from. And then we'll talk about *how* companies must respond to this demand, if they want to remain competitively viable.[2]

For the most part, the business authors who've written about trust in the past have developed their own taxonomies to catalog the various elements that make up trustworthiness, ranging from dependability and reliability to honesty and authenticity. In synthesizing these ideas and joining them to our own, we're going to suggest that the most direct way to think about trust is in terms of a combination of *good intentions* and *competence*. In other words, being *trustworthy* requires:

Doing the right thing. And doing things right.[3]

Peter Drucker referred to doing things right as "management." (That's the competence piece.) Doing the right thing? He called that "leadership," and that's the piece that's all about good faith, playing fair, and best intentions.[4] We'll be talking a lot more about these elements as the book progresses, as well as about a new way to think about what it means when a company creates value—and how that drives the need for Extreme Trust. Mostly, if you want to succeed, you will need your customers to see you as reliable, dependable, credible, helpful, respectful, open, responsive, and honest. Whether you're any of these things or not, they'll still be telling their friends about you. You'll succeed when you generate ease of mind in helping your customers succeed.

Ultimately, our goal is to help you figure out how your business should adapt, as technology inevitably ushers in an age of extreme transparency. Extreme Trust is our answer. Being proactively trustworthy. Treating your customers just the way you would want to be treated if you were in their shoes.

Chapter 5

As Interactions Multiply, Trust Becomes More Important

Trust has always been touted as important, certainly. But one of the most important implications of a more highly interconnected world is the increased level of trust and trustworthiness we expect from others. The fact is that trust is becoming a more essential attribute of human culture, for several reasons, as people connect with one another more efficiently. First, of course, is the simple fact of transparency. The more interacting we do, the more transparent things will inevitably become. From WikiLeaks and the Arab Spring[1] to a cable TV repairman asleep on your couch[2] or an airline's luggage handlers mistreating bags,[3] people will find things out.

It's important, however, not to confuse transparency with trustworthiness itself. Transparency increases the importance of trust because if something can be transparently exposed to the light of day without causing undue embarrassment then it must be considered inherently trustworthy and ethical. On the other hand, *the reverse is not true.* Keeping a secret might be valid for reasons of discretion, privacy, or competition, and not exposing everything all the time does not necessarily imply unethical or untrustable behavior. Businesses and governments have legitimate reasons for keeping secrets, and often these reasons are even enforced by laws and regulations. If your marketing department, for instance, were to voluntarily release its confidential pricing plans for a new product, tipping off your competitors, your executives could be jailed for collusion.

But this doesn't change the fact that the world *is* becoming more transparent and that this *is* raising the stakes when it comes to trying to keep secrets!

> Transparency increases the cost of hiding the truth. More efficient interactivity exposes truths that used to be inexpensive to hide.

Take a look at www.megafood.com. In the often-criticized food supplement industry, MegaFood not only encourages customers to leave candid comments for each other but also features live camera feeds 24/7 in each of the stages of the manufacturing process; you can watch the product being made.

In addition to the issue of increased transparency, trust also plays an important role in helping people deal with the burden of information overload. We are all inundated with a cacophony of messages, information, data, and opportunities to engage with others. For most of us, trust is one of the most important filters for deciding what messages or interactions deserve more of our attention. Which messages are from the most trustworthy sources? Which interactions involve the most trustworthy people? Which e-mails are likely to affect us the most or to contain the most reliable, useful information? How can we make sense of the flood of information being unleashed by technology, and how can managers make better decisions by deploying more reliable and trustworthy tools and analytical capabilities?

However you look at it, trust is probably the single most important ingredient in any personal interaction or relationship. After all, if what you learn from someone else can't be trusted, then it's not worth learning, right? And if you want to have any kind of an influence with others, then what you communicate to them has to be seen as being trustworthy. Short of threat of job loss or brute force, in fact, being trustworthy is the *only* way your own perspectives, suggestions, persuasive appeals, or demands can have any impact on others at all. Whether you're telling or selling, cajoling or consoling, what matters most is the level of trust others have in you.*

So the technology steroids that are now supercharging our social nature are also supercharging our expectations for trustworthy behavior in others. Moore's law is not just driving technology; it is driving the trust we demand from friends, relatives, bosses, colleagues, sales reps, or spokespeople. It should be no surprise that every single business how-to book on dealing with social media emphasizes the importance of participating in an honest, transparent, and straightforward way.[4]

> Transparency may be the most disruptive and far-reaching innovation to come out of social media.
> PAUL GILLIN, THE NEW INFLUENCERS[5]

The penalties for untrustworthy behavior in a highly interactive and transparent business world will be severe and immediate—loss of credibility, for one, and the loss of social or economic value—while the benefits of sharing, collaborating, and cooperating in a more trustworthy way can be immense. The end result is that the more interactions we all engage in, the more trust will be demanded. The more social we are, the more trustworthy we must be if we want to participate credibly. Because everybody can now hear from everybody, the only ones who will be heard will be those who are *trusted* by somebody.

Every organization and business requires *people* to make decisions and to carry out policies. Employees are people. They are social, like you, and they have empathy. They can be outraged at untrustworthy behavior. Sooner or later, outrageously untrustworthy behavior on the part of any organization is likely to be "outed" by an employee of that organiza-

---

* Whether you're working face to face in person, one on one online, or one-to-many online, it may help to have a look at Ed Keller's books: *The Influentials: One American in Ten Tells the Other Nine How to Vote, Where to Eat, and What to Buy* by Edward Keller and Jonathan Berry (Free Press, 2003), and *The Face-to-Face Book: Why Real Relationships Rule in a Digital Marketplace* by Ed Keller and Brad Fay (Free Press, 2012).

tion. And there are literally dozens of websites available to air such outrage—just try Googling "whistle-blower."

The truth is, most real businesses don't abuse customers' and prospects' e-mail addresses or mobile phone numbers. They don't violate their customers' trust like this for reasons that have little to do with the patchwork of regulatory restrictions enacted over the last two decades. In the transparent world we live in, this sort of behavior would inevitably be exposed. So except for rapacious and disreputable fly-by-night marketers, companies refrain from doing these kinds of things at least partly because *they would be found out*. Even if there were no regulatory penalty at all, to be found abusing any person's contact details would immediately tarnish a company's reputation.

But even more important, *it is in a company's own economic self-interest to be trustworthy*. Companies cannot simply ignore the reputational damage they would do to themselves if they were to resort to spamming or rampant telemarketing, and as interactivity accelerates, and trustworthiness becomes even more important, it won't just be spamming that damages a reputation.[6] Untrustworthy activities will cause genuine economic harm to a business, and its cost is likely to dwarf whatever short-term profits a business might have been able to generate. We'll take up the economics of trust later in the book, so stay tuned. Because while economics may not be everything, when it comes to operating a profit-making company with a payroll to meet and shareholders to satisfy, it's *almost* everything. It's extremely important to realize, therefore, that while acting in a customer's interest will often require a company to incur a short-term cost, it will nearly always be economically beneficial for the firm in the long run.

The security and stability of your life depend on people and things you can depend on. Trust is an important part of that: people and groups with whom you don't feel you have to watch your back all the time. Whether it's a true friend, the regular guy behind the deli counter at your local grocery store, your high school teacher who helped you get into college, your buddies at the club, your business partner, your spouse, your parents, your kids—if you're lucky, they're not just trustworthy; they are *trustable*. Someone who is truly on your side has your interest at heart, takes your perspective, won't manipulate you into doing something that you wouldn't want to do, and doesn't stay quiet while you mistakenly hurt your own interest or forget to do something important to protect it. A true friend empathizes and watches out for you. That's what trustability is.[7]

Honesty, transparency, empathy—all the qualities anyone would associate with a true friend, a business will also need to demonstrate, just to stay in business.

It has never been possible to succeed for long with a business that offered substandard product quality or uncompetitive pricing. A business might generate extra profits for a brief period by cutting back on quality or raising prices above the norm, but as customers acquire the information needed to compare one company's offerings with others, it is inevitable that lower-quality, higher-price companies will lose out to higher-quality, lower-price competitors.[8]

One of the hallmarks of any free-market economic system is that price and quality information are conveniently available to all customers. Until recently, however, information about a company's service reputation, or about the overall customer experience at a firm, was not as conveniently available. Social media and mobile technology have revolutionized this, allowing customers quick and easy access, 24/7, to what other customers are saying about a brand or a business.[9] Other customers' opinions on all aspects of their relationship with a company are widely available online, and growing even more available at the speed of Moore's law and unprecedented interconnectivity. "Facebook" became the new hot topic, surpassing even "sex" as a search topic on Google.[10] And one key part of any company's overall service reputation has to do with whether it can be expected to act in the customer's interest. Is the firm really trustable?

Whatever your company does, good or bad, will be spread at Internet speed:

- Everywhere ("online" is ubiquitous)

- Immediately (news travels fast)

- Permanently (not enough lawyers on the planet to take stuff off the Net)

The Screen Actors Guild (SAG-AFTRA[11]) standard contract for assigning rights binds actors and studios to terms that cover "all media current or yet to be invented, on earth or anywhere in the universe." And anywhere in the universe your company does business, the degree to which you respect your customers' interests will now be every bit as visible to customers and prospective customers as your address, your credit rating, and your product's pricing and quality.

Chapter 6

Basic Principles of Trustability in a Business

If you want your business to be trustable, and to succeed in a more transparent, hyperinteractive world, then you had best commit these three basic principles of Extreme Trust to memory:

- **Do things right.** Be competent. Manage the functions, processes, and details right in order to make it easy for customers to do business with you. And pay attention to the customer's experience, not just the company's financial performance.

- **Do the right thing.** Ensure that the way your organization makes money aligns with the needs and best interests of your customers. You can't be trustable if you're entirely focused on the short term. Customer relationships link short-term actions to long-term value.

- **Be proactive.** Knowing that a customer's interest is not being well served but *not* doing anything about it is untrustable. *Not* knowing is incompetent.

Chapter 7

The Trustability of Things

While visiting a website is easy to understand as an interaction with a company, the truth is that all sorts of physical products today are being embedded with information and decision-making capabilities. Scientists and others call it "The Internet of Things." Information technology is permeating our existence. When a car beeps as you shut the door, reminding you that your keys are still in it, is that any less representative of the carmaker's intentions than when software prompts you to avoid a mistake in ordering something on the Web? And why shouldn't a refrigerator, or a microwave oven, or even a cordless drill prompt you to remember that the warranty period expires in thirty days?

Obviously, when you speed down the highway at fifty-five miles per hour in your car, it goes without saying that you trust the product to keep you safe. That's what a competent product should do.

But trust involves more than competence, more than simple product quality or good execution. Trust also implies that the entity being trusted also has *good intentions*. Although good intentions are a distinctly human attribute, residing solely in the human mind, we still evaluate the actions of companies and organizations as if they had minds of their own, with good or bad intentions. We observe a company's actions the same way we would observe a person's actions, and then we decide for ourselves whether these actions evidence goodwill or not. In effect, we evaluate the actions of a company as if they had been organized by some person, and then we try to infer that *person's* intentions.

So when iTunes reminds you that you already purchased a tune you were about to buy, or when Amazon reminds you that you already bought a particular book, even though these reminders are completely automated

27

and there's no human being typing out the keystrokes to protect you from making a mistake, we still see the message as an indication of the company's good intentions. This is the Trustability of Things.

None of this means, of course, that people aren't involved. Of course they are. Software doesn't spring into existence by itself, after all. In effect, the people responsible for programming how these websites respond to customer interactions have created a set of rules designed to protect individual customer interests. The programmers, or the people who directed their efforts, clearly had good intentions toward you.

The company has simply automated these intentions.

Chapter 8

"You're Gonna Need a Bigger Boat"

That's what actor Roy Scheider said in the movie *Jaws* as he got a good look at the immense size of the shark they were dealing with. And it's our advice for businesses now grappling with the rising importance of trust. You're gonna need a bigger boat. Earning and maintaining your customers' trust is a much bigger issue than you thought.

The demand that future customers will make for genuine trustability in the companies they deal with will have a dramatic impact on the structure, operation, and management of businesses. Businesses will need to think much more clearly about balancing their short- and long-term economic interests as they seek to maintain their own level of trustability. Untrustable businesses squeeze every last penny out of each immediate financial period, while trustable ones recognize that customer trust is a highly valuable—and measurable—financial asset, so they place more emphasis on balancing the short-term revenue from customers with the long-term value of their customers, their brands, and their reputation in the marketplace. The problem is that a great deal of money today is being made by *not* respecting customer interests. So the economic consequences of trustability are not going to be trivial.

Companies will also have to figure out how best to acknowledge and accommodate the spontaneous, user-generated customer communications that are likely to become the principal "voice" in the marketplace for any brand. Advertising and sales pitches are low on trustability, while collaboration and relationship building are more trustable. The ubiquitous availability of inexpensive tools for interacting with other people has given rise to a whole new way of creating genuine economic value: social production, often referred to as the "sharing economy."[1] Open-source software, Wikipedia, online reviews, and other valuable information-based products and services are forms of social production, regularly made available for no exchange of economic value at all. In this burgeoning field of online activity, people volunteer, they create, they contribute, and (importantly) they *police* one another—all without formal remuneration. Instead, they take their compensation in the form of recognition, or pride of accomplishment, or general participation.[2]

More recently technology has generated yet another new business model, which we will refer to as the "trust platform." Becoming prominent in just the few years since the hardcover edition of this book first went to press, trust platforms are epitomized by companies such as Uber, Airbnb, and TaskRabbit. This kind of business depends on using interactive technology to connect willing buyers with willing sellers, while relying on crowd-sourced feedback to ensure mutual trust. Rather than a "sharing" economy, trust platforms facilitate an "initiative" economy, based on the entrepreneurial initiatives of thousands of individuals, all seamlessly connected to the larger network.

And finally, we have to realize that social interactions are not as manageable as a company's marketing and other functions are. The social interactions you have with customers and other people can't be directed the same way advertising campaigns or cost-cutting initiatives can. Instead, in the e-social world, companies are likely to find that top-down, command-and-control organizations are not trustable, while self-organized collections of employees and partners motivated by a common purpose and socially empowered to take action are more trustable.[3]

These are *cataclysmic* changes for the business world. These changes will turn most businesses entirely upside down and inside out. We are not just talking about making nice with customers here. We are talking about a technology-driven tsunami of human interaction that will wreak holy havoc with nearly every principle taught in business schools today.

As with all disruptive change, it will be the new companies and start-ups that lead the charge against the established order. These rebels will

be wielding honesty and trust as lethal competitive weapons to steal customers from their more established but less trustable rivals. By contrast,
the firms that have already enjoyed the most success and profitability
are the ones that will find it hardest to adapt. Some will try to become
more trustable but will only grudgingly relinquish the significant cash
flows generated by untrustable business practices. Only those firms that
see the issues clearly and make a more determined attempt at genuine
transformation will succeed, and even for them the process will still be
painful and difficult.[4]

It won't be easy, but eventually our entire economic system will be
transformed by this revolution, in the same way that interactivity itself has
so dramatically transformed us over just the last twenty years. And while
Extreme Trust may be the competitive motivation fueling the revolution,
what you're going to find is that in order to use this fuel you may need to
adjust your business's entire engine.[5]

You're gonna need a bigger boat.

2

Why Your CFO Will Learn to Love Trustability

No one would remember the Good Samaritan if
he'd only had good intentions. He had money, too.

MARGARET THATCHER

Chapter 9

Trustability Increases Profits

Okay, enough with the unicorns and fairy dust. The clash between trust-ability and a company's own short-term financial interest is real. It is a serious and continuing obstacle to be overcome, and we don't want to minimize it. Urging companies simply to "do things right and do the right thing, proactively" isn't likely to change how management sees the world. The profit motive does that. So in part 2 we're going to demon-strate why trustability is actually a tool for generating the kind of profits that ought to be beloved by any good capitalist.

Our company, Peppers & Rogers Group, fielded a research survey to develop some top-line insights with respect to how customer trust affects the mobile phone category. The study involved more than 2,400 respon-dents, who were all U.S. residents and customers at one of the five major U.S. mobile operators: AT&T, Sprint, T-Mobile, U.S. Cellular, or Veri-zon.[1] We began by asking respondents how much they thought their mo-bile services provider could be trusted. Some rated their carriers fairly high on trust, others fairly low, and others in between, and we divided our respondents into three groups of roughly equal size: the trusters, the distrusters,[2] and the neutrals. (The distrusters were actually the largest group, but not by much.)

We found very significant differences in group attitudes on a variety of issues that add up to a great deal of money for a business. Trusters were much more likely than distrusters to say that they would buy more things from their carriers without hesitation, including new data services, ad-ditional lines, and upgraded phones. Trusters also said they would be more likely to remain as customers for a longer period, citing a strong sense of emotional loyalty to their mobile carriers. In addition, far more trusters than distrusters said they felt no need to search for alternatives and would recommend their carrier to others and defend it from criticism.

Some additional findings from the research: First, the single most important statement distinguishing trusters from distrusters was "My mobile services provider focuses on doing the right thing for its customers." Even though competence matters, in other words, the primary determinant of customer trust, at least in this study, was the customer's interpretation of the vendor's intent. Second, several of the attributes that consumers associate with being trustworthy are actually "free" to the mobile carrier. Being "warmly greeted" by a call center representative, for instance, would require virtually no investment to implement. Third and most significant, participants said *they would be willing to pay about $11 more per month*, on average, for a mobile carrier consistently demonstrating a higher level of trustability.

> So let's do the math: If you run a telecom company and your customers would be willing to pay you an additional $11 per month, twelve months a year, then for every ten million customers your company has, you are face-to-face with a potential revenue increment of more than *$1.3 billion*. Only a fraction of this would be needed to accomplish most of the trustable actions described earlier. The rest would drop to the company's bottom line, increasing customer satisfaction in the short term and loyalty in the long term.[3]

Additional research indicates health-care insurance customers would be willing to pay an average of $25 more a month to do business with a company they trust.[4]

This research also demonstrated that with the right analytics it may actually be possible to know which of a firm's customers trust it and which do not. In other words, a company should be able to identify individual trusters, distrusters, and neutrals, giving it the ability to treat different customers differently and greatly improving the efficiency with which a company can implement policies designed to promote trust.

The overall conclusion of our research is that although the financial benefits of earning the trust of customers may or may not show up in current-period results, there can be little doubt that trustworthiness and its higher standard, trustability, have the potential to return significant benefits over the long term. More research will follow, and you can check updates and studies in additional industries at:

www.extremetrustpaperback.com

Chapter 10

Trustability: Capitalist Tool

We're lucky that trustability is a very big tool, because the profitability issue is a very big nut to crack. The U.S. retail banking industry generated $32 billion in bank fees in 2013 alone, following a high of $37 billion in 2009, according to a Moebs Services report. It means nearly half of all the industry's income comes from fees![1] And the FDIC says fee income at banks has soared 44 percent in the past ten years. Not all the fees that banks levy against customers are untrustable. But no one believes that customers have begun to violate good banking practices 44 percent more than they used to!

Banking may be an extreme case, but large and attractive profits can also be generated from unsuspecting or misinformed customers in the mobile phone industry, retailing, credit cards, and most other categories as well. Billions of dollars are at stake just in the "breakage" of prepaid and gift cards. Businesses have a lot of profits at risk when it comes to treating customers fairly. It shouldn't be a surprise to anyone that becoming a genuinely trustable enterprise may look to be a very costly undertaking for many businesses.

This doesn't mean they won't attempt it, however. Regardless of the expense, trustability will inevitably develop in commerce. Even if it were to cost billions of dollars in real money, trustability is still going to become a dominant characteristic of business competition because the rise in consumer expectations with respect to trust and trustworthiness is being fueled by the steady, irresistible drumbeat of technological progress. The world will become ever more interactive and transparent, and competitive pressure will compel companies to adjust their business models to be more trustable.

But when we examine it closely, trustability is in fact financially attractive for a business even though in many situations it may cost money up front in the form of forgone profits or newly incurred expenses, as many business improvements do. If current-period earnings were the only criterion by which Amazon ever evaluated its financial performance, it would never do anything so "stupid" or "irrational" as refusing to make a profit from a willing (if forgetful) customer. But the fact is that when Amazon warns you before you forgetfully buy something you probably don't want, the company gains something far more financially valuable than the profit they could have made one time off of your forgetfulness. In addition to the increased likelihood that you'll recommend Amazon to friends and colleagues, they'll be solidifying your loyalty and continued patronage (after all, you'll now want to buy all your books from Amazon so they can prevent you from accidental repeat purchases, right?).

The clue to understanding why trustability can be financially attractive to a firm is recognizing that many of its economic benefits don't come immediately but over time, as returning customers buy more and as a company's solid reputation continues to generate more new business. Quantifying these benefits—including the value of increased customer loyalty, referrals, and additional sales—requires a robust customer analytics capability, as well as a financial perspective that fairly balances short- and long-term results.

Chapter 11

Short-Termism: Don't Worry About the Long Term, IBGYBG

Unfortunately, however, at the heart of most companies' untrustable behavior is a nearly manic obsession with short-term financial results and almost total disregard for longer-term financial implications. Short-termism generates many dysfunctional and even self-destructive business practices, as profit-oriented companies dismiss the long-term consequences of their actions in order to generate current-period profits—profits that feed the bonus pool, pump the stock price, and meet analysts' expectations. Short-termism stinks of unadulterated self-interest and directly conflicts with trustability, but it is still easily the most pervasive and destructive business problem on the planet today.[1]

But don't take our word for it. Do your own survey. Ask any ten senior business executives at ten different companies if they think their business often makes mistakes because it focuses too narrowly on short-term financial results or costs. And don't be surprised if your survey returns a *unanimous* guilty verdict. As businesspeople, we all know deep in our guts that we should do what's right for our company in the long term, but at most businesses the pressure to make the current numbers—to show concrete financial results, *right now*—is just too overwhelming. In one survey of 401 chief financial officers (CFOs) of large, publicly traded companies in the United States, for example, 78 percent of them confessed that they would be willing to give up actual "economic value" for their firms if that was necessary in order to hit the quarterly numbers.[2]

Short-termism like this emphasizes the "selfish" aspect of free-market competition, without allowing room for the empathetic, nonselfish side of every person's nature. Elinor Ostrom, the first woman to win the Nobel Prize in Economics (2009), has suggested that "when we assume people are basically selfish, we design economic systems that reward selfish people."[3] Obviously, there's no longer any question that a free-market system is much more efficient and fair than any state-controlled system could ever be, but the "greed is good" philosophy that animates so many is testimony to the fact that it offers its biggest rewards to the most selfish people.

The truth is, however, that short-termism only reigns supreme at most businesses because *the financial metrics we apply to business are not economically true measures of success*. They never have been, and they haven't substantially changed since being introduced at the beginning of the Industrial Age. The way most businesses "do the numbers" to document their financial performance focuses entirely on the past—that is, on the most recent financial period. Most companies' financial reports to shareholders include absolutely no consideration of the way the most recent performance has either helped or harmed a firm's prospects for generating future profits, leaving this detail to the stock market analysts and others to figure out.[4] Yes, a good business will track customer satisfaction or maybe NPS or customer lifetime values,* and as Orkun Oguz, former managing director of North America operations, Peppers & Rogers Group, says, this allows the company to "gauge the impact of customer experience on business outcomes."[5] Ultimately, though, these figures *should* have more effect on how earnings are calculated. Unfortunately, today earnings from the most recent financial period are the Supreme Performance Metric, the KPI to beat all other KPIs.[6]

Managers sometimes take comfort in the sophistication and precision of their short-term financial metrics, ignoring the long-term effects simply because they can't be as precisely defined. But this is like the classic joke about the man who lost his car keys late one night and is now

---

* Net Promoter Score® (NPS), developed by Satmetrix Systems, Inc., Bain & Co., and Fred Reichheld, is a popular measure of the difference between customer satisfaction and dissatisfaction based on a customer's willingness to recommend a product, company, or brand.

looking for them near a street corner, even though he lost them half a block away, closer to where his car was parked. When a police officer asked the obvious question—Why?—the man glanced up at the street lamp illuminating the corner and said, "Because the light's better here."

The simple fact about business metrics: If you aren't measuring the right things to begin with, you're not going to get better results by measuring them more accurately.

> When your headlights aren't on, the best rearview mirror available isn't likely to improve your driving.

Nowhere was this no-headlights philosophy more in evidence than during the run-up to the 2008 Great Financial Crisis, a global disaster brought about by rampant, overconfident short-termism. Short-term metrics and incentives, when they are applied to businesses based on current-period financials, almost inevitably end up promoting the interests of commission seekers, bonus-earning senior managers, and short-term investors. Usually this is directly counter to the legitimate interests of a company's shareholders, not to mention its customers, employees, partners, and other stakeholders.

In his book *Saving Capitalism from Short-Termism*, Alfred Rappaport argues persuasively that the inordinate focus on short-term results by corporations is due to the fact that business managers, fund managers, and others have personal interests that are in direct conflict with the interests of the organizations they are paid to manage or represent. A professor at Northwestern's Kellogg Graduate School of Management, Rappaport calls this "agency capitalism," which he contrasts with "entrepreneurial capitalism," the kind of business structure that characterized most companies in the early twentieth century. It used to be that businesses were managed by their principal owners, rather than by professional managers paid to serve as agents for the shareholder-owners. As hired employees, a company's professional managers are paid salaries and incentives that rarely align well with the best interests of the shareholders or owners of a company. You can hardly blame a manager for trying to maximize his bonus, even though in doing so he might sometimes risk his shareholders' capital.

Moreover, the conflict between the interests of professional managers and shareholders is exacerbated by the fact that most shareholders themselves are now also represented by agents, in the form of fund managers. In just the twenty years from 1986 to 2006, for instance, the proportion of shares directly owned by individual investors, as opposed to institutions and managed funds, declined by more than half, from 56 percent to 27 percent. And, according to Rappaport, forty-one of the fifty largest financial funds are themselves owned and operated by even larger financial conglomerates. So not only have company managers become agents, but even the shareholders themselves are now agents.

In effect, the kind of agency capitalism that Rappaport says now characterizes the Western world's economy involves managers managing other people's companies, which are owned by other people's money being managed by others. In this environment, even though everyone is *supposed* to be acting in the interest of someone else (their principals), we shouldn't be too surprised that the actual result is an orgy of self-interested wealth transfer, as company managers and fund managers alike respond quite rationally to their own self-serving economic incentives.

No matter its origins, short-termism terribly distorts a company's view of the economic reality of its situation. During the run-up to the 2008 financial crisis, individual bankers were earning irresistibly attractive bonus and commission checks for packaging mortgages—that were less and less sound—into securities to be sold to investors who were less and less discerning. If you aren't from the investment banking industry yourself, you may not be aware that a high proportion of the individual traders and bankers involved in this death spiral knew (or strongly suspected) that the increasingly hectic traffic in mortgage-backed securities was based on a precarious idea and likely to implode sooner or later. You can watch it at the movie theater in *The Big Short*, based on Michael Lewis's book.[7]

In addition, because the investment banks orchestrating these deals had largely transitioned themselves from private partnerships to public companies during the 1990s, the bankers now doing deals were gambling their shareholders' money, rather than their own capital. Even if shareholders lost in the long term, these bankers' bonus payments and commissions would not have to be returned.* One account of the run-up to the crisis tells the story of two private investors who each made a killing by betting *against* housing prices and mortgage bonds. They bet against the trend because they were highly skeptical about the deals being done, and in January 2007 their skepticism was confirmed at a convention of investment bankers in Las Vegas. At one point the investors approached a banker from Bear Stearns and asked him what was likely to happen to these securities in seven years or so. Weren't they almost inherently doomed, in the long term? The banker's answer: "Seven years? I don't care about seven years. I just need it to last for another two."

IBGYBG is a text-messaging acronym, like "LOL," or "OMG," and was shorthand for a phrase passed between individual bankers to allay pangs of conscience. When two bankers putting together a securities deal or a trade stopped to think more carefully about it, one might worry about the deal's long-term consequences, in which case the other might console him with the advice that you can't worry about the long term, because in the long term IBGYBG—"I'll be gone, you'll be gone."

Somebody else will have to pay the price. Later.

---

* In the business of financial trading, being trustworthy in the eyes of the other party clearly has some benefits, in terms of being able to act swiftly and efficiently. However, *proactively* acting in the interest of the other party is never likely to be the norm because the two parties to a trade have directly antithetical interests. Concealing information and trying to get an edge over the other party to a trade are integral to each participant's success, and this situation is unlikely ever to change, as long as there is a trading industry—in financial instruments, commodities, or anything else. It is highly unlikely, therefore, that genuine trustability—in the form of proactively protecting the interests of the other side of a trade—will ever become the norm. But proactively protecting the interests of your own investors or shareholders—the people whose money you are responsible for—is likely to be more and more expected.

Chapter 12

Taking the Long-Term View

Today's most successful firms focus on the long-term value of their customers, and the importance of maintaining their trust and confidence, despite the fact that sometimes the actual economic value can be difficult to quantify. In his portrait of one such forward-thinking firm, *Googled: The End of the World as We Know It*, Ken Auletta tells the story of how its founders approached their IPO (initial public offering):

> . . . *Google's two 31-year-old founders were driving the company with a clarity of purpose that would be stunning if they were twice their age. Their core mantra, which was echoed again and again in their IPO letter, was that "we believe that our user focus is the foundation of our success to date. We also believe that this focus is critical for the creation of long-term value. We do not intend to compromise our user focus for short-term economic gain."*[1]

And Google has shown again and again that it remains focused on earning the trust of its users by acting in their best interests, no matter what the short-term attractiveness might be for doing otherwise. The company's goal has traditionally been to not accept money for a search result or a higher search ranking, for instance. And rather than trying to "capture" users and keep them on the website, Google's philosophy is driven by the goal of setting its users free as soon as possible, so they can quickly navigate to any of the search results shown. On search results pages the ads are ranked primarily in terms of the number of clicks they generate from users. The more clicks, the more relevant or attractive an ad is to users, and so the more prominently it is displayed. No amount of money (short-term benefit) can generate a higher-than-justified prominence for an ad unless it's designated as such (long-term erosion of trust). We checked, and although there are a zillion articles describing how to bump up your listing on Google, none of them says "Pay Google some money, and they'll do it."

And in *The Facebook Effect: The Inside Story of the Company That Is Connecting the World*, author David Kirkpatrick repeatedly makes reference to the fact that the company's founder is not consumed with making money in the present but with creating lasting value:

> *They all knew Zuckerberg only approved projects that fit into his long-range plan for Facebook. "Mark is very focused on the long run," says one participant in the meetings. "He doesn't want to waste resources on anything unless it contributes to the long run . . ." While Zuckerberg had been forced by circumstances to accept advertising, he did so only so he could pay the bills. Whenever anyone asked about his priorities, he was unequivocal—growth and continued improvement in the customer experience were more important than monetization.*[2]

To forward-thinking online companies like Google and Facebook (not to mention Amazon, Apple, Zappos, and other successes), it is the customer relationship that links long-term consequences with short-term actions. These companies are following a course of action that is intuitively obvious to them even if it might be difficult to quantify mathematically. Don't forget: Jeff Bezos was monomaniacally focused on Amazon .com's ultimate success even though the company lost money for twenty-eight consecutive quarters after it was formed.[3]

We're not saying that Google and Facebook and Amazon are perfect. Like all innovative firms—even those with the best of intentions—they've made mistakes. But it's interesting that they are managed by *owners*, not just *agents*. That is, when we talk about the long-term vision of Sergey Brin, Larry Page, Jeff Bezos, the late Steve Jobs, or Mark Zuckerberg, we are discussing the visions of the company founders—people who maintained a very substantial personal ownership stake in their own companies. Many analysts think that online companies are better able to see the direct link between customer experience and shareholder value because they have a more direct connection with their customers, with less interference from channel partners and more efficient customer interactions. But while the nature of the online business model is undoubtedly an advantage, we can't overlook the fact that online companies are also more likely to be managed by their actual owners, simply because they are newer, and as a result they are less subject to the short-termism of agency capitalism. (One implication for this line of reasoning is that as technological change and innovation continue to accelerate, we may see more frequent examples of successful entrepreneurial capitalism, while companies under the direction of agent-managers may fall victim to creative destruction even more rapidly.)

Regardless of how it happens, a trustable company has to be managed with the discipline and foresight to focus on creating long-term value by earning the trust and confidence of customers rather than going for the instant gratification of a temporary sales bump. Being able to delay gratification in order to achieve a more important objective is a key factor in anyone's emotional maturity. It's one of the key markers used to assess how "grown-up" a child is. So in that sense, a trustable company could be thought of as more "emotionally mature" than a nontrustable company, which would be more "immature."

Chapter 13

Customer Relationships: A Link to Long-Term Value

When it comes to understanding how trustability creates financial value for a business, there are basically two approaches to the issue: a simple, philosophical approach and a quantitative, analytical approach. Both start with customers, for one simple reason: *By definition, all the revenue you will ever generate will come from the customers you have now and the ones you will have in the future.* (Take note: Brands, products, patents, logos, sales regions, and marketing campaigns do not pay money to a firm; only customers do.) The simple approach is to state your company's value proposition as a straightforward quid pro quo:

1. You want each customer to create the most possible value for your business.

2. On the whole, a customer is likely to create the most value *for* you at about the point he gets the most value *from* you.

3. The customer gets the most value from you when he can *trust* you to act in his own interest.

Therefore, to maximize the value your customers create for your business, you need to earn and keep their trust—that is, to act in their interest and to be seen doing so.

The quid pro quo model for justifying trustability is a commonsense approach that can be usefully employed by any business, not just high-end, billion-dollar online firms. Simply choose whatever action is most likely to generate a customer's trust.

A homebuilder we know has applied this model very profitably. When you build a home for sale to someone else, some states require you to guarantee the structure for some period of time (usually twelve months or more). During this warranty period the builder is required to fix all structural flaws or defects at its own expense. Homebuilding is a business that has very few repeat customers, but this particular homebuilder generates about twice as many referrals of new customers as his competitors do simply by acting in his current customer's best interest. When a home warranty period has thirty days remaining until expiration, the builder contacts the homeowner and reminds him or her. Then he suggests that he can send a team over to examine the house for any defects, in order to ensure that they are repaired within the warranty period.[1]

The reason a quid pro quo like this works is not that it generates current-period earnings, because it doesn't. In this case, it clearly costs the homebuilder something to fix defects that his customers might otherwise have forgotten to ask about until after the deadline, when they'd have to pay to make corrections on their own. But the quid pro quo generates immense long-term value. Customers have memories. Whether you remember them or not, *they* remember *you*. So when you treat a customer well today—say, by reminding him that his warranty is almost up or by preventing him from inadvertently paying too much—the customer will remember this in the future and will likely change his future behavior as a result, perhaps buying more from you himself or referring friends and acquaintances to you.

It is your relationship with an individual customer, in other words, that provides the "missing link" between your company's short-term, current-period earnings and its long-term, ongoing value as a business enterprise. Apply this philosophy to enough customers and you'll be able to overcome the temptation of short-termism.

But how much can you really afford to spend *today* in order to create a good deal for the customer, based on her expected future change in behavior? This is a question we have to answer with numbers. If the first approach to the question of how trustability creates financial value is a philosophical approach, the second is a quantitative, analytical approach. Here's how to think about it:

Every business executive knows that customers are financial assets.

> **Each customer is like a tiny bundle of future cash flow with a memory.**

And, as is the case with any other financial asset, every customer has a certain value, based on the cash flow he can be expected to produce for the business over his lifetime.

The usual term for this customer asset value is "lifetime value" (LTV). And while no one can ever know with certainty how much cash flow any particular customer will generate in the future, increasingly sophisticated analytical tools do allow businesses today to model their current customers' likely future behaviors statistically, based on what previous customers have done—that is, similar customers in similar situations. It will never be completely accurate, of course, because no matter how good the analysis is, predicting the future is impossible. But as data become richer and analytical tools become more capable, this kind of modeling has become more and more practical for a variety of businesses.

The inputs for calculating any customer's LTV include, among other things, her loyalty to the brand (or her probable longevity as a customer), her willingness to buy additional products or services from the company, the positive or negative recommendations she makes to her friends, and the cost of serving her. And even though the results of statistical modeling are imprecise,[2] they are still useful enough that you would be hard-pressed today to find any senior business executive anywhere who hasn't at least thought about these facts:

- All customers have lifetime values;

- Customer lifetime values are different, meaning that some customers are more valuable than others; and

- Customers not only spend money today (which changes the company's current earnings), but also the customer experience that any customer has today will likely increase or decrease that customer's lifetime value (which will change the company's future earnings).

It is the third point that we should pause to reflect on for a minute. When a customer changes her future behavior based on the good or bad moment she has with you today, or based on her good or bad feelings about your business today, her lifetime value will go up or down. This increase or decrease in LTV represents economic value that is being created or destroyed by the customer's experience, *today*. So every day, with every customer experience your company delivers, customers are creating and destroying both current value (costs and profits) and long-term value (changes in their lifetime values).

Suppose you have a very valuable customer who calls you to complain about something, and for some reason you don't handle her complaint very well, with the result that at the end of the call she hangs the phone up in disgust. She no longer trusts you. There can be little doubt that her LTV declined as a result of the call. The amount of this LTV decline can be thought of as the shareholder value destroyed by this unsuccessfully handled complaint. You won't realize the actual cash effect of this event until sometime in the future, when the customer doesn't return to buy more things, and maybe some of her friends do less business as well. But the value destruction occurred today, with the phone call. The question to ask is whether the cost saved by not handling the customer's complaint better was more or less than the decline in her lifetime value. And while the statistical modeling can be complex, in the end this is a straightforward calculation.

If you could add up all the lifetime values of all your customers, including those you have now and all the customers you will ever have in the future, the result would be something we can call "customer equity," and it represents the real economic value of your business as a going concern. So for the manager of a company, this means there are two different ways to create genuine economic value for shareholders:

1. You can generate current-period earnings (short-term value), and

2. You can add to your customer equity (long-term value).

Every dollar added to customer equity by a good customer is a dollar added to a firm's shareholder value. Economically, after we apply a discount rate to account for the time value of money, this dollar is equivalent to a dollar of current earnings—it is a dollar of value generated now, although the cash effect won't be felt until some later point. And the link between today's customer experience and tomorrow's cash effect is the individual customer relationship.*

Ideally, you would want to take actions today that feed *both* current earnings *and* customer equity, as when you sell something to a customer and the sales process itself inspires more confidence or trust in the customer's mind, increasing the likelihood that the customer will come back to buy again. In their study published in *MIT Sloan Management Review*, V. Kumar and Denish Shah's research concluded that "certain marketing techniques can influence a company's stock market valuation—if the techniques increase customer lifetime value."[3] However, even when you forgo some current earnings, it may be the case that customer equity is increased by an amount that will more than offset this loss, and using today's metrics and methodologies, this increase in customer equity is documentable. Sometimes it's even acknowledged by stock market analysts. In 2006, for instance, an analyst for American Technology Research, Shaw Wu, said of Apple's first-quarter slump, "We are not too bothered" by the dip because, "from our checks, Apple's sales representatives have been instructed to not push PowerPC Macs on customers who

---

* Serious readers are encouraged to turn to *Return on Customer: Creating Maximum Value from Your Scarcest Resource* (Currency/Doubleday, 2005), by Don Peppers and Martha Rogers, Ph.D., for a comprehensive discussion of the statistical, mathematical, and practical issues involving calculation of up-or-down changes in individual customer lifetime values. At an operating business creating value for shareholders, customer equity is virtually the same as a company's economic value, because the economic value of any business is the discounted net present value of all future cash flow yet to be generated by the business.

want to wait for Intel versions. In this day and age where making numbers is important, *we believe Apple is in a rare group of companies willing to sacrifice its near-term revenue opportunity for greater long-term success by developing customer trust.*[4] (Italics ours.)

Earning the trust of customers often does require an up-front investment like this—forgoing the profit on a customer mistake, for instance, or reminding a customer that the warranty is almost up and almost certainly incurring some immediate costs in the process. But these kinds of "investments," done prudently and carefully, can almost certainly return many times their cost in terms of increased customer equity. The increase in your company's customer equity is the financial benefit you will get from earning and keeping the trust of your customers.

In a nutshell, two different kinds of current-period business success are on every company's menu, and it's critical to know the recipe for both:

- Good current profitability, while generating more customer trust and customer equity (have your cake and eat it too); or

- Good current profitability, while eroding customer trust and customer equity (use your cake up so there's nothing left).*

Who will *your* customers flock to when their choices include companies that embrace trustability in their charter and are not driven by an obsession with short-term numbers? And how will your short-term success compare with the long-term value created by companies capable of balancing the short term with the long term?

John Stumpf, the CEO of Wells Fargo & Company, describes the

---

* Look at it this way: If your stockbroker came to you at the end of the year and summarized your dividends and interest payments for the year, but refused to tell you whether the underlying value of your stocks had gone up or down, you'd fire that stockbroker because it would be impossible to make investment decisions based solely on knowledge of current cash flow. And yet, companies that operate only on current-quarter earnings reports without *also demanding to know whether underlying customer equity is going up or down* are basically making the same mistake. See our discussion of these issues in Don Peppers and Martha Rogers, Ph.D., *Rules to Break and Laws to Follow* (Wiley, 2008), pp. 80–84.

period when he entered banking thirty-five years ago as being like the classic Frank Capra movie *It's a Wonderful Life*. Since then, Stumpf notes, trust has declined sharply as many institutions have become "practically anti-customer" and are focused on how to rebuild customer intimacy and trust. For B2B and B2C, he says, trust is the basic element of any healthy relationship. He notes that Wells Fargo is a huge organization; it does business with one in three Americans. A customer with Wells Fargo averages six products and contacts the bank eighty times a month, including ATM, mobile, and online touches. Stumpf says,

> *We owe our team members a full customer view so they help each client get the most from their relationship with us. Our hardest work should be behind the scenes; we should become intuitive about how to help each client. We have to balance our long- and short-term goals; for example, we had to spend a lot on our operating system, but that allows us to see each client completely and individually. It's not a customer's job to become profitable to us; it's our job to get the roadblocks to customer profitability out of the way. For a customer to trust us, we have to take the customer's perspective and also get the details right. Even if we do it right 99.9 percent of the time, if we're down for that one customer, then for that customer, we're down 100 percent of the time.*[5]

And something more to consider: The competition for customer goodwill is already heating up. In the past, your for-profit company has been competing against a bunch of other companies hell-bent (like you) on making their own short-term numbers. But in the future, more and more productive activity is going to take place based on social goals in addition to economic ones. Cooperatives and nonprofits have always existed, of course, but two trends are driving more and more economic activity in this direction. First, as the cost of interaction plummets, volunteer and not-for-profit activity gets easier and easier to organize, and second, people in developed countries simply *want* to give back, to contribute to others, and to make a difference. Whether it's consumers texting on their mobile phones to contribute $3 at a time to aid a disaster recovery effort, or software engineers volunteering some of their spare time to write code, your next "competitor" might just be an organization more interested in the welfare of your customers than you are. Ask Microsoft what it's like to compete with Linux, the free computer operating software created and updated entirely by volunteers, for instance. "Social production" like this is both a threat and an opportunity.

Chapter 14

Trusters and Distrusters

We can already hear the whining. Is it really financially smart to treat each customer the way the customer wants to be treated? What if the customer just wants the product for free? What if the customer doesn't want to pay anything at all, or wants to try everything out without charge, or wants to be able to return every item even if it's been damaged by the customer? Surely there must be some *limit* to a firm's willingness to proactively protect the interest of its customers. There is, and being profitable by being trustable doesn't require that we behave as though every customer is "good" every time.[1]

Protecting the interest of a customer should not mean you have to give up your own economic interest or subject your employees to needless abuse. Some people just don't deserve to be trusted—customers as well as companies.[2]

Research will demonstrate that earning the trust of customers almost guarantees substantial financial benefits. One way to snap a picture of this process is to focus on the different behaviors and attitudes of customers who say they trust a firm and customers who say they don't, and to identify those actions of a company most likely to enhance or diminish a customer's perception of its trustability.

As the paperback edition of *Extreme Trust* goes to press, Martha's company, Trustability Metrix,* where Don serves on the board, is working on research that will investigate, among other things, whether em-

---

* www.trustabilitymetrix.com

ployees believe they are able to trust the company they work for and whether employees believe customers are able to trust the company those employees work for. This is based on research at the Einaudi Institute for Economics and Finance, which found that a better predictor of "corporate integrity" than mission statements from a firm's website was the opinions of employees at different levels.[3]

Chapter 15

There's No Such Thing as One-Way Reciprocity

Good intentions are based on the principle of reciprocity, and there's no such thing as one-way reciprocity. I treat you the way I think you'd want to be treated, assuming that you're treating me basically the same way. If I conclude that you're abusing my own good intentions, then I have every right to watch out more carefully for myself. If I'm a business manager, I have a duty to my other customers, my employees, and my shareholders to do so.

Customers are all different. Most customers (like most people) are good, but some are bad, and some will change their spots on a moment's notice. Fortunately for businesses, computer technology has made it possible to analyze and track customer differences in some detail, and as the world becomes ever more transparent, it's likely we'll learn more and more about how to identify and deal with untrustable customers. Trustability, in fact, may soon become a routine measure of customer value, just as credit risk, transactional performance, and social influence are today. And a trustable company will distinguish their most trustable customers from the less trustworthy ones. When it comes to spending resources, doing too much for untrustable customers, in a misguided attempt to make everybody happy, not only shortchanges shareholders but also shortchanges the very best, most trustable, and most valuable customers, since they'll have to foot the bill.

In ordinary life, empathy is almost always returned in kind, and every business would be wise to keep this principle in mind. Most customers will feel good toward vendors who seem to feel good toward them.

58

Numerous studies have shown, for instance, that the single biggest predictor of medical malpractice complaints is not the technical quality of a doctor's care but the doctor's bedside manner. Caring, empathetic doctors don't get sued so often because patients simply won't sue medical professionals they consider to be friends, regardless of the merits of the case. But whenever doctors (or companies) fail to connect with people, or when they fail to inspire empathy, or to relate to others with a human face, then lawsuits result more frequently.

Reciprocity and empathy have a great deal to do with customer loyalty. When managers consider the issue of customer loyalty, they usually focus on its financial benefits. But there are two ways we can talk about loyalty: "behavioral loyalty," which is demonstrated by a customer's repeat buying, and "attitudinal loyalty," which occurs when a customer has a liking for a brand or company. Obviously, attitudinal loyalty usually leads to behavioral loyalty, but not all behavioral loyalty results from a loyal attitude. For instance, if you're a frequent flier living in a major city, you will almost certainly be "loyal" to whatever airline uses that city as its primary hub, even though you may not have a favorable feeling toward it. Or you might be loyal to your retail bank because you think it would just be too much trouble to switch, or because you think all banks are going to be equally disappointing anyway.

Attitudinal loyalty, on the other hand, is usually driven by a customer's emotions, and emotions can be extremely powerful motivators. An emotionally loyal customer may go out of her way to deal with a particular brand, based on a generally favorable feeling about the brand that might be hard even for her to put into words.

Ken Tuchman is founder and CEO of TeleTech, one of the largest global providers of transformational customer value strategy as well as technology and business process outsourcing solutions, based in Englewood, Colorado, serving large business clients. (Peppers & Rogers Group is now a unit of TeleTech.) One thing Tuchman knows a great deal about is the nature of customer loyalty, because customer loyalty has been the primary metric of his company's success since its founding in 1982. In Tuchman's view,

There is absolutely no question that emotional loyalty is different from pure behavioral loyalty. And while behavioral loyalty obviously pays the bills, the right way for any company to get there is to create a desire in the mind of a customer to do business with it. Companies like Apple, USAA, and Costco—these are companies that "get it" in their bones. These are the kinds of companies that customers trust to do the right thing.[1]

Companies that reach out empathetically to their customers (or to other stakeholders) will usually see the same kinds of empathetic behaviors coming back to them. This will often be reflected in less fraud, fewer service problems, more customer loyalty, and better word-of-mouth recommendations. But sometimes it can be even more dramatic, because reciprocity is a very powerful concept.

Remember our story about USAA, the banking and direct-writing insurance firm whose customers returned their refund checks? USAA built its reputation for trustability over several decades, based largely on a call-center model of direct interaction with customers. (Importantly, the firm also placed a strong emphasis on improving the efficiency and accuracy of its services, focusing not just on "good intentions" but on "competence" as well.) USAA is a company we've cited many times as an example of trustability. (In fact, we dedicated one of our books to US-AA's former leader Brigadier General Robert McDermott.)[2] The company's mantra is to "treat the customer the way you'd want to be treated," and Forrester has ranked USAA higher than any other financial services firm in North America when it comes to "customer advocacy," or "the perception by customers that a firm does what's best for them, not just what's best for its own bottom line." Forrester calls it "customer advocacy," but this is just another way to say "reciprocity."[3]

As technology continues to improve our ability to interact with others, it is likely to promote wider and deeper empathy among businesses, customers, and employees, with more and more companies choosing to imitate USAA.

For instance, while most companies forbid customers to post reviews and comments directly on their websites, Amazon trusts its customers enough to allow them to post uncensored customer reviews of any merchandise they sell. Building enough financial success through mutual trust, they were able to make an otherwise nonsensical offering—unlimited two-day shipping for a yearly flat fee. Is this working? In 1996, executives from Barnes & Noble, a company then worth just under $1 billion, offered Jeff Bezos a chance to sell Amazon to B&N before they started selling books online and creamed Amazon with their better-known brand. As we know, Bezos declined, and in retrospect it appears to have been a good decision on his part. By September 2015, B&N's market cap was the same as it was two decades earlier, while Amazon's market cap had ballooned to $267 billion.[4]

Or consider Zappos, the online shoe merchant. Realizing its customers would have to trust their company to order shoes without trying them on first, Zappos trusted its customers by offering free shipping both ways and no-questions-asked returns. Zappos sold its first pair of shoes in 1999 and sold to Amazon for $1.2 billion in 2009.[5]

Reciprocity in Action: The world's largest credit union with $44 billion in assets and 3.6 million members, Navy Federal Credit Union in Vienna, Virginia, announced in April 2011 a contingency plan for supporting its members in the case of a possible government shutdown. Their major initiatives included covering the April 15 payroll for active military members who have direct deposit of their pay at Navy Federal, expedited approvals for lines of credit, and 0 percent fee balance transfer for credit cards. Members who were concerned about loan payments were invited to call or visit a branch. Navy Federal president and CEO Cutler Dawson said, "For over seventy-five years, Navy Federal has been there to serve its members' financial needs. If a government shutdown does occur, we want [our members] to know that their credit union has programs in place to help them in this time of uncertainty."

Will their members—or their children—ever bank anywhere else?[6]

Recent advertising from Nationwide Insurance makes the point that they are owned by their members, "not by Wall Street," and therefore they can do what's best for members. The short term is certainly seductive, but reciprocity generates truly immense long-term benefits. So the right question to ask now is:

How will you compete against companies that balance making a profit with building long-term business value?

A friend of ours discovered just such a company and agent when she moved to New York, the city of sharp elbows, during the recession. Determined to get a great apartment for a great price, she and her husband met up with a Realtor they really liked. She told the story this way:

Our Realtor, Karen Kelley, with the Corcoran Group, showed us forty apartments. It took days. We had narrowed the choice to three when we got a call from another friend who was selling a classic co-op "by owner." So I called Karen to ask what we should do. She suggested we go see the apartment, which turned out to be wonderful. Despite the fact that no commission was involved, Karen rushed over to join us, armed with lots of useful information about the building's history, maintenance records, tax information—the works. That was before we insisted on paying her the buyer's part of the fee she would have earned, had the apartment been listed. Even before she knew she would make money on this transaction, she wanted us to have the right apartment. Since then we've sent several other people to her— both buyers and sellers. We feel as though we're doing our friends a favor by helping them find a Manhattan real estate agent they can genuinely trust. And of course we're thrilled to see Karen succeed too![7]

Chapter 16

Trustability and Self-Interest: A Paradox

The fact that earning your customers' trust has economic benefits for your business sets up an interesting philosophical conundrum: If you "do the right thing" for customers because it benefits your business economically, aren't you really just being *self*-oriented? Let's put it this way: If trustability requires that your "intent" is to act in a customer's interest, but your real purpose is to further your own economic interest, then doesn't that set up a conflict of interest?[1]

An inquisitive sixth grader might ask it this way of her Sunday school teacher: If you get to heaven by being good, then aren't you just being good so you can get to heaven? In Sunday school this dilemma is easily resolved, because God can see into everyone's heart. But here on earth none of us can actually know what's going through any other person's mind. We can only judge others' intents by observing their actions.

On the other hand, we all know there's a difference between being genuinely concerned with the interests of customers and merely appearing to be. Some companies want to be *seen* as trustworthy even though their deepest motives are entirely selfish and usually have to do with making the short-term numbers. They may look good at first, but before long the cracks begin to reveal that they are willing to bend their stated values to achieve their own economic goals, even at the customer's expense. (Theoretically, if the behavior of a company portrayed constant reciprocity even though the secret wishes of its top decision makers were entirely selfish, we suppose the company could, technically, still be considered "trustable," but we don't think most business managers are good enough actors to pull it off.)

Which brings us right back to our argument about the nature of "good intentions." Trust is as trust does. It doesn't matter at all to a customer whether his interests are being proactively looked after on account of the benevolence of a company's management or on account of their desire to benefit their own shareholders. Either way the customer is better served. It is the firm's actions the customer can see, not what's in the company's heart.

However, motive *does* make a difference *within the firm*. That is, in order to have a company that seriously tries to earn its customers' trust, there must be some unifying message or sense of mission that drives employee behavior at all levels to do this, in the thousand decisions they make every day. This is a tall order because no business rule or line of software code will ever be sufficient to ensure that employees treat customers right. Your employees have to *want* to do that. To have this kind of an organization you have to focus carefully on the corporate culture and on the "unwritten rules" that govern how your employees approach their jobs.

In reality, the issues of intent and action are probably destined to become just as entangled and inseparable for a business as they are for a person. From the standpoint of human psychology, research shows that behavior often leads intent. One surefire way to cheer yourself up, for instance, is simply to force yourself to smile. Physically. *Make* your face form into a smile, *keep* it there for a while, and soon you'll actually feel your mood lifting. It's just a part of human nature: Not only does intention lead to action, but action leads to intention.[2]

And it's highly likely that something analogous would happen in a company as well. If the financially directed mandate is to treat the customer the way you'd like to be treated if you were that customer, simply because this policy best promotes the financial interest of the company, then pretty soon these self-oriented mercenary intentions will likely be supplanted by genuinely good intentions. The mission of the firm will become: Earn the trust of customers. That's what would be in the firm's "heart," if it had one. Or maybe we'll come to a point where we are innovative enough, competitive enough, and smart enough to figure out how our interests and our customers' interests are aligned. We'll succeed when our customer succeeds, and our customer will succeed when we do.

But there's more to it than this. If we're right, and if good intentions really can be grafted into an organization simply by pursuing the goal of creating shareholder value, then even totally self-interested companies may yet find salvation. So as a citizen, consumer, employee, and voter, you should sleep a lot better knowing that companies won't choose to be trustable just because it's the right thing to do, but because they won't last long in a competitive marketplace if they don't.

It would put a new light on the adage that "greed is good." As long as it's an educated greed that's aligned with the best interests of our customers, it really is.

3

Do the Right Thing

We judge ourselves by our intentions and others by
their behavior.

STEPHEN M. R. COVEY

Chapter 17

Serving the Interests of Customers, Profitably

Trust has been defined many different ways, but in the final analysis the trust you have in someone you interact with, or with a company you buy from, can be defined in terms of how you assess two different qualities in that person or company:

1. *Good intentions—Doing the right thing.* Are they honest? Do they intend to act in *your* interest, or do they appear more intent on their own self-interest? Selfishness manifests as the exact opposite of trustworthiness.

2. *Competence—Doing things right.* Are they capable of acting on these good intentions? Proficiency (what we might call "flawless execution") matters, and incompetence will destroy trust just as surely as bad intentions will.

Both these qualities are important if you want to be considered trustworthy; either one by itself is not sufficient. It does a customer no good, for instance, to deal with the best-meaning company in the world if that company doesn't have enough competence to deliver the product on time or in good condition. Even if an appliance manufacturer promises to look after your best interest with a three-year all-inclusive warranty, and even if they contact you to remind you when your warranty is nearly up, if they just can't figure out how to get a repairman to your house when you need it, you still can't trust them. And even if the airline's posted online policy is to display the lowest fare available, if their website just can't access all the different fare combinations, then you still can't trust that you'll get what they promised.

We'll come back to both of these components of trust throughout this book, along with the important emphasis on being proactive, but it should be obvious that trust is a matter of degree, and that all of us will find some people or companies more trustworthy than others.

Let's start with "doing the right thing"—the "good intentions" part of a higher level of trustability. What does it mean, really, when a business has good intentions with respect to a customer?

Perhaps the best way to illustrate good intentions is to contrast them with the bad intentions you find at some companies.

"You've Got Mail": The Wages of Untrustability

"You've got mail" is a phrase made famous by AOL, one of the earliest and most successful Internet service provider (ISP) companies. Formerly known as America Online, at the height of its power AOL had some $5 billion in annual revenue, a market cap of $222 billion, and over thirty million paying subscribers, the vast majority of whom connected their computers to the Internet via AOL's toll-free telephone numbers. In 2000, AOL bought media giant Time Warner, which was at the time the largest corporate acquisition ever.

Over the last fifteen years, however, AOL has been a business in decline. After separating from Time Warner (which remains reasonably healthy), while it did earn some money from selling advertising and operating a few interesting and useful online properties such as MapQuest, *Huffington Post*, and Moviefone, AOL was never more than a shadow of its former self. In 2015, after losing all but 2.2 million paying subscribers, it was acquired by Verizon for $4.4 billion,[1] about 2 percent of its onetime value.

All this would be just another story about the meteoric rise and fall of an Internet company except for one thing: Throughout its history, AOL reaped enormous profits by deceiving its subscribers, tricking them, and fooling them into paying higher fees than they needed to pay. It raked in literally *billions* of dollars over the last twenty years essentially by ripping off millions of its own customers—customers who simply weren't paying enough attention, probably because it never occurred to most of them that a publicly held company with such a well-known brand name would actually stoop to such behavior. AOL would rank very high on any list of technically noncriminal companies earning the bulk of their profit by betraying the trust of their customers. The difficulty of quitting AOL as a customer is infamous on YouTube. Employee moles have sent training materials to customer activists exposing the call-center rep training that makes it hard to leave AOL and describes ways to "Think of Cancellation Calls as Sales Leads."[2] (AOL is not the only company that has done this, unfortunately. Recent complaints abound about eHarmony and Match.com.)[3]

Despite AOL's more or less continuous controversy with respect to customer service[4] and its foray into advertising-supported businesses, at the time it was acquired by Verizon the company still got more than 80 percent of its profits from subscribers, many of whom are older people who have cable or DSL service but don't realize that they don't need to pay an additional $25 a month to get online and check their e-mail.

> "The dirty little secret is that seventy-five per cent of the people who subscribe to AOL's dial-up service don't need it."
> *FORMER SENIOR AOL EXECUTIVE[5]*

Given all this, it shouldn't be a big surprise when we say AOL is just not a firm you can trust. Even though companies have no minds of their own, AOL could serve as a poster child for consciously bad intentions. Suppose for a minute that AOL really were a person. Not a company, just a human being with a funny name. Would you trust Mr. AOL to give you the correct change at the checkout counter? If he offered you a used car for sale, would you believe him when he described its condition to you, hand over heart? If he ran a charity, would you contribute—confident that he wasn't pocketing a big percentage of your contribution as his fee and only sending a fraction of your gift to the cause?

Chapter 18

Banking on Customer Mistakes

Untrustable business models thrive in our economic system today largely because being untrustable can be highly profitable—in the short term anyway—and many businesses are managed almost entirely for short-term results. If you've ever incurred more than one overdraft charge on your bank account in a single day, for instance, then you may be interested to know that this is exactly how some banks like it to work, and what they're doing is legal. Some retail banks clear the biggest checks and charges first, in an explicit effort to maximize overdraft charges. Let's say you have $250 in your checking account in the morning. During the day you withdraw $80 from the ATM, and then use your debit card to buy lunch for $20, then maybe a book for $25, then a new coat for $180. At the end of the day these charges won't be debited to your account in the order you incurred them, but in order of size, with the largest charges debited first.

Your charges, in the order made:	Charge	Balance		The bank's accounting:	Charge	Balance	
Initial balance		$250		Initial balance		$250	
ATM withdrawal	$80	$170		Coat purchase	$180	$70	
Lunch	$20	$150		ATM withdrawal	$80	$(10)	**NSF!**
Book purchase	$25	$125		Book purchase	$25	$(35)	**NSF!**
Coat purchase	$180	$(55)	**NSF!**	Lunch	$20	$(55)	**NSF!**

As a result, even though you only exceeded your account balance one time, with the very last purchase, ending the day with an overdraft of $55 in total, you will incur *three* NSF charges (bank lingo for "insufficient funds"), with fees totaling more than $100 at many banks.

> Miss Piggy—the famous Muppet—once pointed out that all you need to know about bankers . . . is that they attach little chains to their ballpoint pens.
> *JIM HIGHTOWER, ON ALTERNET.ORG*

Now maybe—way back when the majority of retail checking transactions were physical checks that were cashed by merchants and then mailed in to banks in daily batches for clearance—just maybe this largest-charge-first policy was implemented as a service to customers, to ensure that the biggest, most important checks arriving in each day's batch of mail would be paid and not bounced. But this benevolent motive—if ever it was the real motive—has now been completely overtaken by the fact that real-time electronic transactions constitute a lot of retail banking activity. Most bounced-check fees today are incurred through ATM withdrawals and debit card swipes, with each transaction having an unmistakable date-time stamp.

Some banks' intentions can be called into question even more by the services they offer to ameliorate this situation, because many of these services are designed primarily to generate even more fees. Some banks offer their customers the option to cover an overdraft immediately with a credit card, for instance, but whenever such a transfer is made, a cash-advance charge is applied to the credit card, and the minimum transfer may be $100.

Many banks also offer "courtesy overdraft" coverage up to some limit. But courtesy overdraft coverage doesn't mean what it sounds like—that you can overdraw your account as a "courtesy," for free. It just means the bank won't *stop* you from overdrawing your account, unless you exceed the coverage limit. A fee will still be imposed, but you'll be spared the embarrassment of having a debit charge denied. And while it used to be the case that you had to sign up with the bank to get this "courtesy" extended to you, banks are increasingly simply subscribing their customers to the policy automatically, so if you charge something with your debit card that exceeds the money in your account, the transaction will still go through—along with the NSF fee assessed to you later, often exceeding the value of the original charge! In a 2013 survey of the top five banks and savings institutions in each of the top ten U.S. metropolitan areas, the average "courtesy overdraft" charge was $30.[1]

But at some banks it gets even worse. Suppose you have only $50 in your account but you also have courtesy overdraft coverage up to $250. And remember now, the bank may have even signed you up for this courtesy overdraft coverage without your knowledge. Not wanting to overspend, you use the ATM to submit a balance inquiry. The ATM will tell you your "available balance" is $300! This is of course an important figure to know, but the way it's presented by some banks will distract attention from your actual balance.

Even as new legislation suggests reforms in these areas, the result of all these policies is that while banking companies may not have real "intent," because a bank isn't a real person with a real brain any more than AOL is, anyone observing this behavior in a *person* would be likely to conclude that Mr. Bank *wants* you to overdraw, if it is at all possible for him to fool you into it. Mr. Bank *wants* to maximize those NSF penalties by reordering the daily charges to your bank account after they are made.

Still not convinced? Here's what one bank employee said with respect to promoting the use of debit cards, as reported by consumer-advocate blogger and MSNBC commentator Bob Sullivan:

> *Our focus is to get you to start using the debit cards so you can charge up those NSF fees, because the purchases that you make will not show in your account until many days later.*

When Martha signed up for a checking account at a large, well-known bank in New York, she was offered a debit card against it. She adamantly declined, commenting that debit cards are better for banks than for customers. Three days later, she received a debit card in the mail, with a letter that began: "Here is the debit card *you requested*." (Italics ours.) Does it matter whether the debit card sent to Martha after she refused it was sent on bad faith? Or (more likely) because the bank is not competent enough to meet the request of an individual customer? Either way—whether it's bad intentions or incompetence—the customer starts looking for a way to jump ship because clearly this bank is not really trustable.

Not every bank behaves this way toward customers. But—like AOL—many that do would find it very hard to wean themselves off these perfectly legal practices. And if you are a customer, and you know enough to have your choice between two banks—one bank that looks out for itself and maximizes the fees they can charge you in order to make the most they can every quarter, while another bank looks out for you and helps you maximize how far your money will go and makes a decent profit every quarter, *which will you choose?*

Chapter 19

Netflix: Good Guys Who Wavered for a Moment—Bad Intentions? Or Incompetence? Or Both?

Blockbuster, the original giant of the video-rental business, made a lot of money from late fees—so much in fact that its customers grew to detest them. Derisive jokes about Blockbuster and its late fees became regular fare for comedians on late-night television shows. But Blockbuster was addicted to the late-fee revenues, and rationalized that the company itself wasn't to blame for rampant customer dissatisfaction or the resulting abuse their employees had to take; all a customer had to do to avoid a late fee was bring the movie back on time. Blockbuster's business model was based on revenues that infuriated customers, and the company wasn't innovative enough to figure out any other way to make money that didn't include late fees.[1]

But a newcomer did. In 1999, Netflix appeared with a completely different business model: Customers got to choose their level of commitment to renting movies (different pricing levels for different quantities of movies out at a time), and paid a fixed monthly fee to enjoy each movie for as long as they wanted. Send them back fast, get more movies for the same price, but never pay a late fee. Furthermore, Netflix remembered what you liked, made recommendations, and allowed customers to create personalized "queues" that lined up the next movies they wanted to see. The way Netflix made money was aligned with the way customers wanted to do business.[2]

After Netflix had siphoned off about two million customers, Block-buster saw that to remain competitive with the most valuable movie rent-ers, it too would have to adapt. In 2004, the company decided to eliminate late fees in its company-owned stores, despite the projected annual reve-nue loss of more than $250 million, although franchised stores were free to continue charging these fees, and many of them did. But the handwrit-ing was already on the wall for Blockbuster's decline. Netflix had set up a low-priced, customer-friendly alternative in the form of mail-order DVD rentals, and disillusioned Blockbuster customers flocked to it. Hooray! They had found a business that valued customer service, made it super-easy to participate, remembered individual customer preferences, and didn't try to "trick" customers with fees that sometimes exceeded the value of the DVDs being rented. Netflix was *trustable*, even reminding customers if they'd had a DVD for a very long time, in case the customer had forgotten it was lying around somewhere.

But even while it was still competing with Blockbuster, Netflix was occasionally accused of cutting costs by "throttling" its highest-volume, most frequent customers (that is, selectively slowing down the turn-around times on these customers' DVD orders).[3] Nevertheless, its low-price market-entry strategy seemed successful enough on balance, and Blockbuster, which never lived down its reputation for rapacious late fees, filed for bankruptcy in 2010. By 2011, Netflix had established a growing business in live streaming videos as well as DVD rentals, with twenty-five million customers, and its market cap had soared to $16 billion as investors fought over the chance to own a piece of the victor in the U.S. video-rental war.

But then, in the summer of 2011, Netflix (like many companies) got so busy working on its "business" that it forgot the heart of its success: cus-tomers who liked Netflix, who valued what they had taught the company when they got good recommendations,[4] and who trusted the company to provide good product and service at a fair price.

Although its customers liked paying one fee and keeping one "queue" for streaming movies as well as DVDs by mail, Netflix wanted to antici-pate the end of DVD rentals, which it predicted for 2018, and separate itself into two businesses—DVD rentals and streaming videos. This would be more convenient for Netflix but not more convenient for the customers. In fact, the way Netflix reconfigured itself resulted in an effective price increase for customers, as well as a great inconvenience. Customers had to check movie listings on two websites (streaming Netflix and DVD-by-mail Qwikster), feeling as though they were dealing with two companies, and being ripped off in the process. Many customers felt betrayed by this company they once thought loved them.

Netflix provides a parable about what happens when executives put their own business models ahead of how customers want to do business. By the end of October 2011, the company's stock market value had fallen to $4 billion, down 75 percent from its high in July, indicating that investors were still concerned about the direction of the firm's business, and CEO Reed Hastings confessed that it would take more than a year for the company to claw its way back to the kinds of customer satisfaction levels it had enjoyed before the debacle.[5] It took Netflix nearly two years to regain the stock market value it had prior to its fumble.

Netflix benefited directly from Blockbuster's own self-inflicted wounds, and yet less than a decade after trumping Blockbuster's self-interested business model, Netflix put its own preferences for business structure and efficiency, as well as a desire for increasing prices, ahead of the loyalty of its customers. It may as well have started charging late fees.[6]

On one hand, we could argue that this is simply a case of incompetent execution on Netflix's part. It fumbled the ball during a complicated play, trying to shift its business model because of a legitimate and predictable technological change on the horizon. On the other hand, we could also argue that it is a case of bad intentions; that Netflix never really thought of its customers first at all but merely posed itself as a customer-friendly alternative to Blockbuster in a competitive strategy made attractive by the bigger company's own prior missteps. Or maybe it was a bit of both?

Chapter 20

So What Are Good Intentions, Anyway?

We can never really know someone else's intention. Any person's motive is internal to the person. It's in the mind. All we can do is observe their behavior—what they do, how they look, what they say out loud.

It is in our nature, however, to put ourselves in others' shoes and to ascribe motives to people based on what we see them do. We know what goes on in our own minds, we know what *our* intentions would be if we were doing these things, and so we hypothesize about what must be going through someone else's mind to account for their actions. When we trust someone's intentions, we're really just making our own judgment based on their behavior. It may sound like a circular argument, but Henry Stimson had it exactly right when he said: "The only way to make a man trustworthy is to trust him."[1]

Nor should it be a surprise that two different people, evaluating the exact same behavior in someone else, might make *different* judgments. Only a mind reader could be 100 percent confident when the subject involves someone else's intentions.

We make the same judgment calls when it comes to assessing the businesses we buy from, the companies we work for, and most other organizations we deal with. As Seth Godin has pointed out, a "company" doesn't really have intentions at all, because a company has no mind of its own.[2] But this doesn't stop us from viewing a company's behavior through our own anthropomorphic lens and asking ourselves what *we* would intend if we were to take the same actions. This lens may not explain how things actually happen in the world, but as a logical shortcut most of us still find it useful. And since we can't know someone else's actual intent anyway, the shortcut costs us nothing.

We've seen plenty of examples of bad intentions, or simply not caring. Assume that transparency, exposure, and the consumer thirst for retribution for unfair behavior will accelerate and scare businesses straight. What does that mean for the way a business has to think about being deliberately trustable?

- Figure out how to protect customer interests, profitably.

- Understand that betraying customer interests will cost more than it has in the past.

If we've been looking at examples of bad intentions, how would we define good intentions? Without exception, definitions of "trust" require taking into account the other person's best interests when making decisions. This means treating someone the way you'd want to be treated yourself—it's the Golden Rule for Christians and is a similarly revered principle in virtually every other world religion. When people describe "trust," they use words like "playing fair" or "following your conscience" or "showing goodwill." The academic term for this is "reciprocity," meaning that a trustworthy person must understand—have insight into—the best interest of "the other," and then reciprocate with his or her own actions. In order to be trusted by someone, a person must be seen to take account of and respect the other's interests.

The more you think other people are acting only to further their own interests, the less trustworthy you're likely to think they are. One authority on trust, Charles Green (coauthor, with David Maister and Rob Galford, of the very well-respected and widely quoted book *The Trusted Advisor*),[3] suggests that a person's trust in another is inversely proportional to the degree of "self-orientation" he perceives in that other person's actions. The more you think my actions are driven primarily by my desire to benefit myself or to achieve my own goals (say, making a profit this quarter), rather than by my desire to do what's in your interest (say, telling you the best prices available right now), the less inclined you will be to trust me.[4]

In real life, it's easy to recognize the conflict between trust and self-interest. We don't trust transactional salespeople who have everything to gain from our purchase and nothing to lose from our dissatisfaction. We are *least* likely to trust someone who smiles and says, "Trust me."

We don't trust advertising and marketing messages because each is designed with a particular, self-oriented purpose in mind: to improve the bottom line of the company doing the communicating. Advertising costs money, and while no one holds it against a brand for trying to recoup this investment, it does mean that every ad carries a point of view—an inherent bias. Surveys show that consumers place far more trust in their friends' opinions, and even in the opinions of complete strangers whose reviews they read online, than they do in the claims made in advertising. They tend to trust "a person like me" or an objective expert the most.[5] Ads have a bought-and-paid-for point of view, but your own friends—and even uninvolved strangers—have no such agenda. If you ask a friend his opinion, he's likely to give you his most honest assessment because he's your friend. Right or wrong, his assessment is not going to be biased. If he's a true friend, his opinion will be delivered with no hidden agenda in mind at all. (Haven't you ever tried on anything at a clothing store and had a genuinely honest salesperson—one who really wanted to help you look good—say, "That doesn't really flatter you. Try this instead"?)

Being self-oriented, self-centered, or self-obsessed is simply not the way to earn someone's trust. Selfish people aren't considered trustworthy. Selfishness is antithetical to trustability.

Chapter 21

Is Your Company Trustable? Or Merely Trustworthy?

A company can be trustworthy largely by doing what it says it will do. But it can only be *trustable* by genuinely considering the customer's interest and balancing it with its own. Obviously, a trustable company still wants to make a profit, but not by deceiving or fooling the customer, or taking advantage of the customer's lack of knowledge.

> Many companies, following their current business models, can be "trustworthy" in the sense that they are legally operated and do what they promise. But until they change their underlying strategy, which often depends on customers' not paying attention or not knowing enough to make the best decisions, they can't be considered "trustable."

Trustable Companies Do Things Right. A trustworthy firm will do what it promises but may only do it in the most basic way. It will be competent enough to answer the phone when you call, but it may then measure the performance of its "service" reps solely by how many calls they can handle per hour. A *trustable* company not only means to do well but cares enough about this objective to execute well also. Keeping its own profit in mind, a trustable firm is always trying to understand what it's like to *be* the customer, and then to make that experience as hassle-free and satisfying as possible. In most cases, of course, this will also create a great deal of value for the company itself, in the form of customer loyalty and additional patronage.

———————

Trustable Companies Do the Right Thing. A trustworthy firm will do what it promises to do, but a *trustable* company, like a friend, will do what's best for a customer even if the customer isn't really paying attention or isn't as well informed or knowledgeable as the company is. Importantly, this means that a trustable company must find a business model that allows it to create shareholder value by acting in its customers' interests. It won't—and shouldn't—sell its products or services at a loss, but to be trustable it must be sensitive to the customer's point of view and try to deliver a fair deal. In the past, companies assumed a gap between what's good for customers and what's good for profits. The trustable company sees no such gap, but—starting from scratch if necessary—figures out how to use what works for customers as the basis for developing its business model and strategy.

> *A friend ordered a three-piece desk online. Two of the pieces were delivered without a hitch, but the third piece wasn't there a week later. Thomas called the company to ask about the missing piece and discovered that the piece had been taken by the delivery company to the wrong delivery center and was in the wrong city. The online retailer's rep immediately solved the problem: "Sir, I am so sorry this happened. I'm going to sign you up for an even exchange and send you the missing piece in overnight delivery so you will have it tomorrow." Our friend had been ready to express his annoyance but was disarmed by this completely fair treatment. When the rep said, "And we're going to credit your credit card an extra twenty-five dollars for the inconvenience," Thomas pointed out that it was not the retailer's error but the transportation company's mistake. "Don't you worry about that," he was told. "We just want to make sure you are working at your new desk tomorrow." Is this good customer service? Good intentions? Competence? Who cares? This is a company you can count on, a company that is completely trustable.*

Chapter 22

How Trustable Companies Use Customer Insight to Improve Customer Experience

It's a reasonable bet that very few customers would *want* to pay a monthly fee for a dial-up ISP subscription they don't need and never use, and don't really know they're paying for. And most likely no one would actually *want* to incur NSF charges (overdraft fees) by accident. There may be times a person would choose to incur such fees, and (who knows?) some people might simply choose to pay for AOL's dial-up service just so they can say they do, but on the whole, we don't think we're going too far out on a limb by saying neither Mr. Bank nor Mr. AOL is "doing the right thing."

Once we dispense with such obvious examples of untrustability, however, we will find that the task of acting in the interest of a customer is considerably more complex. Obviously, since I can't be any more certain of your motives and interests than you are of mine, it's possible my company might not respect your needs simply because I don't fully understand what your needs are. How can any company genuinely know what's in the best interest of a particular customer when customers clearly have different tastes and preferences?

Even though no company can ever be certain what's in any particular customer's mind, companies today do have much more capable technologies for analyzing their customers' needs and protecting their interests. Sometimes, all that's required is for a company to use its own processes to help a customer avoid a costly and preventable mistake. Peapod, the online grocery service, for instance, has software that will check with you about a likely typo before you buy something highly unusual ("Do you really want to buy 120 lemons?").[1]

And the best companies are also using their greatly improved IT capabilities to do a better job of remembering their customers' individual needs and preferences. A trustable company will remember what it learns about each customer, becoming smarter and more insightful over time, and then using this insight to create a better customer experience. Sometimes, all that's required is for a company to use its own database of past customer transactions for the customer's benefit. Remember: If you order a book from Amazon that you already bought from them, they will remind you before they process your order. Same with iTunes. These are examples of genuinely trustable behavior. In each case, the company's database gives it a memory that can sometimes be superior to the customer's memory. It would not be cheating for Amazon or iTunes simply to accept your money, thank you very much. God knows, Mr. AOL and Mr. Bank certainly would. Rather than using their superior, computer-powered memory to *take advantage* of the customer, however, Amazon and iTunes use it to *do the right thing*.

And note that "the right thing" to do, at least in this case, is mutually beneficial. Even as Amazon offers you the chance to opt out of a purchase you've already made, they also reduce the likelihood that you'll receive the book, realize you already have it, and return it. And when iTunes warns you you're about to duplicate a song you already own, they are making it less likely they'll have to execute a labor-intensive and costly refund process, or that you'll think badly of them aloud on Twitter. This is exactly how "reciprocity" is supposed to work—as a win-win.

Ironic—isn't it?—that some banks use their customer databases and analytics tools to craft highly sophisticated pictures of their customers' and prospects' value, profitability, and credit risk and then bombard them with two billion credit card solicitations every year.[2] Why don't more of them do what Royal Bank of Canada (RBC) has done? RBC has used its superior insight to extend automatic overdraft protection (with no fee!) to low-risk customers (that is, *most* customers). That way, the customer gets a break—and so does the bank; instead of having to pay a service rep to handle a call from a reliable customer who demands the fee be rescinded, the bank chooses instead to send a note explaining "this one's on us" and how to avoid this in the future, reducing their own costs in the process. Rather than incurring costs and resentment, and then netting no fee anyway, the bank saves the costs, builds goodwill, and *then* nets no fee. During the first ten years after instituting this approach, RBC increased per-customer profitability by 13 percent.[3]

Chapter 23

Empathy, Self-Interest, and "Homo Economicus"

One of the problems with the idea that trustability and selfishness don't mix, just in case you haven't already picked up on it, is that it calls into question the moral legitimacy of free-market economics itself, which is built on the principle that people acting in their own self-interest will, collectively, create a better standard of living for everybody. The "neoclassical" economic model assumes that people *always* act in their own self-interest, and that these independent, self-interested actions collectively create substantial economic value. As Adam Smith famously suggested in *The Wealth of Nations*, "It is not from the benevolence of the butcher, the brewer, or the baker that we expect our dinner, but from their regard to their own interest."[1]

It turns out that neoclassical economics is flawed, however, in the way it defines human motives, because pure, absolute self-interest in any person is not the norm but an aberration. Very few people are ever completely self-oriented, never doing anything that might undermine their own interest. People like this are called psychopaths, and what makes them aberrations is that they're completely immune to the feelings of others. The rest of us have empathy. Concern for others' feelings is hardwired in our brains. You don't have to "learn" empathy. Newborn babies, a few days old, will cry when they hear other newborns cry. Toddlers unable to speak will try to help adults in accomplishing tasks. So while Adam Smith's description of the baker's motive may be *generally* correct, if one of the baker's close friends was starving, or if the baker was contributing to a community dinner, or if he was particularly proud of one of his confectionary creations, then he would not be likely to look solely to his own financial interest in selling his goods.

Nearly all of us are born with such a strong sense of empathy, in fact, that we can barely tolerate the idea of killing or inflicting pain on others, even when dealing with outright enemies. During World War II, U.S. Army brigadier general S. L. A. Marshall surveyed several thousand U.S. troops immediately after they had been involved in combat. What he found was astounding: Fewer than 20 percent of all American combat troops actually shot at the enemy, even when they were being attacked! In Marshall's words, "It is fear of killing, rather than fear of being killed, that is the most common cause of battle failure in the individual."[2]

By the end of the twentieth century, social science had persuasively demonstrated that people have strong empathetic motives, and that these motives directly conflict with rational, economic self-interest. These findings are partly responsible for the rise of the entirely new discipline of behavioral economics, a field of study that combines psychological and emotional factors in human decision making, along with the rational calculations of self-interest posited by the neoclassical model. As one academic study summarized,

> Over the past decade, research in experimental economics has emphatically falsified the textbook definition of Homo economicus, with hundreds of experiments that have suggested that people care not only about their own material payoffs, but also about such things as fairness, equity, and reciprocity.[3]

One of the most widely cited behavioral economics experiments demonstrating empathy is called the "dictator game." Designed to examine people's willingness to be generous with others—indeed, their *need* to be generous—it's not actually a game at all, in the strictest sense of the word. It doesn't involve any interaction between people, so there is no strategy to it, nor is there any decision making based on outsmarting or second-guessing some other player. Instead, in the dictator game two people are identified who don't know each other and are unlikely to have any future contact. The first is designated as the "dictator" and given a sum of money by the experimenters. The dictator then decides how much money, if any, he or she will give to the second person, and the experiment is concluded. The second person makes no decision at all, and the only role he or she plays is that of a passive recipient of the first person's largesse. The question being explored with this experiment, of course, is just how large a typical person's largesse is likely to be, under a variety of different circumstances. A purely self-interested, nonempathetic dictator would give nothing, keeping all the money himself. But repeated experiments under varying conditions show that a majority of people do not choose to keep all the money but freely share some portion of it, averaging around 20 percent.[4]

It's almost certainly an evolutionary advantage for our species that individual human beings have empathy, making it easier and more efficient for us to cooperate in finding food and preserving our joint lineage. Empathy plays a major role in the fact that we are social animals to begin with, and it is the fact that we are social that accounts, more than anything else (more, even, than our individual intelligence), for our civilization and technology.

In *How We Decide*, Jonah Lehrer reports on another dictator game experiment in which brain imaging was used:

> . . . *a few dozen people were each given $128 of real money and allowed to choose between keeping the money and donating it to charity. When they chose to give away the money, the reward centers of their brains became active and they experienced the delightful glow of unselfishness. In fact, several subjects showed more reward-related brain activity during acts of altruism than they did when they actually received cash rewards.*

Lehrer adds: "From the perspective of the brain, it literally was better to give than to receive."[5]

So science has demonstrated fairly conclusively that empathy is a key motivation for human beings, having evolved in us for some reason almost certainly related to furthering our success as a social species. People have empathy not just because they expect to benefit themselves, per se, and not just because of some complex calculation or rational assessment of their own long-term self-interest, but also because empathy is a natural impulse. It is an *instinct*, hardwired into the human brain.[6]

The same technology that is driving up our rate of interaction is almost certainly raising the general level of empathy we have for others as well. Concern for others increases as people become more interdependent and a society gets to be more advanced. In primitive societies, genuine empathy might be limited to blood relatives or maybe tribe members. With the Industrial Revolution and the invention of the modern nation-state, patriotism became a widely respected virtue, while tribalism was disdained as backward. And as we continue to become ever more electronically interconnected, with geographic boundaries declining in importance, we can already see that patriotism itself is losing some of its former luster. There can be little doubt about the direction of change. Some sociologists point out that modern advocates for animal rights are an example of empathy being extended beyond our own species.[7]

Still, it will be a gradual and uneven process. Even today, tribalism weighs heavily in many African and Middle Eastern societies, while family ties remains the primary glue for many modern Asian business organizations—even giant ones. And we can't forget that for some reason about 1 to 2 percent of people get severely shortchanged in the empathy department. These are the people who are born with so little natural empathy as to be considered borderline personalities (that is, on the border between sane and psychopathic). It's interesting that when "normal" people encounter psychopaths and borderline personalities, they are usually astounded. They just cannot fathom how it could be possible for someone to show no feeling for the impact his or her actions have on others. They don't "get it," and so they don't believe it could be true. In *Evil Genes*, Barbara Oakley argues that "the worst of all human crimes—genocide—often occurs simply because people can't believe that heretofore noncriminal humans can perpetrate horrendous acts such as mass murder or gratuitous torture." Healthy, empathetic people fall into two classes, according to Oakley: those who have been personally victimized by a nonempathetic person, and those who have not. Only the victims, she says, truly grasp the ruthlessness and self-interested "evil" that a complete lack of empathy represents.

You don't have to be psychopathic to be a mobster, or a con man, or a drug trafficker. There are many gradations of empathy. Prior to the 2008 financial crisis there were some on Wall Street who cynically benefited from the financial bubble while fully expecting the party to end painfully for others, but this doesn't mean they were psychopathic, or even borderline. As an emotion, empathy is based on many nonrational inputs. Our empathy for someone else will depend partly on the closeness we feel to them and the type of action being considered. Taking home a big bonus for putting together a securitized bundle of subprime mortgages even though it's likely to go bad in the future is one thing, while raising your M1 rifle, aiming at another human being's head, and pulling the trigger is another thing entirely.

The fact that empathy is a natural and increasingly important driver of human behavior overall doesn't change the fact that people are diverse, and some have less empathy than others. (We've been advocating customer differentiation for years. Perhaps now, instead of looking only at the ways customers are different in (1) their values to the organization, and (2) their needs from the organization, companies will eventually be looking for ways to predict which current and future customers have no conscience, in order to protect the organization's employees, other customers, and shareholders from these personalities!)

As interesting as all this is, it only becomes compelling when we come to understand what it has to do with our business strategy. We'll see that more clearly in the next few chapters.

Chapter 24

The Social Role of Empathy and Trust

Normal, empathetic people crave social connection and trust so much that they become upset, irritated, and sometimes outraged when confronted with what they perceive as lack of empathy in others, in the form of unfair or unjust actions. Most of us are not only willing to punish others who aren't trustable, but we take pleasure in it. Social, empathetic people derive satisfaction from righting or avenging wrongs, and this human tendency contributes immensely to the success of our social structures. It's also one of the reasons trustability is going to emerge as the primary structural issue facing brands, marketing, and boardrooms.

The structure of a social network can be made more stable and trustable—and therefore more productive—when there is an appropriate mix of roles played by its participants, from producers of value or creators of content, to editors and curators, to punishers and enforcers. The right mix will ensure that cheaters and bad operators—the nontrustable few—never get too far before being restrained by the "system" or the network. In a stable social system, untrustable participants aren't able to gain traction as fast as those who are trustable. Over time, as interaction continues to reinforce and feed on itself, empathy and trust will inevitably increase in value to everyone. The result is that the companies we buy from will be held to an ever higher standard, and this new standard will probably materialize much faster than most companies are ready for today.

The world we live in and raise our children in just works better—for us, too—when we play fair in it. Here's how Martha explained it to her son when he asked how it could work at the newsstand where people paid $2 on the honor system and picked up a newspaper. She told him that if they just stole a paper this week, as they surely could, they'd get a free newspaper for a day or two. But in exchange for cheating the newsstand out of a few bucks, they'd pretty much guarantee that in the future, once they had to pay the $2 again, they'd have to stand in a long line to do it. And, whether they were ever found out to have stolen the paper themselves or not, they'd have to live with the uncomfortable knowledge (a "guilty feeling") that they were personally responsible for having imposed the same inconvenience on dozens or hundreds of others as well.

Although this book is about proactive trustability in business settings, we could have long discussions about the applicability to governments, nonprofit organizations, schools and colleges, and other human institutions. Seattle often makes the list of top ten most livable cities in the United States, cited for having a high percentage of residents who recycle, volunteer, and learn CPR—all activities you engage in to make lives better for the collective, not just for yourself. And Japan, one of the most socially cohesive of all national cultures, showed a remarkable spirit of community following the earthquake and tsunami in March 2011. Rather than the looting and the breakdown in civil order that often follows such a disaster, Japanese citizens actually returned wallets and safes that had washed up onshore, with the cash still in them! More than $48 million in wallet cash and $30 million locked inside some 5,700 safes were voluntarily returned by the finders to their rightful owners.[1]

Our own well-being is wrapped up in the well-being of our society, and empathy for others is a social stimulant, a catalyst for collective welfare. As a result, the more technology facilitates the "social" aspect of our lives, the more selfless most of us will become. Being able to feel others' pain unconsciously is one of the most important building blocks of empathy, and for everyone but the psychopath it is a natural-born ability.[2]

Chapter 25

Psychopathic Capitalism

Human beings may seldom act out of purely "rational" self-interest, but what about companies? A corporation is legally chartered to create wealth for its owners, and failing to work on behalf of creating shareholder value would seem to be an abdication of management's fiduciary duties. However, in any modern economy a successful company is also a complex organization with multiple stakeholders, including not just shareholders but also employees, customers, and the communities in which it operates. From a practical standpoint, a company must be careful not to ignore the interests of its nonshareholder constituents precisely because doing so could threaten shareholder value. Abusing employees, the community, or the environment could easily lead to costly regulations or legal conflicts.

While there is no union movement or environmental group championing the rights of customers, the discipline of competition has always been considered a sufficient check. Fail to respect your customers' interests, and you will be competed out of business, or so the argument goes. And for the most part it's proved correct. Case in point: AOL's steep decline, which as we've noted was almost certainly hastened by its aggressively self-interested dealings with customers. At the height of its fortunes several years ago, in an effort to overcome the looming technological obsolescence of dial-up connections, AOL tried to reinvent itself as an advertising-supported content company. Regardless of the technical merits of this effort, the initiative didn't pay off very significantly, and the company certainly wasn't helped by the poor state of its customer relationships.

By contrast, consider how a trustable company might have fared when faced with such an existential threat. Apple, for instance, has had no trouble at all moving its business into music retailing, interactivity, and even mobile phones. And Amazon's original bookselling business is now just a small part of an enterprise that includes all sorts of other retailing categories, as well as a considerable range of business services. It's doubtful that either of these companies could have made such transitions without having first earned the trust and support of their customers.

A trustable firm will find empathy returned by the customers themselves. You don't have to count your change when you're dealing with a real friend. When an untrustable company pursues immediate economic gain to the exclusion of all other considerations, however, we could make a direct analogy with the human psychopath, oblivious to how his actions affect the feelings of those around him. And while only a few of us may ever have been victimized by a psychopathic person, all of us interact regularly with at least a few "psychopathic" companies and brands. We have become so accustomed to nonempathetic customer "service," in fact, that we do not even consider it abnormal. But as standards improve, nonempathetic companies will become rare, then rarer, then endangered, and eventually extinct.

A trustable company with policies in place that demonstrate good intentions toward its customers is likely also to have those good intentions reflected in other domains as well—human resources, investor relations, community participation, and so forth. The surest way to teach managers and employees to deal with customers the way they'd like to be dealt with themselves is to have them practice by treating each other in the same empathetic way.

Untrustable companies, on the other hand, see customers first and foremost as objects with pocketbooks, rather than as close business partners with individual needs. Customers are simply inanimate steppingstones on the way to generating the immediate profits that feed the company's own interest. And in the psychopathology of an untrustable company, it's not too far a step from treating customers as objects to treating its employees or its communities the same way—or even, in extreme cases, the shareholders themselves.

Michael Schrage has recommended a litmus test for companies that are thinking about trustability. Are your best and most valuable customers dumb, uneducated, or not paying attention? (If the answer is yes, then you should engage in a little self-analysis of your business model.) AOL may like 'em stupid, but no trustable company should.[1]

At this revision, the latest demonstration of psychopathic capitalism is being dissected in the press as Volkswagen scrambles to recover the customer and shareholder trust it squandered by installing software intentionally designed to cheat on diesel emission tests. The company has just announced it will be recalling 8.5 million cars in the European Union, out of an estimated 11 million cars sold worldwide with the emissions-cheating software (including nearly 500,000 cars in the United States). The cost of this recall will be enormous, of course, and the company may also find it necessary to compensate customers for the loss in value of the cars they bought in good faith from this iconic brand. Dealers were harmed as well. Preliminary reports indicate that over a period of at least seven years the company intentionally altered emissions-cheating software programs so as to modify the testing data for four different engines. There is no reliable estimate yet of how many people at the firm knew of this deception, but it had to have involved dozens, if not hundreds, of engineers and technicians, financial executives, and managers. What is remarkable is that the cheating was eventually discovered by an outside party, and not revealed by an inside whistle-blower at some point in the last seven years.[2] When employees and senior managers team up to defraud customers, they are undermining the very purpose of their business, and scandals like these call into question the long-term wisdom of incentive compensation plans based on sales, profits, and other short-term financial metrics.[3]

This kind of psychopathology on the part of businesses is no longer tolerated by customers, who take delight in exposing and punishing the unfair or nonempathetic actions of companies they discover to be untrustable. According to one survey, more than 60 percent of those who read about a bad customer service experience online stop or avoid doing business with the company involved. Another survey showed that 79 percent of customers who had a negative customer experience told others about it, 85 percent said they wanted to warn others about their bad experiences, and 66 percent wanted to dissuade others from doing business with the offending brand. Some 76 percent indicated that word of mouth had influenced their purchasing decisions.

In the e-social world, companies will be expected to act toward their customers the way most people act toward other people—with empathy. Violators will be prosecuted.

What do trustable companies look like?

■ Jacquielawson.com, a clever e-cards site, invites you to sign up for automatic renewal with your credit card, but pings you before your credit card gets hit with the renewal: "Your membership of jacquielawson.com is due for renewal on 28 July. When you last joined or renewed, you selected the option for automatic renewal, so unless you instruct us otherwise we will renew your membership using the same card details as before. The annual membership fee is $14.00 and this will be charged to your card on 28 Jul. For further assistance, including instructions on how to change the credit card details we hold for you, please go to http://www.jacquielawson.com/help_7.asp."

■ At Ally Bank (formerly GMAC Bank), customers are proactively reminded if they have funds in an account that could be earning higher interest, no depositor is ever charged for moving money from a savings account to a checking account in order to cover an overdraft, and the bank reimburses customers for ATM fees charged to them by other banks. According to Sanjay Gupta, former chief marketing officer, Ally Bank's "three pillars" of customer service are to "do right, talk straight, and be obviously better," and it would hardly be possible to define a brand's positioning in a more trustable way.[5] As a nationwide direct bank, without brick-and-mortar branches, Ally Bank doesn't take cash deposits but provides postage-paid envelopes for mailing checks in for deposit, and it allows customers to scan their checks and e-mail them to the bank for immediate deposit.[6] Every page on Ally Bank's website has a toll-free 24/7 phone number clearly displayed, along with an estimate of "call wait time," and one of the very first options when calling in is to speak to a live person. In addition, Ally Bank has introduced customer reviews for all its various banking products and services.[7] According to Gupta, the process had to be vetted in order to ensure that customer reviews were authentic, nonabusive, and so forth, but a "Customer Review" tab now shows on all product pages on the bank's website, and there are literally hundreds of reviews available.[8] Asked how it was that Ally Bank seemed able to sustain its business following the implementation of new consumer-protection regulations without having to raise fees or introduce new ones, the way other banks had tried to do (including Bank of America's highly publicized $5 debit card fee, for instance, later withdrawn due to overwhelming consumer outrage),[9] Gupta explained: "We just set out to build a business model that didn't depend on fees. We take deposits and we lend out money, and we make money on the spread. I guess you could say we have old school values but leverage today's technology."[10]

■ A friend's daughter was moving a few blocks to a new apartment in Chicago. Her rental truck was due back to the garage at 5:00 P.M., but at 4:30 Kate was caught in afternoon traffic, still needing to unload the last of her things and get the truck back to the rental company. Her cell phone rang. "How's it going?" asked the rental company. Kate was dreading the need to pay another day's fee for being a few minutes late. "Don't worry," said the company rep. "Drive safely. Take your time. We'll be here till six and don't need the truck before then." Who does Amanda recommend to her friends who are moving?

■ At a speaking event we did in Mexico City, a teenager ran up to us and enthused, "I know what you're talking about! I got a text

from my cell phone company that said my mom could save money
if I were on a different plan since I send so many texts! Can you
believe it? They helped us save money!" Telcel would have to really screw up to lose this customer, who tells everybody how fair
the company is and will be a loyal customer for decades.

Customers who trust companies remain loyal to them. According to
Forrester Research, the attribute that creates more customer loyalty than
any other is "the perception on the part of customers that the firm does
what's best for them, not just for the firm's own bottom line."

Chapter 26

Putting on a Human Face

And so we return to where we began this section: with the fact that trust is as trust does. Your ability to trust a company can be inferred only by observing its actions.

The argument we've been making about good intentions requires us to examine a company's actions as if the company were really a person, with a mind of its own, rather than just a legal entity. If a firm appears to demonstrate empathy for others, if it appears to consider their interests and not just its own, then people are more likely to conclude that the company is trustable. This means appearances do matter. No matter how good the management team's *actual* intentions are at a company, if no actions can be observed, there will be no basis on which customers can judge the company to be trustable.

There is an important lesson here for companies trying to figure out how to appear to be more trustable to customers, so as to compete more successfully with other companies: In order to look trustable, you must put on a human face. You have to behave in a way that demonstrates empathy, and this means your managers and employees have to behave this way. When thinking about customers, try thinking about them as your partners in a relationship that benefits both of you. When you make decisions for your company, you must ask yourself: What action would a friend take toward a friend in this situation, and is there any reason your company shouldn't proceed this way?

Raj Sisodia, David B. Wolfe, and Jag Sheth, authors of the book *Firms of Endearment*, suggest that one important aspect of demonstrating your firm's essential humanity is not to shy away from showing vulnerability when that's appropriate.[1] We don't normally expect companies to talk frankly about their own problems, or to admit to their own vulnerabilities.

The problem is that admitting vulnerability or any kind of fallibility at all is anathema to most companies, leading to something that consultant and business author John Hagel has called "the trust paradox." He suggests that the very activities a company undertakes to improve its trustworthiness in the eyes of its customers and prospective customers have the perverse effect of undermining their trust. When a brand promotes only its benefits, he says, while simply ignoring any problems or weaknesses, it defies belief, and asks:

> . . . what is our reaction when someone presents an image of great strength and complete control, with no weaknesses? We don't trust them . . . If someone only presents strengths and accomplishments, we know they are not sharing with us the full picture. If they don't trust us enough to share their weaknesses and vulnerabilities, why would we ever trust them?[2]

We can't blame companies for being reluctant to share weaknesses with customers, because exposing a weakness in the wrong context can sometimes lead directly to a lawsuit. But as direct interactions between companies and consumers increase in number, with blogs, Twitter, Facebook, YouTube, and other mechanisms, consumers have shown an increasing willingness to give the benefit of the doubt to those companies that do show a more "human" face to their customers.

There's a bonus to putting on a human face. When you do, your employees will be proud to be part of your organization. Your employee turnover will go down, since your employees, for the most part, *prefer to do things in a trustable way*, and as you expect them to behave more trustably toward customers, your employees will trust your company more.

But if a psychopath is someone who can't *be* trusted, then what would you call someone who can't *trust*? Control freak. Psychopaths and control freaks are flip sides of the same disorder. *Nobody* can trust a psychopath, and control freaks can't trust *anybody*. However, e-social technologies raise the general standard of trustworthiness for all of us, no matter which side of the interaction we're on. Trustability is an incoming tide lifting all boats. It happens a little unevenly, perhaps, generating a few bumps and collisions here and there, but this incoming tide is driven by Moore's law, and no man can resist Moore's law.

Extending trust to others is a particularly scary idea for executives and managers, stirring up nightmares of cheating, disengaged employees and litigious customers. You can't take the "manage" out of "manager" without creating a feeling of insecurity. Inevitably, the power equation governing commercial transactions will be upended by this incoming tide. As transparency increases and customers know more and more, every advantage a business used to have as a result of one-sided information flow will evaporate. Companies can no longer control the knowledge that gets "out there."

We're going to suggest that business success in the transparent, trustable future is likely to depend just as much on extending trust to others as on being trustable yourself.

4

Do Things Right: Honest Competence

Chapter 27

Competence and Good Intentions Are Joined at the Hip

Good-Nature and Good-Sense must ever join;
To err is human, to forgive divine.

ALEXANDER POPE[1]

On the surface the two primary components of trust—good intentions and competence—would seem to be two completely different and independent qualities. Intention is a state of mind, and as we've already said, since we can't read minds, the only way we can get any indication of someone else's intent is by inferring it from their words and actions. We judge their intent by what we would intend ourselves, if we were to speak or act in a similar way.[2]

"Competence," on the other hand, is not a state of mind at all but a demonstrable talent or capability. A competent firm executes well, has reliable and disciplined people carrying out its policies, and doesn't make stupid mistakes. Proficiency and competence are directly observable. And they are an important part of the "customer experience"—how it feels to be a company's customer. Delivering a better, more frictionless customer experience is the reason you connect your siloed databases in the first place. It's why you send your people to seminars on mobile best practices, and increase your company's efficiency so you can save your customers time and help them find and get what they need without any roadblocks, at a fair price.

The truth is, however, that while competence may seem to be more visible than good intentions, it is still a quality that has to be deliberately built over time. Companies don't just spring into existence fully capable of good service, high-quality production, and customer insight. To become competent requires some amount of deliberation and intent on the company's part. Without good intentions, it's doubtful that a firm would actually go to the trouble to build up enough competence to treat customers fairly, or "do things right."

Or, turning the question around, suppose you buy from a company that promises it will always respect your interest, but when dealing with their customer service representatives you find that they don't understand your problem, they can't answer the phone in less than five minutes, their right hand doesn't know what the left is doing, they can't remember your specifications from last time, or they treat every customer exactly the same, you included. They screw up a lot, and even though they act nice and *mean* well, it's just too difficult to do business with them. There's so much friction in their customer experience that you can't rely on them. In this situation, you'd have to find yourself asking just how good their intentions could actually be, right? If they *really* intended to protect your interests, wouldn't they have made a little more effort?[3]

Consider Netflix's fumbled effort to separate the DVD and streaming video business in 2011 while also introducing a significant price increase. What aroused customers' ire was the fact that the company appeared to have disregarded customer sentiment altogether in making its pricing move. It might have been incompetence, or it might have been bad intentions, but customer trust evaporated almost overnight in any case.[4]

In retrospect, Netflix could have done things differently, and the outcome might not have been so bad for them. In the first place, every junior marketer knows that price reductions should be dramatic and significant, while price increases should be small and incremental. It's almost a certainty that Netflix's own marketing people would have argued strenuously in favor of that kind of a strategy, but the technologists and engineers running the company (including CEO Hastings, a mathematician and computer scientist himself) must have overridden this advice. More important, however, all Netflix's customers are monthly subscribers, most of whom were at the time actively engaged in mailing DVDs back and forth to the company, or connecting directly to the company's website in order to schedule their streaming videos. In other words, Netflix's customers interact with the firm on a regular basis. Some had already subscribed for years, having deserted Blockbuster for a company they felt was more reasonable (and more trustable), but Netflix never once acknowledged this loyalty or familiarity. Here was a direct-marketing business with vast details on people's movie-viewing habits, behaviors, and tastes, and yet, when the change came, Netflix treated every customer exactly the same as every other customer! Instead of treating everyone the same, what if Netflix had announced its price increase with even a rudimentary amount of special treatment to provide a small benefit to the customers who had been with the company the longest, or who had used it the most, or who had recommended other customers? What if the announcement from Hastings had said something like: "Hey, in two months we have to increase our prices, but if you've been our customer for two years or more, then we won't increase *your* price until this time next year, and thanks for your loyalty!" Even a nominal offer like this, had it been aimed at those customers most involved with the company, would have had a dramatic impact on how Netflix was perceived by everyone.

Or, once the social conflagration flared up, consider what might have happened if, in his apology e-mail, Reed Hastings had said: "We at Netflix want to continue the DVD-rental business economically, but our pricing for DVDs and for streaming videos needs to reflect the very real fact that our costs are quite different for providing those two types of service to you. We're going to put off any price or service change for six months, and during that time we'd like your support in helping us to design a different business model that will be able to support both DVDs and streaming video, so our customers can continue seeing movies the way each of you wants to. If you'd like to help us work on this problem, we'd greatly appreciate your ideas. The job doesn't pay anything, but if you are the first to suggest any idea that we end up using, we'll give you a lifetime membership. . . ."

Whether Netflix fumbled the ball on account of bad marketing advice, or bad planning, or simply arrogance, or most likely just getting caught up in the day-to-day interests of the company and putting that ahead of the interests of the consumer, customers looked at the result and just scratched their heads, many of them more mystified than irate. They didn't want to believe that this company they once loved had had selfish intentions all along. They wanted to give it the benefit of the doubt. But competence *does* matter. You can't maintain your customers' trust if you aren't even competent enough to handle a simple price increase. And as Netflix learned, once you violate your customers' trust, it could take years before you get your mojo back.

Because a company's intentions can be inferred only from its actions, it has to be at least somewhat competent in its actions if it wants people to be able to see its good intentions. If it stumbles in an obvious or careless way, or if its actions show little regard for the competent serving of customers and respect for customers' needs and time and effort, then its intentions will definitely be called into question. Competence and good intentions, in other words, are not separate ideas at all; they are joined at the hip.

Chapter 28

Product Competence and Customer Competence

To remain competitive, a company needs to make and deliver a quality product or service, and it needs to understand and relate to the customer being sold to. We can call these two basic capabilities *product* competence and *customer* competence, and both are critical. Product competence means your company delivers a reasonably good product or service, on time, in such a way that it doesn't need a lot of maintenance, repair, correction, or undue attention from the customer just to meet the need or solve the problem it is designed to handle. Customer competence requires your company to understand the customer's individual needs and address them, and interact with the customer smoothly and efficiently.

Do things right.

When we talk about product competence, we're not just talking about the physical product, if there is one, but we're including whatever service is required. Fashioning the "offer" for a customer requires organizing the firm, procuring the resources, running a factory, scheduling jobs, managing and training people, keeping the books, evaluating investments, and deploying capital. There was a time, perhaps, when product quality varied so much among companies that simply delivering a quality product could often differentiate a business, and history is full of well-meaning companies that failed on account of product incompetence.

Today, however, no business can persist for long without having relatively high-quality products—that is, products that do what the firm says they're going to do and don't break or malfunction with normal use. There are varieties in terms of quality and pricing in most categories, but competition is a great leveler. Without pricing differences, it would be impossible to remain in business with lower-than-normal quality. Instead, a company has to have product and service quality that is generally on a par with its immediate competitive set, and this standard has increased enough over the last century that it's hard today to find truly substandard products in most developed economies. Subquality products just aren't around long enough to be an issue. If you don't have at least a basic level of product competence, your business won't be operating for very long and, of course, no one is going to trust you either.

Instead, the sort of competence most often lacking in a business nowadays has to do with *customer* competence—insight into what the customer actually needs (as opposed to what he's buying), how he sees the world, and how he's different from other customers, along with the ability to act on that insight by treating different customers differently. In short, most businesses are just not very competent when it comes to *empathizing* with their customers.

When a customer decides to buy a product or service of any kind, it's not because he is enamored with the physical product or the elements of service. It's not because he loves your store or your website or even your friendly people. The basis of the customer's motivation is that he has some need to be met, or some problem to be solved, and he believes you have the competence to do it. Your product or service is simply his tool for accomplishing the task. As Clayton Christensen famously suggests, your customer is simply hiring your product to do a job. Customer competence involves the skill to truly understand what job the customer is actually trying to get accomplished, *from the customer's own perspective.*[1]

When Cigna made a commitment to become a more "trusted" organization, the health-care industry was not particularly in popular favor. So making a shift to build advocacy for and by customers promised to become a serious journey. The first step Cigna took was simply to consider the customers' point of view about the language used in the company's communications with customers, which didn't match the vocabulary Cigna employees usually used. For example, customers like to be called "customers," and not "patients." And rather than hearing about a "health-care provider," customers would rather use the words "doctor" or "nurse." More than two hundred terms required similar replacement and overhaul, and internally Cigna employees docked each other when someone used the old terms instead of the customer-friendly ones. But the results were dramatic: The number of customers who understood how Cigna's business worked for them more than doubled, increasing in excess of 100 percent, while the volume of explanatory materials Cigna had to send out to members fell by more than 50 percent, reducing costs and improving the customer experience.[2]

One innovative health insurance company in South Africa, Discovery Life, offers a special program called Vitality, which members purchase to get deep discounts on wellness benefits, such as free gym visits (which are only free provided the member makes a certain minimum use of the gym!). According to Kenny Rabson, deputy CEO of Discovery Life, "The positive impact of Vitality on mortality and morbidity is significant, and it is in fact exceeding expectations, particularly in the first years of a policy's lifetime." Discovery encourages healthy behavior that reduces long-term health-care costs by rewarding members for improving their health, and it's been clinically proved that Vitality members have lower health-care costs than nonmembers. In the United States, Humana has teamed up with Discovery to launch a similar program, "Humana Vitality,"[3] providing incentives and rewards to members in order to encourage them to maintain healthier habits and lifestyles. In essence, a trustable health-care company will be expected to make recommendations to customers that will improve their health and *reduce* their premiums, something that makes more economic sense for payers following the passage of the Affordable Care Act.[4]

Before assembly lines and mass production, when virtually all commerce involved face-to-face interactions with merchants, the best merchants were those who maintained the strongest relationships with their customers, remembering their personal specifications and attending to their needs with care. The highly efficient mass-marketing disciplines that characterized most of the last century meant that this sort of personalized service became far too expensive to be competitive, but computer technology has once again made it possible. Today we might call it customer experience management, or managing customer relationships, or CRM, or one-to-one marketing, or customer value management, or customer centricity—but no matter what you call it, the fact is that to be competitive today a company has to have some degree of customer competence, *in addition to* product competence.

To be competitive today, a company needs to be able to empathize with customers more effectively, to take the customer's perspective, to know what it feels like to "be our customer." What it *should* feel like.[5] As with product competence, competitive success doesn't require a firm to be the very best at remembering and interacting with customers individually, but it does require that it not be significantly behind its competitors.

Although we just said that simply maintaining a par performance for product and customer competence should be good enough, we should also stipulate that *most* firms could still generate a substantial financial benefit for themselves simply by improving their performance in either area. Both types of competence are required in order to satisfy customers. And consumer research shows that while improvements in customer satisfaction do generate modest improvements in customer loyalty, what *really* generates greater loyalty and therefore financial return is reducing or eliminating customer *dis*satisfaction. Rather than figuring out how to do a better and better job of "surprise and delight" for customers, in other words, most firms would be better advised to concentrate simply on eliminating the friction in their customer experience—obstacles, nuisances, redundancies, or extra work on the customer's part. To be trustable, a company needs to empathize, take the customer's point of view, and figure out how to make it easy to be a customer.[6]

Forget about "surprise and delight." Just don't screw up.[7]

Most companies that customers see as being "competent"—as "doing things right"—either have already embraced customer centricity as a primary business driver or are in the process of doing so now. They recognize that customers are the only source of revenue (by definition), that customers are a scarce asset (likely the scarcest and least replaceable), and that customers create long-term value as well as short-term value. If you want to be customer-competent enough to be trustable, then you must:

- Treat different customers differently, based on what they need from you and what their value is to you;

- Rather than focusing on one product at a time and trying to find customers for that product, focus on one customer at a time and try to find products for that customer;

- Get smarter over time with customers, by building Learning Relationships—that is, by steadily enriching the context of your relationship with each individual customer;[8]

- Ask what customers want and would be willing to pay for that they can't get from anyone for any price (not you, not your competitors); and

- Build customer-based metrics, including lifetime value, customer profitability, and customer equity, into the evaluations of employees and business units.

There's more to it than this, of course. All we're talking about in the bullet points above is the *stuff you have to do*. We haven't even addressed the issue of *how to get it done*, and that's a very big issue to address. When clients ask us difficult questions about how to get this stuff done, we often tell them that no matter how good your computer systems, analytics, and work processes are, you can't just write a line of code or a process requirement that will result in earning a customer's trust. Customers don't trust processes, business rules, or bureaucracies. Customers trust people.

So one aspect of trustability is simply putting on a more human face—
a face designed to show empathy, to be fallible, to embrace creativity and
humor, and to relate to others. But another aspect of it is having the kind
of people at your firm who *want* to be trustable, who embrace the goal of
being trustable and will push your organization toward it.

Chapter 29

Honest Competence Requires Honestly Competent People

Culture eats strategy for breakfast.

WARREN BUFFETT[1]

You can't earn the trust of your customers with a policy statement. You can earn trust only with actions. The problem is that the "actions" your company takes are taken by employees, not by the CEO or the board of directors. As far as a customer is concerned, the ordinary, low-level customer-contact employee he or she interacts with on the phone or at the store—that employee *is* your company.

If you want to ensure that your company treats each customer the way you'd want to be treated if you were the customer yourself, then you need to think about the way individual employees deal with and interact with customers. Obviously, policies and practices will be involved, but by themselves they won't be sufficient. What you really need is a culture within your company that celebrates earning the trust of customers. Or as Susan Whiting, former vice chair at the Nielsen Company, says:

> *Connect "do good" with your brand. Make it business as usual to secure the website, be a good citizen, achieve sustainability. And do it right. For many companies, that will be even harder than doing the right thing. But it's impossible, really, to separate the importance of serving shareholders from the importance of serving the customers. How can you make life better, simpler, easier, more rewarding for clients?[2]*

The problem is that "culture" is one of those things that is very diffi-cult to pin down exactly. A lot of management teams latch on to the idea of "culture" and try to codify it and popularize it within the firm, but writing a values statement for your company is not at all the same thing as living it, nor will it have much impact on your real-world culture. We once visited a company that had a written set of official company values, and these values were posted throughout headquarters, along with the company's mission statement. You've probably seen stuff like this before (who hasn't?), but to protect the identity of this client, we'll just para-phrase the top line of the posted "statement of values," which went some-thing like this:

We always do the right thing for customers.

Now doesn't that sound just terrific? That's a great attitude to take to-ward customers, the market, and the business's overall purpose. It's a marvelous statement of values for a forward-thinking, customer-oriented company. Yet the more employees and middle managers we met, the more it became clear to us that everyone in the organization was focused on one thing: Make this quarter's numbers at any cost. These managers' daily actions and decisions supported a different set of values—a set of values that weren't written down and posted on the wall but which per-meated the culture and dominated how the company decided which ac-tions were right and wrong. The *real*, unwritten value statement, if it had been posted on the wall, would have read:

We always do whatever it takes to make this quarter's numbers.

So far, we haven't read about this firm being involved in any kind of scandal, industrial safety failure, or customer service meltdown. But our guess is that the only reason we haven't is that the company just hasn't encountered any serious threat to its quarterly bottom line yet. Sooner or later, however, the company is likely to meet such a problem, and when it does, it will fail the test. And then everyone will wonder how a company with such marvelous values could have acted in such a self-centered, uncaring fashion toward its customers, employees, or shareholders.

The culture at your firm will reflect how you measure success, how you reward people, what tasks you consider to be important, how quickly and effectively you make decisions, and who approves decisions. Your culture will reflect how friendly people are to others, how trusting they are, how much disagreement is tolerated, and what actions are considered out of bounds. Your company's culture will trump any rules, defeat any controls, and trample over any conflicting processes. "Culture, more than rule books, determines how an organization behaves" is how Warren Buffett put it. In other words, you can write down your firm's values, and even codify them in an employee manual, but if you want the company to live up to them, then you'd better ensure not just that your systems, rules, and processes are aligned with your values but that your *people* really believe in them and are rewarded when they act on them. Really.

A company's culture can be either good or bad for the business, either a "long-lasting competitive advantage, difficult for your competitors to duplicate, or a giant albatross with bad breath hung around your corporate neck."[3] It is your company's culture that maintains the permanence of your organization. People will come and go, business initiatives will thrive and perish, but the unspoken rules that permeate your company are a *social* phenomenon, passed on from employee to employee, aided and abetted by compensation formulas, expectations, and social protocols. Dov Seidman says it is through their cultures that "companies have the opportunity to grow more varied and diverse while simultaneously remaining tightly aligned in a common purpose."[4]

Although culture permeates an entire organization from top to bottom to top, what a company's senior managers expect of employees, what they say, and how they behave will have a pronounced influence. Creating a culture in which honest competence will succeed requires leading by example.[5] If you want employees to treat customers the way they'd like to be treated if they were the customers, then treat your employees the way you'd like to be treated if you were the employee.

Company "culture" is what employees do when no one's looking.

As a leader, you should never shrink from an opportunity to stand up for your company's values. Consider the hypothetical effect of the alternative:

DEAR ABBY,

A colleague in my company is responsible for selling professional services to our corporate clients—usually large companies. He's very successful and has built his division into a high-growth business in just the few years he's managed it.

But there is something very unsettling to me about the way my friend deals with his clients. When I'm with him and he gets a business call on his cell phone, he has absolutely no regard for the truth when it comes to telling his own managers what to say to a client. In pricing negotiations, for instance, I've heard him suggest complete and utter lies, such as "tell the client this is absolutely our biggest possible discount, because the head office forbids us to undercut the rest of the company" (untrue), or "tell them the hourly rate can't be reduced on this contract because of our prior contractual obligation to this subject matter expert" (also untrue).

I've noticed that even in our casual discussions, when so much as a minor inconvenience is threatened, my friend might make up a totally bogus excuse for dealing with it. To overcome a scheduling conflict I've heard him tell his secretary to call the client and tell them he got delayed on his flight (he didn't), or that his boss unexpectedly convened a must-attend senior-staff phone meeting (not so). What bothers me most about these overheard comments is the complete casualness with which my friend bends, twists, and undermines the truth. Not only does he show no remorse whatsoever, but in many cases I've heard him suggest a lie when it wouldn't really have been much more trouble just to explain the truth carefully.

Am I a prude here? What should I do?

Signed, Honestly Stumped

Chapter 30

Self-Organizing Employees and Trust Platforms

In the hyperinteractive, e-social future, the only kind of company or organization that will be able to survive will be one that is fueled by the trust and empathy that flow among independently acting human employees. This will mean less reliance on top-down, hierarchical, command-and-control management principles and more on bottom-up, values-based self-organization. When a customer problem occurs, and a number of employees zero in on it, take ownership of it, and figure out on their own how to solve it with no top-down direction or management intervention—that constitutes "self-organization," and mutual trust among employees is a minimum requirement.

Forward-thinking companies are already doing this. In 2015, one financial services company in Australia tested a highly original idea with respect to empowering rank-and-file employees to take action on their own initiative. Basically, when a problem arises that might require an exception to prescribed policy in order to satisfy the customer, the worker trying to solve the problem is encouraged to come up with a creative resolution that he or she thinks is appropriate, even if it might be "out of policy."[1] But then, before being authorized to apply that solution, the worker is required to seek the agreement of at least one other customer-facing employee, who will also sign on to the action. The company says that whenever two customer-facing employees both agree that a particular unique or different solution to some customer issue is the right way to proceed, even if it is technically out of policy, then the solution will be automatically approved by the company and reviewed later to see if it might have broader application. It's a test program for now and hasn't yet been rolled out to the whole employee population, but as this paperback went to press, the results were promising.

The truth is, employees are very insightful about whether companies are trustable and how to make them better. They know whether they trust the companies they work for and whether customers should trust the company the employees work for. (At Trustability Metrix, we measure these employee perceptions as one way of understanding company integrity, confirmed by Professor Luigi Guiso of the Einaudi Institute for Economics and Finance.*)

Ultimately, of course, the plummeting cost of human interaction will not just change the nature of a corporation's activities but *will call into question the need for the corporation at all.* Companies exist because they enable people to interact more efficiently for the purpose of creating value collectively. But we're already seeing that as frictionless interactivity increases, the number of tasks directly taken on by companies is declining. The dramatic upsurge in outsourcing and partnering with other firms (including, sometimes, direct competitors) is only the beginning. Over time, firms will increasingly divest themselves of tasks not directly relevant to their most central corporate missions. And in some business arenas, we're already seeing the complete displacement of corporations. Corporate organizations are simply no longer necessary to provide many services.

The year *Extreme Trust* first went to press as a hardcover edition, Uber launched its mobile app in San Francisco.[2] Uber, Airbnb, TaskRabbit, and similar operations are "trust platforms," bringing willing buyers and sellers together while using social commentary and customer feedback as mechanisms for enforcing quality, as we discussed earlier.

Trust, transparency, and punishment have become the key drivers of

---

* As reported in HBR Blog Network by Andrew O'Connell, July 7, 2015, a team led by Luigi Guiso reported that there is no correlation between the stated "values" of companies on their websites and the firms' performance, but that high employee assessments of companies' integrity are associated with higher productivity and profitability.

all kinds of high-growth trust platform business models in just the last few years.

Trust platforms are possible today because interactive technologies efficiently match buyers and sellers of goods or services directly. Each party's ability to trust the other depends not so much on the brand or on some government agency's rules and regulations, but on how other parties have rated them in the past. The system is set up to prevent any ratings trickery. In many cases, the rating is part of the payment process itself. Before you can take your next trip on Uber, for example, you have to rate the previous driver, and this builds a rating for this driver that is immediately accessible to all his or her future riders. Importantly, the driver also rates you, the passenger. So bad behavior by a passenger (for example, trashing the backseat or making a driver wait at the pickup point) will also incur punishment, as future drivers become a bit more wary of doing business with this passenger in the future. (Martha won't get into an Uber whose driver is rated below 4.5. And drivers in a rush-hour snowstorm will only head for the customers who have high ratings too.)[3]

It won't be the company with rules, structures, and detailed compliance mechanisms that succeeds in the future, but the one with employees who *want* their company to succeed—employees (and contractors) who *trust* their company and have *empathy* for its customers.

Competence matters, and you can't be a trustable company if you aren't customer-competent.

Nor can you be trustable for very long if the quality of your product and service isn't on a par with that of your competitors. You should be better, but at a minimum you should be comparable. In many business categories, simply not causing customers grief will go a long way toward making you tops in trustability.

But what if your product really isn't up to par?

Chapter 31

True Confessions: Domino's and the Transparent Pizza

If the customer experience is bad, customers will still talk about it. They'll let others know. But don't expect acknowledgment from the brand. Yes, the marketing department would encourage their company to take steps to improve the experience, but no, no, NO—if the experience isn't good, they certainly won't broadcast the fact. No sane marketing executive would ever call a flawed customer experience to anyone's attention.

In today's highly transparent world, however, an ugly fact like a bad customer experience will no longer go unnoticed just because it isn't advertised. Whether the marketing department acknowledges it or not, people will know. Immediately. Everywhere. Forever.

In April 2009, a couple of rogue Domino's Pizza employees posted a video on YouTube showing one of them doing disgusting things to prepare food, even sticking cheese up his nose before putting it on a pizza.[1] The video was viewed more than a million times in just a few days and soon dominated Google's search results for Domino's Pizza, as well as becoming a trending topic on Twitter. But he who lives by the Tube dies by the Tube. Within hours of having posted their videos the perpetrators were identified by bloggers and others as Kristy Hammonds Thompson and Michael Setzer, employees at the Domino's outlet in Conover, North Carolina. Although the two maintained that none of the food filmed in the video was actually delivered to a customer, they were summarily fired and handed over to Conover police to face felony charges. Moving rapidly to contain the PR disaster, Domino's CEO Patrick Doyle immediately posted his own YouTube apology.

That would have marked the end of the episode, just one more social media headline for a day, except that a much bigger story was about to unfold. More than a year before this incident, Doyle and his marketing people had begun wrestling with the thorny problem of Domino's seemingly poor and outdated product quality, from the blandness of their standard pizza's taste and the processed appearance of its cheese to the sloppiness of its delivery. Domino's had developed a reputation among pizza consumers as the "pizza of last resort," the kind of food delivery you might order if you didn't have enough money to get a good pizza or if there was no Pizza Hut or Godfather's near enough. So, to celebrate the chain's fiftieth anniversary, the company rolled out a completely new and revamped product. More than that, however, to publicize the upgraded product, they launched a television ad campaign frankly admitting to the error of their (past) ways. One of the new commercials, for instance, played clips from focus groups in which participants lambasted their product as "the worst excuse for pizza" they'd ever had, before cutting to CEO Doyle's confession that while his company's pizza had been below standard for years, Domino's was now determined to do better.

Even though the new and improved pizza would still not be confused with a gourmet product, and Domino's certainly wasn't in the same league as some of the trendier, pricier pizza boutiques offering features such as whole-wheat crusts and all organic ingredients, people were nonetheless intrigued by the company's candor.* According to one college senior, for instance, who had himself participated in one of the focus groups panning the previous product, "those ads resonated with me in a way I didn't expect. I mean, they're right: Their pizza's bad. But to be honest like that—it makes you reconsider for a second."[2]

And there was more to come. Six months later Domino's announced it would stop using retouched photos to promote its pizzas, relying instead on straight camera shots, honestly taken—and appealing to customers to

---

* Candor is an important topic in the quest to understand the trustability of companies. See Laura Rittenhouse, *Investing Between the Lines: How to Make Smarter Decisions by Decoding CEO Communications* (McGraw-Hill, 2013), pp. 93–97.

send in their own photos for use in its ads. (*Adweek*'s story about this was headlined: "Domino's last week introduced an industry first: A transparent pizza."[3]) The fact is that Domino's had embraced the power of social media early on, and company executives were already convinced that what customers said to one another mattered more to the brand's product reputation than what the company itself tried to say with its advertising. In the e-social era, they knew that no amount of gloss or bright paint would be able to cover up a weak product. According to Doyle,

> *. . . trying to spin things simply doesn't work anymore. Great brands going forward are going to have a level of honesty and transparency that hasn't been seen before.*

The "Pizza Turnaround" campaign gave Domino's revenues and profitability a nice lift as well, with U.S. same-store sales increasing by nearly 10 percent the following year, a phenomenal increase for the large chain. In fact, it was the first full year of positive growth since 2007, and for at least the first half of 2011 those higher levels of domestic same-store sales were maintained or increased.

Domino's was taking on a serious obligation when it decided to confess its sins. If the newly designed product had not been judged to be of higher quality, the brand's credibility would have plummeted even further and perhaps never recovered. As Doyle himself noted early on, while he was confident that the new product was good, "we also know this works once, and only if the claim is true." Good intentions are important, in other words, but competence still matters. And when you state your intent so openly, you have to be certain that your company has the competence to deliver on it.

As Domino's gained confidence from its policy of transparency, it continued to push the envelope. In an effort to publicize its "Domino's Tracker," an online tool allowing customers to follow the progress of their pizza delivery orders, the company conjured up a unique demonstration of transparency for the summer of 2011. For a full month, from July 25 through August 23, Domino's took over a lighted billboard above Times

Square in New York City and ran a near-real-time feed of candid customer comments about its pizza, taken from the online tool. In announcing the program, Domino's said simply that customer comments made the company better—so both positive and negative comments were going up on the billboard for the whole world to see. And sure enough, while a large majority of comments were positive, sprinkled among the positives were a significant number of negatives as well.[4]

Chapter 32

Fallibility and Trust

Domino's counterintuitive approach to marketing involves a frank admission of fallibility, along with a promise to do better. For traditional marketing professionals, this seemed just crazy, but the craziness itself was something they found appealing. They liked the initiative's novelty, but they still weren't sure it made sense for any company to air its dirty laundry so publicly. In critiquing the Times Square billboard initiative, for example, a columnist for *Adweek* colorfully labeled Domino's broader marketing strategy "stridently self-flagellatory."

And one widely recognized positioning consultant's perspective perfectly illustrates how traditional marketing spin differs so substantially from trustability. Noting first that a marketing strategy promoting authenticity did have its benefits, she referenced the "Real Thing" campaign for Coca-Cola. But, she said, Domino's claim had been undercut by its own Pizza Turnaround effort. "What's more inauthentic than admitting you had a crappy recipe?" she asked. (Interesting question. How about: *not* admitting it?)

The traditional PR and marketing approach to a bad product or service accusation would be to follow the classic CIA dictum: "Admit nothing. Deny everything. Make counteraccusations."[1] If you're a traditional marketer, the basic problem with the whole idea of publicly admitting any kind of error is that the admission undermines whatever artificial reality you've crafted with millions of dollars' worth of spin. Whether or not it's justified, it undercuts your investment. But the only reason an inauthentic—even deceptive—communications strategy has ever actually succeeded in the past is that until recently people mostly *didn't* know your product needed work. So even if *you* knew there was a problem (after all, it's your product, you have most of the research, and you're the one with the satisfaction statistics), admitting to it would simply alert a lot of otherwise in-the-dark customers. In such a world, any admission like that is damning. Deny everything. Make counteraccusations.

Today, however, the world has become so transparent that everybody will already know your product is "crappy," so refusing to admit it yourself is not just inauthentic but downright delusional. In the real world—the *non*marketing world inhabited not by business gurus and marketing experts but by ordinary people constantly interacting with other people—fallibility is the most direct route to trustworthiness. Admitting one's own vulnerability is the first step in earning someone else's trust.

The converse of this, by the way, is that admitting to errors is more acceptable in a more trusting environment. Therefore, if you want a resilient culture at your firm, making your organization capable of innovative experimentation and constant self-improvement, then you would be well advised to create a work environment in which errors are viewed not as political or personal liabilities, but as learning opportunities. Consider, for instance, the unexpected outcome of one study of U.S. nursing home practices during the 1990s. A Harvard Business School researcher found that in those nursing homes characterized by the most respected leadership and the closest, most trusting relationships among workers, the reported error rate was *ten times greater* than in other, comparable institutions with less trusting work environments. The reason, she found, was not that the quality of work was lower. In fact, the actual quality of work was *higher*, but because workers trusted management and each other, they weren't afraid to report mistakes. There were almost certainly many more errors in the nontrusting work environments, but they weren't reported.[2]

An honest work environment—a culture in which people share a unifying set of beliefs and are encouraged to share opinions and self-organize—is the secret sauce of a trustable organization. It is the primary ingredient of organizational competence, and competence is just as important as good intentions in earning the trust of customers.

5

Be Proactive

Chapter 33

Proactive Refunds

Refunds are costly. When you sell a product or service to a customer, you generate revenue from the sale, and some portion of that revenue amounts to profit, which improves your bottom line. But when you issue a refund, often 100 percent of the refund will directly reduce the bottom line. So minimizing the cost of refunds has driven businesses to erect obstacles, such as requiring customers to produce paper receipts, or to go through multiple website screens, or to pay restocking fees, or to call in by phone and wait on hold, rather than engaging in an online session.

Nor will most companies provide a refund unless the customer actually requests one, navigating first through whatever obstacles have been put up to minimize their success rate. When something goes wrong, many companies want to minimize refunds by maximizing the breakage—that is, the refunds that would be payable to customers but go unclaimed, either because they didn't know about their right to a refund, or they forgot about it, or didn't qualify for it, or didn't know how to claim it, or just didn't want to go through the hassle.

Has something like this happened to you? Don's Internet and television signal was on the fritz one evening, and when he called the cable company he got a recorded message saying there had been a disruption in his area but that service would likely be restored sometime after midnight. The next day he called the cable provider to be sure his bill that month reflected a credit for the previous day, when the service was out. The service rep confirmed that the service had indeed been out in his area, and that his account would be credited, no problem. Out of curiosity, however, Don asked the rep whether his company had already planned to give him the credit, since they knew he was one of the hundreds of households that experienced the outage. The rep's answer: "No, we only give refunds to those who call in to ask for them."

This cable company—not unlike all other cable companies and subscription-based businesses—is minimizing the cost of issuing refunds, not by denying them to people who are entitled, but simply by requiring people to request them first. So out of every thousand refunds that might be due, it's likely that only ten or twenty will actually be paid, amounting to an extremely high "breakage" rate.

But this method for handling refunds is less and less satisfactory to customers, who are used to having their needs met and their problems addressed in a more automated, frictionless fashion. And this is exactly what Amazon has begun doing. In his 2013 letter to shareholders, CEO Jeff Bezos explained that Amazon no longer waits for a customer to contact the company with a complaint.[1] When Amazon's computer system detects that a video ordered from the company doesn't stream well, for instance, or that a purchased product became available at a lower price, the company simply e-mails the customer a credit without even waiting for the customer to detect the problem or call in about it.

And we're noticing that other companies are starting to issue refunds proactively, also. A friend of ours was on a JetBlue flight that experienced mechanical problems before takeoff and ended up almost six hours late. Everyone was terribly inconvenienced. As passengers exited the plane at the destination, however, each one of them was handed a memo from Jet-Blue apologizing for the delay and notifying them that because of the incident they were entitled to compensation under JetBlue's Customer Bill of Rights. The amount of refund or payment due to each passenger depended on how much had been paid for the ticket and whether it had been purchased with money or with TrueBlue points (JetBlue's frequent-flier currency).

What stood out about JetBlue's action, however, was that rather than asking its passengers to mail in their boarding pass, or to log in to the airline's website and fill in their flight information and confirmation number, the airline said passengers didn't need to do anything at all to claim their refunds. Just wait a couple of days and the appropriate credit would automatically be posted to each passenger's "Flight Bank" at Jet-Blue, to be immediately available for use on future bookings.

Proactive refunds are likely to become ever more common, as companies try to provide ever more frictionless customer experiences, and as customers themselves continue to share these more and more frictionless customer experiences with their friends and colleagues.

Chapter 34

Sharing: Not Just for Sunday School

Have you ever used Wikipedia? Pinterest? Skype? These are just a few of the thousands of examples of "social production," in which products and services become available through the voluntarily shared efforts of unpaid, individual contributors, working collaboratively with little or no top-down direction.[1]

■ Millions of individuals now generate their own content and upload it to the network for others to read or view on a wide array of hosting websites, from Yahoo! and YouTube to Flickr and Facebook. (London's Science Museum surveyed three thousand people to ask what they could not live without. Facebook came in ahead of flushing toilets and fresh vegetables.)[2] Peer-to-peer networks such as Skype and BitTorrent eliminate the need for hosting servers altogether. And nearly a million new blog posts are uploaded daily to the more than 130 million blogs around the world tracked by Technorati.[3]

■ Wikipedia, a poster-child example of social production, offers more than nine million articles in 250 languages and is today one of the world's most used references. It was created and is maintained entirely by unpaid contributors—nearly 300,000 of them altogether.[4]

■ The Mozilla family of Web applications, including the Firefox browser, is "open-source" software, free for anyone to use, and maintained by a small army of volunteers who continually update and improve it. Apache software, another open-source application, is used by about 70 percent of corporate Web servers, including those for many high-traffic commercial sites. And large companies like Google, CNN, and Amazon power their websites with the GNU/Linux operating system, which is also open-source and free.[5]

"Crowd service" is augmenting traditional self-service for many firms, especially when they sell more complex products or services. Go to the customer service section of Verizon's website and ask a question about installing a home network or programming a high-definition television, for example, and the answer may come from some other customer—a completely unpaid volunteer. Other companies, including Apple, Best Buy, Linksys, Cisco, HP, Nintendo, AT&T, and iRobot (makers of the Roomba robotic vacuum cleaner), also facilitate crowd service on their own customer service websites, and for some a majority of service inquiries are answered by other customers, rather than by company employees.[6]

Why does this matter to the success of your business? Stay tuned.

Chapter 35

Value Creation: Invented by Somebody, Owned by Nobody, Valuable to Everybody

"Social production" as discussed in the previous chapter is an entirely new way to create economic value that has only become practical on such a large scale with the advent of cost-efficient interactive technologies. The fuel for commercial production is money, but the fuel for social production is trust. People volunteer, they collaborate, and they *share* their own time and energy with others, not in return for some market payment, but for the personal satisfaction of creating and sharing, or enjoying the goodwill of others, or simply feeling more connected.

During the political debate between left and right that dominated economic discussion throughout the twentieth century—with the right advocating more free-market solutions and the left advocating more government regulation—social production was never considered. The very idea of it would have seemed preposterous, like proposing to boost GDP with a series of barn raisings. But now that the technology is available, unpaid volunteers are in fact creating billions of dollars' worth of time savings, entertainment, instruction, new information, and knowledge, through a wider and wider variety of social production enterprises.[1]

This is what your customers do in their spare time.

And social production can often prove far superior to commercial production. Presumably, billion-dollar firms like Google and Amazon don't power their Web servers with open-source software because it's free, but because it's good. According to SourceForge.net, a kind of registration site for open-source software projects, there are now more than 260,000 such projects involving more than two million registered users, all of whom, more or less, are volunteer software coders.[2]

Clay Shirky estimates that, globally, our collective free time amounts to about a trillion hours each year, so even a minuscule portion of it, if properly organized, could generate immense productivity and actual value. Recently, for instance, it took online readers just hours to annotate an unsigned album of World War II snapshots, including identification of the photographer.[3]

There are many reasons why people spend time documenting their opinions for others they have no connection with, or improving software they have no commercial interest in. Empathy is a good catchall category for giving vent to your urge to help others. But there are additional motivations at work too, many of them more akin to pure self-interest. It takes time and effort to share an opinion, so why do it at all? Because we *enjoy* sharing our perspectives or ideas, that's why. Some of us feel fulfilled by offering helpful advice, and some of us get a thrill from influencing others' opinions. If you're a revolutionary protester in the Middle East, China, Brazil, or Myanmar, you want the world to know what you're going through.

In addition to a satisfying sense of accomplishment, you can earn the respect of others, you can validate your own importance and significance, and you can improve your personal status. One reason often given by computer programmers for volunteering their efforts to an open-source project, for instance, is simply "to have control over my own work"[4]— something more difficult to obtain from working at the direction of an employer. The choice between plodding along with the status quo or feeling good helping others and making things happen is a no-brainer.

It's obvious that social production is entirely different from for-profit production or government-mandated activity, but frequently it can still be harnessed directly to serve the interests of for-profit companies or governments. In his book *Remix: Making Art and Commerce Thrive in the Hybrid Economy*, Lawrence Lessig maintains that the *dominant* form of organizational design in the future is likely to be some kind of hybrid that combines for-profit or government-mandated action with social, volunteered action. Lessig says one example is Red Hat, a software service and consulting firm that earns a profit by helping its clients get the most out of their GNU/Linux software.[5] Even though any user can dig into the source code for GNU/Linux and tinker with it, there's no support system if help is required,* which is the gap Red Hat sought to fill. Red Hat has been very successful, and IBM purchased a minority interest in the company a number of years ago.[6] In fact, even though IBM holds more software patents than any other company in the world, Red Hat actually earns more money from servicing the unpatented, open-source Linux operating system (through Red Hat) than IBM earns from all its software patents combined.[7] And Red Hat has spawned a whole industry composed of firms that now compete with it to do the same thing—that is, to provide professional services to help maintain GNU/Linux.

Sometimes social production can make the difference between success and failure for a profit-making firm. Case in point: eBay. Pierre Omidyar's going-in assumption when he founded eBay was that "people are basically good," but within weeks his venture was on track to become a complete failure as a result of rampant fraud and cheating. Rather than hire the staff required to check credentials and vet contributors from some central office, however (an extremely costly, likely unfeasible task), Omidyar decided to enlist his own customers, who cheerfully chipped in. For free.[8] By incorporating a voluntary ratings system that allowed buyers to evaluate the trustworthiness of sellers on an objective basis, eBay became successful.[9] Without the volunteered "social" part of the eBay business model, the company would have failed, but now it is a publicly traded enterprise generating more than $3.5 billion of annual profit for its shareholders,[10] not to mention the tens of thousands of small and large businesses that rely on eBay to generate their own revenues. The reason eBay succeeded

---

* Many large firms with mission-critical computer systems (like a phone company, say) use Linux because if their servers go down, they can drill down into the system themselves and fix the problem immediately. If they use a commercial operating system, they can't do this because vendors keep their code a secret to protect their patents, so the client company has to wait for the vendor to deploy resources to fix the problem. As a result, many such firms consider open-source software a necessity.

was because the company figured out how to get its own users to create a system that made it possible for total strangers to trust one another—and it works, nearly all the time.[11] Violators of trust are outed, punished by the society. The pleasure generated by meting out vengeance to a wrongdoer is something we can all relate to, and this biological phenomenon itself is important for maintaining social order.

It shouldn't surprise us that most social production initiatives are not launched by big businesses or governments in order to accomplish complex tasks (like supercomputing), but by ordinary citizens accomplishing ordinary tasks. Some social production initiatives grow large, like Wikipedia and Mozilla, but more often they stay small. In Lahore, Pakistan, for example, some teenagers mobilized via Facebook to pick up trash around the city—a task apparently beyond the capability of a corrupt and listless city government.[12] And in Oakland, California, in the wake of a racially charged court verdict, several citizens relied on Twitter and Ushahidi, an open-source disaster-mapping platform from Kenya, to minimize violent rioting, saving lives as they alerted police and tracked events in real time, scooping the media on most stories by twenty to thirty minutes.[13] Elsewhere around the world, people increasingly turn to the network in order to mobilize their efforts—to find bone marrow donors for a leukemia victim in Israel,[14] or to collect money and organize gifts for their friends, or to expose and publicize a dictatorial regime's heavy-handed policies in the Middle East.

Chapter 36

Trust, Punishment, and the "Monkey Mind"

■ A man born without arms entered a bank in Florida and tried unsuccessfully to cash his wife's check. He was refused because, although he could provide two forms of identification, he couldn't provide a thumbprint. The story circulated on the Internet and in mass media.[1]

■ When a customer's DVD, recently and legally purchased from an electronics store, did not work, the manufacturer told him to return it to the retailer. The retailer told the customer to return it to the manufacturer. The customer spent $20 and ninety minutes on the DVD and still didn't have anything to watch, vowing to pirate content in the future. He's in his twenties and recommended the same to all his friends on Facebook.

■ Our colleagues were given a $100 gift certificate for their wedding. Right after the ceremony, they moved to Costa Rica, where they worked on assignment for their company for the next eighteen months. When they got home, they took the gift certificate to the store to use it but discovered that it had expired after twelve months. Turns out companies offering gift and rebate cards make a big profit from the 10 to 20 percent of cards that regularly go unredeemed, forgotten, or lost. Our friends vowed never to buy another one, from anybody.

■ In Canada, a young boy accompanied by his mother entered a bank to start his first savings account. After he waited in line with his jar of carefully saved change, the lady behind the counter wouldn't open the account because the coins had not been counted and wrapped before the little boy came to the bank branch. He was so upset that his father, the CFO of a major business, transferred the company's business to a different bank that welcomed the little boy's loose coins. The story was told at the next international banking association meeting, where it quickly passed into the blogosphere.

■ Four men in Belgium, completely fed up with the lousy customer service and impenetrable call center of a large telecom provider, decided to protest. They set up a call center of their own in a large shipping container and had the container delivered to the telecom company's main office, thereby blocking the entrance. When the company security guard called the phone number on the side of the container, he was subjected to the same kinds of impenetrable phone trees and unhelpful call handling the company's customers have to endure. The pranksters managed to drag out a simple phone call requesting them to move the container to a three-hour telephone "service" ordeal, in their attempt to simulate the company's own treatment of customers. The story has become a hilarious YouTube vignette.[2]

This list could go on for pages. In fact, we bet you already have your own stories to add to this list.

Dan Ariely, Duke University's respected behavioral economist, suggests that "revenge, even at personal expense, plays a deep role in the social order of both primates and people." He describes an experiment involving two chimpanzees placed in neighboring cages with a single table of food just outside the cages but still within each chimp's reach. The food table is wheeled, and either chimp can reach out to pull it closer to its own cage (and therefore farther from the other's). However, a "revenge rope" leading out from each cage is rigged so that if either chimp pulls it the table will collapse and spill all the food onto the floor, out of reach of both of them. Use of the rope is carefully demonstrated to the chimps, so they each know that it destroys any possibility of either of them reaching the food. Researchers have found that if both chimps share the food, all goes well in this experiment. But if either chimp rolls the table too close to its own cage and the other can no longer reach it, then that other chimp will sometimes explode in a rage and yank the rope, collapsing the table for both of them.[3]

> . . . among people who design software for group use, human social instincts are sometimes jokingly referred to as "the monkey mind."
> *CLAY SHIRKY, HERE COMES EVERYBODY*[4]

As human beings, almost all of us are hardwired to expect empathy, to the point that we get upset or angry when we see others not showing it. It may not sound polite to say this in public, but taking revenge on people who violate your trust (or the trust extended to them by others) is actually a good way to improve society's overall functioning.[5] When any member of a group can punish any other member who behaves unfairly, the result is more trustworthiness in the system, with a fairer and more just social environment for everyone.[6]

Trust and trustworthiness will increase over time, not because *every* company and individual will always be trustworthy, but because technology empowers punishers more and more to keep untrustworthy behavior in check. Punishment makes our social world go 'round and serves as the ultimate enforcer of trustworthiness, whether it's twenty-five to life for murder or a low review for a lousy product. Punishment keeps psychopathic capitalism in check:

> The easier it gets for customers to seek revenge, the more trustworthy businesses will *have* to be, for their own survival.

Chapter 37

Death by Tweet

However we frame the issue, punishing unfair behavior is an essential part of being social. And there's a reason for the phrase "sweet revenge." Behavior that is too selfish or "not fair" is the opposite of trustworthiness. Our human urge, our emotional impulse based on all our social biases, is to punish it. To seek revenge or payback of some kind even if it costs us something. To upset the food cart.

Nor is trustworthiness purely an animal instinct. At least in humans, having empathy for others and getting upset at injustice are also learned cultural traits. Studies show that the desire to punish injustice varies from society to society, with the citizens of more highly developed and interconnected economic cultures having a much higher sensitivity to injustice than members of less advanced cultures.

Online technologies allow us to avenge wrongdoing in a highly social, highly interconnected way. Revenge has never been easier or more satisfying, and it can be far more long-lasting and punitive. Reminder: Once an opinion about you hits the Internet, you may as well count it as immediate, ubiquitous, and *permanent*. As one advertising executive said, "You can't un-Google yourself."[1]

Or, in a more picturesque image relayed by one influential blogger:

> Dude, you can't take something off the Internet . . .
> that's like trying to take pee out of a swimming pool.[2]

We've all been entertained by the creativity and effort of victims exacting revenge by YouTube on companies and brands that have wronged them, and as word-of-mouth communication among consumers continues to accelerate, you can expect that the punishment imposed for poor service or a less-than-acceptable product will arrive ever more swiftly.

Case in point: Sacha Baron Cohen's movie *Brüno*. Even though a lot of people usually like Cohen's movies, *Brüno* was different. Released to theaters in the United States on Friday, July 9, 2009, this movie was apparently *so* tasteless, *so* over-the-top, and *so* overbearing in its self-conscious need to violate every possible taboo that people walked out of it in large numbers on that very first night. And that's not all. As they walked out, they were using their smartphones to text and tweet their friends, advising them not to bother seeing it. Stay away. The result: *Brüno*'s box-office receipts on Saturday were down by an astounding and unprecedented 40 percent from Friday's.[3] Before Twitter and Facebook and other status-updating social media platforms, word of mouth on a movie just didn't get passed around so fast. One reviewer noted, "even if they had a turkey, [studios] used to get two weeks of business before the stink really caught up to the film. Now they have twelve hours."[4]

It's important to maintain the right balance in a system, and sometimes the feedback loops have to be adjusted in order to ensure continued viability. We mentioned before how eBay became viable only because of the reviews volunteered by users. But as the company flourished and users became accustomed to shopping for sellers with the best reputations, the sellers themselves began trying to game the system. More and more, some sellers would rate their buyers high even *before* the sale transaction actually occurred. This action on a seller's part was specifically designed to influence the buyer's rating of the seller, and apparently it was having an effect. As a result, in early 2008 eBay changed its system so that sellers would be allowed to give positive ratings *only* to actual buyers. The company's action was designed to keep its system in balance— to keep it trustworthy.

As people become more and more efficiently interconnected, they will inevitably become more social; so the "prosocial" motivations that drive us, including empathy, reciprocity, and avenging injustice when we see it, will rise steadily in importance in all our dealings—not just with other people, but with the companies and brands we buy from as well.[5] We may never know exactly what motivated any particular customer service rep to blow the whistle on any particular company, but it's a safe bet there are employees at virtually every untrustable company in business today who also don't like having to come to work with the goal of tricking customers out of their money. And as technology continues to drive us closer together socially, they will like it less and less, and talk publicly about it more and more.

David Kirkpatrick argued in a 2011 *Forbes* cover story that every company in business today has become vulnerable to the judgments and actions of its customers and employees, who are now able to mobilize themselves using social networks. According to Kirkpatrick, "companies and leaders will have to show authenticity, fairness, transparency and good faith. If they don't, customers and employees may come to distrust them, to potentially disastrous effect."[6]

The role that trust plays in our everyday, routine interactions with others is an important driver for the "sharing economy" and social production. But doesn't trust's role directly conflict with the role that self-interest plays in the market economy? Now that we understand social behavior, sharing, and our strong tendency to play the role of punishers, we'll discuss how and when to apply the principles of empathy, sharing, and trust, versus the principles of self-interest and monetary incentives. And we'll discuss why "proactivity" is important to building customer experiences that will make your CFO smile.

Chapter 38

What Would Proactive Trustability Look Like in Your Business?

In chapter 3 we used the mobile phone category to illustrate the contrast between proactive trustability and doing business the traditional way. But what about other businesses? What about nonsubscription service models, or product manufacturers, or retailers, or financial services firms? Here are our ideas for how some of these businesses will operate competently, fairly, and proactively in the near future, as their customers come to demand more trustability from them:

Trustability in Prepaid Cards. Many retailers and other marketers have adopted "stored value" cards as a marketing and promotion vehicle. Sometimes these cards are sold as gift cards at face value, and sometimes they are distributed as rebates or refunds, or in lieu of loyalty points. Retailers like prepaid cards because studies have shown that a consumer typically spends more than the value of the card when redeeming it.

Manufacturers use prepaid cards to lower the effective price of their goods in a retail store, doing so in a way that puts them in direct touch with consumers whose identities they would otherwise perhaps never learn. Buying a new flat-screen television for $499.99 "after $100 manu-facturer's rebate" means that you pay the initial purchase price of $599.99 and mail your receipt in to the manufacturer along with the UPC code clipped from the packing box, and the manufacturer sends you a $100 rebate. When the rebate comes, however, it isn't a check but a stored value card with $100 stored on it. Unlike a gift card, most rebate cards aren't limited to a particular brand or store but can be used more generally, as a kind of debit or credit card.

So far, so good, but the problem with a prepaid card is that it can also serve as a vehicle for retailers and manufacturers to profit from mistakes that consumers make. For one thing, a substantial portion of the "stored value" in prepaid cards goes unclaimed by consumers, because while accounting rules have historically required businesses to put an expiration date on a card, the customer may neglect to use it before it expires, or the card itself might get lost or misplaced before all the stored value is claimed. So for many customers, there is no straightforward way to collect the rebate.

New legislation may reduce this problem for companies and consumers, but if you buy a $50 Starbucks gift card and send it to your friend for her birthday, there's still a good chance she'll lose it or forget about it before she claims the full $50 worth of value you purchased for her. In fact, of the $125 billion in gift cards issued in the United States annually, the "breakage"[1] (industry lingo for the amount issued to consumers but unclaimed for any reason) averages as much as 20 percent, a loss to consumers that rivals all debit card and credit card fraud[2] combined. In other words, when a marketer sells a gift card, it is actually *better than cash* (for the marketer). But customers have a new way to fight back. More and more, they can keep track of their gift card details on their smartphones and keep more of their cash!

In addition to the risk of expiration, loss, or misplacement, however, customers often encounter service fees assessed by issuers on the use of prepaid cards. In response to consumer complaints, Congress passed the Credit Card Accountability, Responsibility and Disclosure Act of 2009, or "Credit CARD Act,"[3] which puts limits on these activities, banning the imposition of "inactivity fees" during the first year after a gift card's issuance, for instance, and requiring at least five years' wait time before a card can be deemed to have expired.[4] But of course these legal restrictions were only necessary in the first place because many card issuers were using fees and expiration dates to keep the money of inattentive or unsuspecting customers.

A retailer or manufacturer that wants to be trustable with its rebate or gift card policy would link the card issuance to customers' identities in order to notify them if the card hasn't been used after some period of time, or if there is money remaining on a card that hasn't been fully claimed. It would be relatively simple and risk-free for a trustable company to offer replacements to customers who lose their cards. (Many competent retailers already keep electronic receipts so customers don't have to keep up with paper slips just to return or exchange a purchased item. And the truth is, there's a benefit to the company for this, as well as to the customer. Just for doing the right thing, proactively, the company gets to connect identity data to purchase or other customer behaviors, and thus is able to learn more about a customer. This enables a relationship-building company to create a better experience for a customer, which creates a more loyal customer, and so goes the virtuous circle.)

At a minimum, a trustable company should proactively send the customer an e-mail notice a few weeks before imposing any sort of service fee or expiration action. And any *competent* gift or rebate card issuer will have in place a convenient mechanism for capturing the customer's name and e-mail address or other contact details when the card is issued in the first place.

Trustability in Financial Services. How would a genuinely trustable retail bank operate? What would it do differently? How would it operate if it wanted to demonstrate trustability?

While there is obviously no requirement for any financial institution to extend credit to a customer (or to cover an overdraft without charging a fee), a large proportion of "penalty" fees are incurred by customers who are in fact creditworthy. A genuinely trustable retail bank would use easily available information to assess customers automatically for their creditworthiness, eliminating many such charges and possibly offering an automatic e-transfer among accounts when such a transfer is available but just hasn't yet been elected by the customer. At present, most banks reserve this kind of service for high-balance customers only, but there's no business reason it couldn't be more generally available.

A genuinely trustable retail bank would also disclose its fees in a way that is more obvious and available to consumers. Even though U.S. banks are already required by law to disclose their fees, multiple studies show that the majority of banks make information about fees either completely inaccessible to consumers or difficult to find.[5] Small banks and credit unions are more likely to disclose fees, but in the transparent future even the large, publicly held financial institutions that are so notoriously devious today will be forced by competitive pressure to do so. (Note that the question is not whether the company formally discloses the information—perhaps in small type in a long document—but whether customers know it.)

And any genuinely trustable financial institution would allow its customers to post their own reviews of its services and products (including comparisons with other companies' offerings) on the company's own website, making these reviews freely and impartially available to other customers.

We once met an insurance manager whose company offered "freeze damage" insurance to contractors and homeowners. Freezing weather in the manager's Florida region is very rare, but when it hits, it can ruin all the plumbing in a home and create a great deal of damage. Some customers bought the coverage, and some didn't. Nevertheless, whenever freezing temperatures were predicted, this manager had his agents call *all* the company's policyholders—even those who had not bought freeze-damage coverage—to warn them *proactively* about the impending freeze and educate them about how to prevent damage. In this way, he not only minimized damage to the properties he would have had to pay to repair, but he also helped the policyholders who hadn't even paid for the coverage (at very low cost to the company) and who obviously trust him more as a result.

So here's an Extreme Trust idea for retail banks that might at first sound just as foolish as serving customers who haven't bought your product but could have similarly beneficial effects in terms of securing your reputation as a trustable company: One of the hassles involved in switching banks is setting up your electronic bill payment system. Once you've gone to all the trouble of inputting dozens of business names, addresses, and account numbers for your bank's online bill paying system, the very idea of having to start over again at another bank is wearying. But if, as a bank, you were truly confident in your ability to serve customers well and always act in their best interests, then you could offer a service to do just this. That is, if a customer ever decides to leave you for another bank, you could provide all the customer's bill payment files in some kind of format for the new bank to load automatically.

What you would be saying to customers with this policy is that you are always on their side, no matter what, and if for any reason they feel they'll be better served somewhere else, then doggone it, you're going to help them. Don't hold your breath for most banks to do this kind of thing, but it wouldn't be too big a surprise for Navy Federal, Ally Bank, USAA, or maybe RBC to offer a similar service someday. *And then how will everyone else compete?*

Trustability in the Automotive Category. What would it mean for an automotive company to be proactively trustable? This depends on which type of automotive firm we're discussing. In most countries manufacturers or importers procure the physical product and are generally responsible for its quality, while retail auto dealers sell, deliver, and service the product, having many more day-to-day interactions with consumers. As a consumer, however, you are more likely to hold the *brand* accountable for both product and service failings, as well as for its "intentions" toward you. So a genuinely trustable brand would have to involve a close, competent relationship between dealer and manufacturer. When a brand-name dealer's service doesn't live up to the car brand's advertised standard, it's a recipe for customer disappointment with the *brand* as much as with the dealership.

A trustable car dealership would probably try to compensate salespeople based not just on how many autos they sell but on how much customer satisfaction is actually generated. One idea might be to pay a "lifetime commission" on new car sales. Whenever a salesperson sells a car to a customer who is new to the dealership, the dealer would tag that customer with the salesperson's name, and every time that customer spends anything with the dealer anytime in the future—for service, for buying another car (new or used, even if bought from a different salesperson)—then the original salesperson would get some kind of commission. This would give the salesperson a vested, proactive interest in the continued satisfaction and loyalty of the customer, and it would also help ensure that a dealer's most productive and valuable salespeople remain loyal themselves.

There are some obviously untrustable behaviors in the auto category ("Would you buy a used car from this man?"), but increasingly we'll find that untrustable practices will be "outed" by social media commentary and online word of mouth. Even today it isn't hard to find out, for instance, whether a dealership has a reputation for unnecessarily expensive servicing, or for overly aggressive up-selling of features and options. And as transparency continues to throw light on this and every other business category, such practices are likely to prove less and less financially attractive.

A trustable car brand would proactively e-mail or phone you thirty days before your warranty expires, so you can bring the vehicle in for any needed repairs while the warranty is still valid. And to improve its reputation for trustability during the sales process, a brand might want to consider helping customers to make direct comparisons with competitive vehicles. At a minimum, a trustable auto brand would host objective online reviews by authenticated owners and drivers of multiple brands, and it might even consider arranging test drives right at the dealership. Imagine a BMW dealer allowing a customer to test-drive a Cadillac, Infiniti, Tesla, or Audi, for instance.

Carmakers know that consumers will explore different brands. So why not facilitate a process that will occur anyway and, in effect, be "present" for a greater portion of the customer's overall shopping experience, with the opportunity to get smarter? This would simply be acknowledging what should have been obvious all along: providing objective, unbiased advice to customers will earn their trust, and trust is highly valuable for the brand.

Think about it: if a company thinks it *isn't* in its own interest to provide good, objective advice to customers, then what is the firm really saying?—that it prefers to take revenue from unknowledgeable or unsuspecting customers before they acquire enough information to make more intelligent decisions? That its business model depends on customers who don't make smart decisions?

In one event like this, what one car company found after a similar test-drive program was that "After the test drives [including competitive brands], vehicle consideration was increased by 20 percent and sales were increased by 11 percent."[6]

Trustability in the Credit Card Business. How would a proactively trustworthy credit card company operate? For one thing, rather than encouraging spending and borrowing, a trustable credit card business would counsel its customers to spend wisely and use the card prudently. (Think of the utility company urging you to turn off the lights or adjust the thermostat when you leave the house, for instance.) It would provide incentives for customers to pay off their balances, perhaps reducing the interest rate applied when a balance is reduced. Such a company would be careful not to earn too much of its profit from late fees, which would indicate a flaw in the business model; in fact, it might provide extra incentives for on-time payments.

Imagine being offered a credit card by a highly trustable issuer. Rather than exploiting your instant-gratification bias, such a trustable credit card company might even use this bias to craft an incentive to promote more long-term saving. For instance, it could offer you a savings account fed by an extra charge applied each month to your bill, so that the more you spend in the present, the more you save for the future. What if, for every dollar you charged on your card, an additional five cents was charged on your bill, to be put into your savings account (or you could specify some other amount)?

To help you rein in your own spendthrift ways, a trustable credit card company might ask you to set a monthly spending budget and then text you during the month to keep you apprised as you "use it up." If you get to the middle of the month and you've already spent more than your planned budget allows, at least you'd know.[7]

To operate in this way, a credit card company would have to make some changes to its business model. There is a lot of short-term profit to be made by encouraging consumers to borrow and spend, regardless of their own interests, so a trustable credit card issuer wanting to remain in business must figure out how to make money from more customer-friendly activities.

As far as we know, right now there aren't any fully trustable credit card companies like the one we've just described. We predict there will be, sooner or later, however, because rising levels of transparency make it virtually inevitable that some credit card company somewhere *will* find a profitable way to turn trustability into a competitive advantage. Once that happens, other credit card issuers will have to figure out how to offer a similar level of proactive trustworthiness—of *trustability*.

And already we can see glimmers of hope. Discover's Motiva Card, for instance, has allocated some of its "cash back" rewards program to an incentive for simply paying each month's bill on time.[8] And Citi's Simplicity Card, launched in 2013, doesn't charge late fees or penalty interest rates, although it doesn't offer miles or points or other benefits, either. That's because the simple truth is that credit card companies offering airline miles and other benefits are really just giving your own money back to you.

Chapter 39

Becoming More Trustable to Large Enterprise Customers

When selling software or SQL server installations to large enterprise customers, it has always been Microsoft's practice to provide, free of charge, a number of vouchers allowing the customer to send key personnel to special Microsoft training courses, which are conducted through the firm's network of certified partners. Training is one of Microsoft's most important value-added services, because it is designed to appeal especially to the kind of enterprise customer more likely to want a collaborative, long-term commercial relationship. But a few years ago, Microsoft was wrestling with the challenge that fewer than 20 percent of these vouchers were being redeemed by customers. Four out of five vouchers simply languished in customers' desk drawers, never to be used. The marketing people at Microsoft had mixed emotions about the low redemption rate, however. Even though they knew that such training could help cement the firm's relationships with its largest customers and would also likely improve customer experience with the product, the fact was that high levels of voucher breakage were good for the marketing budget, because every dollar of training not redeemed was money that could be used to fund other marketing activities.

Chris Atkinson, a vice president of Microsoft, decided that customers who were not redeeming their training vouchers were just not getting the most benefit from Microsoft's products, and even though it cost money, his unit began sending out reminders to those customers proactively. Atkinson noted,

There were absolutely no strings to these reminders, which were simply notices to customers that they should be sure to take maximum advantage of the training vouchers they had been provided and not yet redeemed. This program immediately doubled the redemption rate in the Southeast Asia region and caught the attention of Microsoft corporate product marketing in Redmond, as well, with the result that it is now standard practice around the world to send out reminders to enterprise customers who have unredeemed training vouchers.[1]

Soon redemption rates for Microsoft training vouchers around the world soared, as did trust in the Microsoft brand among these valuable customers. Reminding a customer that she is due for a benefit or service she may have overlooked is certain to build your brand's reputation for trustability, and Microsoft earned this benefit in the same way as the homebuilder we cited in chapter 13 did, when he began reminding his customers when their new-construction warranties only had thirty more days to run.[2]

Chapter 40

Every Frequent Flier's Dream: The Trustable Airline

Trustability in the Airline Industry. Airlines are seen by most consumers as highly self-oriented and untrustable, partly on account of their complex and hard-to-understand pricing policies. Airlines do need pricing flexibility because their inventory is perishable. Like a phone network, an airline has an extremely high ratio of fixed to variable costs, and an airline seat flying empty (like network capacity that goes unused) is revenue lost forever.

Airlines have, over the last thirty years or so, greatly improved the science of revenue management, constantly evaluating the ebb and flow of demand for every flight as its departure time nears. When revenue management is combined with tariff rules for discount fares that require things like Saturday-night stays, no refunds, or advance purchase restrictions, the plane will fill up with passengers who have actually paid many different fares and are subject to many different restrictions.[1] And, while there is nothing overtly wrong about this type of pricing, the system is so complex for passengers that many simply don't understand whether they're being treated fairly or not.

An airline could deal with this problem in a number of ways. It could, for instance, heavily promote a low-fare offering, and then (if the flight isn't yet filled) promote an even lower fare closer in to departure. While this might appear highly cynical on the airline's part, it is in fact the practice of at least a few airlines. But even if the initial low fare (later to be undercut) is not specifically advertised or promoted, reducing the fare at a later point to fill a plane at the last minute might still seem unfair to many of the early planners, unless the last-minute fares have some significant and rather onerous restrictions or conditions.

A genuinely trustable airline, on the other hand, would go to great lengths to try to ensure that customers didn't end up paying a higher fare just because they were unknowledgeable or unlucky.[2] If you book a ticket at one price, and the price for a similarly restricted ticket on that flight later drops, a trustable airline would either refund you the difference automatically or offer to allow you to exchange your ticket for one at the lower price (with different restrictions). It's one thing to manage your seat capacity scientifically, but it's an entirely different proposition to make money by playing a shell game with customers.[3]

Some travel delays are unavoidable in the airline business, for reasons that have to do with random weather patterns and maintenance issues. But different routes are subject to different patterns of delay, with some more likely to be affected than others. The FAA keeps accurate statistics with respect to the historic patterns of travel delays by airline and route, and any passenger could turn to www.fly.faa.gov to look up an itinerary he or she is planning, but why wouldn't the airline itself display a travel-delay likelihood score for each flight segment? In fact, it would be a relatively simple thing for an airline's online travel reservations system to tap the government's database and display a "likelihood of on-time arrival" figure for any particular itinerary booked, maybe pricing accordingly, allowing passengers to choose whether to take a more expensive flight that is usually on time, or a cheaper flight that is often late.

Airline frequent-flier programs are useful vehicles for earning the trust of customers, provided that they aren't relegated to serving purely as marketing come-ons. If an airline promotes the fact that it "only" takes twenty-five thousand miles to make a trip but then heavily restricts the availability of eligible seats, it's just playing the same kind of airfare shell game with passengers, only this time with mileage redemptions.

Most airlines allow their frequent-flier miles to be redeemed for car rental days, hotel stays, or merchandise, and miles have become a kind of promotional currency, bought and sold in a variety of different ways. One way an airline could immediately boost its trustability in the eyes of its frequent fliers might be to let them redeem their miles on *other* airlines, including even direct competitors. As long as Airline A can buy miles from Airline B, it wouldn't be difficult for A to allow its own frequent fliers to redeem their miles for flights on B. Such a program would provide evidence to customers that Airline A is actually on their side and not just trying to line its own pockets with customer patronage. In addition, of course, the air carrier would acquire valuable insights into the flying preferences and off-route travel habits of its most frequent customers, a benefit somewhat analogous to the insight a car company would get from allowing customers to test-drive a variety of different car brands.

And if something doesn't work—there's no seat light for reading on a night flight, or the entertainment system doesn't work, or the seat won't lean back—the proactive airline will not only apologize but will also make sure the flight doesn't cost the same as it would if the full value were available to the passenger.

Airlines, in the end, are just as much a high-end *personal service* business as hotels or restaurants are, where the smiling face or warm touch of a competent and caring maître d' or concierge can immediately generate a feeling of trust and confidence. If you fly frequently on United Airlines, you are likely to have one of two very disparate views of the airline, depending on the culture of the employees who handle your flight. For example, Martha avoids United Airlines because, she says, "On every flight, they yell at a passenger. On a good day, it's not me." On the other hand, Don likes United. Recently he found himself on a plane captained by John McFadden, a veteran pilot based in Chicago.[4] After the passengers had boarded, and while the plane was still at the gate, Don noticed that the pilot himself came out to make an announcement to passengers, using the microphone usually handled by flight attendants. While it was unusual, he thought nothing more about it until, two hours after takeoff, flight attendant Diane Johnson began distributing McFadden's business cards to about twenty different passengers in first class and coach, each with a brief thank-you note hand-written on the back:

> **Dear Donald Peppers (1F): Thank you for your business! How can we exceed your expectations?**
> *JOHN McFADDEN*

McFadden says he began giving out these thank-you notes to high-value passengers during a period about ten years ago when United was going through a rough patch and says he almost always gets favorable feedback for the initiative, including innumerable e-mails from passengers when they complete their trips. When Don asked him why he began doing this, he was stumped. But in a few hours he sent an e-mail:

> *As we flew to SFO [San Francisco, the next destination], I reflected on your question—"Why do you do what you do?" That is a question I am asked quite a bit. The simple and straightforward answer is—If I try to teach my kids (16-year-old son and 13-year-old daughter) to treat others as I would wish to be treated, it is crucial that I put that "golden rule" philosophy into action. I know that may sound somewhat simplistic. The truth is, I really believe in living my life this way.[5]*

In the final analysis, McFadden values empathy and reciprocity above everything else. He refuses to be just an employee. He insists on being a human. Imagine how many more loyal, valuable customers United might have (Martha?) if the company built a culture of proactive trustability and more people saw behaviors like those of Captain McFadden.

6

How to Build a Trustable Business

Chapter 41

What Do We Do Every Day?

JetBlue Builds Trust into its DNA

When people ask very frequent fliers, "How was your trip?" the best answer we can give is "Fine. I won't remember it tomorrow." But JetBlue handles things differently. They were founded based on the idea of "bringing humanity back to air travel," according to Nancy Elder, vice president, JetBlue Airlines.[1] "There are 18,000 crew members who ask themselves every day 'What would I want in this situation?'" such as in a flight delay or cancellation. So ground crew and on-board personnel help families with small children proactively find a place for the kids to sleep, and proactively refund money or miles when things don't go just right. Recruitment, and training, and a culture that is not about a "program" but is all about asking "What can we do to help?" provides the support for this kind of on-the-spot experience:

■ A passenger at JFK near New York really wanted her latte at Starbucks, but to make her flight, she had to hurry to the gate and skip the longish line at the coffee shop. Once she arrived at the gate at the far end of the concourse, she discovered the plane was delayed a few minutes and she could have gotten her coffee and still made the flight. Darn! She tweeted about it—just another one of the little stings of modern travel. The tweet made its way back to the JetBlue personnel at JFK. Obviously, they can't do this every time, but that day they were able to get the Starbucks coffee and bring it to the passenger as she boarded the plane!

■ JetBlue, sensitive to nut allergies among passengers, does not serve peanuts. But a popular vendor at the New Orleans airport does. The mother of a child with a peanut allergy, noticing at the gate that quite a few passengers had bought peanuts from the

vendor, asked for help. Ground personnel were able to reseat
several passengers to create a buffer between the child and the
passengers enjoying their treats.

But JetBlue's trustability goes beyond personal interaction, and is
actually an integral part of the company's approach to doing business.
When two police officers were killed in New York, JetBlue's leadership,
asking "How can we help?," offered any police officer anywhere in the
country a free round trip ticket to attend the memorial service. After all,
they reasoned, we have the planes to do it, and we can help. Nearly five
thousand officers took them up on their offer. JetBlue did not announce
this move—it was not for public relations. The news got out, but JetBlue
tried to keep a low profile on it. Maybe it's because the founders are still
wandering around the company, influencing the culture. Maybe it's because every two weeks, the CEO shows up at training programs at The
Lodge facility in Orlando in order to meet every new employee. Maybe it's
because the leadership at the company cares more about the long-term
value of the company than about what the short-term stock analysts will
say about the company's deep customer care, pet-friendly approach, and
helpful attitude—and has an analogous devotion to the company's great
employees.

Nancy described one of the many times the empathy that JetBlue
shows its customers paid off. (Remember, there is no such thing as one-
way reciprocity.) She was the designated "supervisor" at a counter in the
airport, and was trying to help a customer who just could not be satisfied
with any of the offers Nancy made, and was frankly complaining very
loudly about it. Not one but two passersby came up to speak to Nancy
during the sensitive moment. Both said something akin to "I just love Jet-
Blue." These customers were supporting her, taking sides with the airline
they knew would look out for *them*.

In the next few chapters, we will outline some of the very real phe-
nomena that are changing the way customers relate to each other and how
they will expect to relate to your business. As you read through this section, you may wonder what each of these points, ranging from evidence-
based management to the e-social ethos to sockpuppeting to the power of

an apology, have to do with making your business simultaneously more trustable and more profitable. What we have tried to do here is to summarize for you the changes that are affecting your customers, your employees, your bosses, your shareholders, your government regulators, and all the other people who affect the success of your business. Every step you take will create better customer experience, which will increase customer value, which improves shareholder value.

Chapter 42

The E-Social Ethos

In addition to reciprocity, empathy, and the desire to avenge injustice, our social interactions are subject to a whole set of customs and "unwritten rules" that have developed over untold generations of people conversing with each other. Your customers know these as well as you do. They aren't fooled by faux adherence to the rules either. You know that when you discuss something with a friend, colleague, loved one, or stranger, you're supposed to adhere to these customs even without thinking: Don't interrupt. Listen first, show an interest. Respond to what others are saying.

But there are subtler principles as well. Suppose, for instance, a good friend were to ask your help in getting a job at the company where another friend of yours is a vice president. All he really wants is an introduction. He's your friend, and he would certainly do the same for you. But what if, in asking for this favor, your friend also offered you $100 to make the introduction? Or $500? Wouldn't you be totally put off by this? Maybe he's not really your friend after all, you might think, because this certainly isn't how friends deal with friends.

This conflict represents one of the most important differences between how we interact in a commercial setting versus in a social setting. The commercial economy is characterized by people freely exchanging money with other people. You buy from me, I sell to you, and if we do it right we both consider ourselves better off. Nor does this seem out of line to any of us. We all expect to pay for the things we want. When you pay the grocer $6 for a twelve-pack of Diet Coke, you don't begrudge him the money. You expect to pay. You wouldn't even consider asking the grocer to give you the soda for free. And if the grocer asked you for a favor—say, stopping in to help restock the shelves some evening—you would be just as baffled as if a friend offered you money for making an introduction or do-ing a favor, or demanded money for spending time with you.

With the rise of modern, free-market capitalism, these two domains of human activity—social and commercial—became quite distinct and sep-arate, but technology seems to be smashing them together. Social produc-tion, for instance, combines features of both domains, being fueled by social interaction, trust, and sharing, but generating real economic value as well. Whether the sharing involves someone's free time, honest opinion, computer coding, editing and curating, or computation cycles on their computer hard drive, the end result is genuine economic value, worth real money.

Over time, the e-social "ethos" that comes to govern our online in-teractions will develop as a set of purely informal and unwritten customs, much like the customs that have already developed to govern our offline social interactions.

Regardless of the legal and regulatory protections or mandates even-tually enacted, however, it is clear that *trust* will be a dominant guiding principle in the e-social ethos, because maintaining trust is essential for the smooth functioning of the overall system. An ethos that rewards and encourages trust—and punishes untrustworthy behavior—is inevitable, because it will always succeed more efficiently than one that doesn't.

As a result, the importance of trust and trustworthiness is continu-ing to increase as interactive technologies continue to improve. Over the last several years, as more and more people have become familiar with and participated in various social production activities by uploading, col-laborating, and volunteering, we have already come to rely more on shar-ing and trust. And while the task of policing trustworthiness used to be in the hands of just a few offline organizations—the Better Business Bu-reau, *Consumer Reports*, the newspapers, the FDA, the NYC Taxi and Limousine Commission (TLC)—already this task is being performed more efficiently online, and everybody participates. People share their opinions, and they punish unfairness, socially. We are more trustworthy, and we trust more.

Chapter 43

How Friends Treat Friends

The unfamiliar workings of the e-social ethos can easily trip a business up when it tries to deal with social media simply as a new channel for marketing or to generate positive word of mouth, because most marketing and business tactics that make sense in the commercial domain just don't apply in the social domain. You can buy advertising exposure with media dollars, you can buy better customer insight with data and analytics, and you can buy Facebook "likes" with sufficient discounts or giveaways. But you can't *buy* meaningful word-of-mouth recommendations or social influence. That's just not how friends treat friends.

In an early violation of e-social trust, a blog appeared in September 2006 entitled *Wal-Marting Across America*. It featured two intrepid RV owners, known only as Jim and Laura, who were driving from Walmart to Walmart across the United States, visiting stores along the way, and interviewing a whole stream of ever-upbeat Walmart employees. It turned out that Jim and Laura were fictitious, not real people driving their motor home around from store to store; they were actually paid contract writers for Walmart, hired by Edelman, the company's PR firm, to create a series of glowing articles. This ignited a firestorm of protest from others in the blogosphere, with people lashing out at both Walmart and Edelman. Walmart's initiative perfectly illustrates the single biggest error most companies commit when they try to operate in the social media space: Rather than respecting the e-social ethos, they think they can treat social media just like any other marketing "channel," in this case using it to create a kind of advertising message. ("I'm not a motor-home owner, but I play one on TV.")[1]

To the PR agency's credit, CEO Richard Edelman jumped

immediately into the fray, personally and vigorously, with multiple online apologies and mea culpas, answering most of the angry inbound e-mails and social media postings himself. He knew that in an age when anyone at all can comment publicly, "no comment" has become a confession all by itself. It's no longer possible simply to run from mistakes or to hunker down and wait for the furor to subside.

(Once the pee gets into the pool, the only possible remedy is adding more and more clean water.)

What Walmart learned was that even though the social domain can serve as a marketing channel, the social ethos still has to be respected. You can advertise to viewers using a fictional story to entertain them on television, but you don't lie to your friends and call it "advertising."

We're not saying you can never launch a pure marketing initiative that uses a social media platform like a "channel." Many companies do this, and they can get good results from it, but it's not a *social* strategy, and it shouldn't be portrayed as one. Most brands' Facebook fan pages, for instance, serve primarily as vehicles for disseminating discounts, coupons, and other goodies to their customers. There's nothing at all wrong with a brand using Facebook or Twitter or other social platforms to disseminate rebates or incentives, or to publicize sales, but *selling* is not *friending*. Selling is a *marketing* objective, not a social objective, and the consumers who become "fans" of a commercial brand fully understand this. Boosting the number of Facebook "likes" or Twitter users who follow your brand bears little similarity to generating the kind of goodwill or positive reputation that comes from having genuinely social relationships with customers— relationships that are based on friendship and trust.

Disney figured this out almost the moment the company started dabbling in social media. At one industry conference on social media, two Euro Disney executives related that their firm had discovered it needed to use completely different rules for selling in the "marketing space" to consumers who had enlisted for one of the company's e-mail newsletters, as compared with selling in the "social space" to consumers who had friended one of Disney's many characters on Facebook. While offering cross-sell deals and other promotions to e-mail newsletter subscribers was fine, they found that if they tried to make such offers to Facebook friends, a large number of them took offense. It wasn't just that the response was lower. The response was *negative*, because marketing offers, when made in the social space, can actually generate ill will.[2]

So forget ROI when you violate the social ethos with your marketing campaign. It will be worse than no marketing at all.

Chapter 44

Trustability and Social Influence

But even though money and other commercial inducements aren't appropriate for social interactions, you can still have a positive effect in the e-social domain as long as you respect the ethos and concentrate on the *noneconomic* things that people value—the social things.

If you want to influence social sentiment, but in a trustable way, start by trying to think about what actually motivates an influential blogger or Twitter user—someone whose opinions matter to thousands of followers. Yes, most key influencers would be offended if you offered to compensate them for a favorable post, but they are still human beings, and like all the rest of us, they have ambitions too. They want to be noticed and to increase their own influence. They want to write better, more original and authoritative posts. And there are a number of noneconomic services or benefits you can provide to key social media influencers that will help them achieve some of these ambitions. If you're a student of employee motivation, what we're talking about here is focusing not on "extrinsic" benefits, such as compensation and perks, but on "intrinsic" benefits, such as appreciation, encouragement, camaraderie, and fulfillment.

And before delving into the intrinsic benefits that influencers will find most appealing (see sidebar), a quick word of caution: Be sure you understand your influencers' own perspectives. The overwhelming majority of social influencers do not consider themselves to be experts on any particular business category, company, or brand, per se. Rather, they think of themselves as having an authoritative point of view with respect to some particular issue or problem of concern to them and their followers. It might be a business issue or a health issue or a relationship issue, but it's unlikely that they will think of their own central mission in terms of rating or evaluating the products and services offered by you or your competitors. Their central mission is to be of value to their friends and followers—those who depend on their opinion and thinking. Talking favorably or unfavorably about your brand or product has to be seen in this context—as a service they are performing for the benefit of their own network of friends.

INFLUENCING THE INFLUENCERS

The intrinsic benefits social media mavens value most can be categorized in terms of acknowledgment, recognition, information, and access. You can remember these benefits easily if you remember the mnemonic "ARIA," as in the solo sung by your favorite opera star.[1]

ACKNOWLEDGMENT: Simply identifying influential bloggers or social media influencers and acknowledging them with your own message will go a long way toward having a positive influence. If you haven't yet assigned people in your organization the task of identifying those tweeters and bloggers with the most credibility and influence in your particular category, then it's time to do so. When you identify someone important, reach out to her, and do it genuinely. Post a comment on her blog, retweet a smart update, e-mail her with a thoughtful (but non-self-serving) suggestion. Acknowledge her existence, and by implication her significance, by letting her know that *you* know she exists and that *you* are paying attention.

RECOGNITION: Bloggers, product reviewers, and others who become expert in your business's category want to be recognized as such. Recognition is a key motivator for all of us, but it's even more crucial in the social media world, where monetary compensation is completely inappropriate. So be sure to recognize a key blogger by forwarding the link to his or her website on to others. You might even consider mentioning very authoritative bloggers in your own press communications, providing not only recognition to the blogger but also additional sources for whatever reporters or other commentators follow your firm. If you have a crowd service system that relies on some knowledgeable customers handling the complicated inquiries of other customers, be sure to recognize the most expert contributors or the most prolific participants with special badges, emblems, or status designations. Everyone wants to be platinum in something.[2]

INFORMATION: Information is power. Think about it. More than anything else, *information* is exactly what influential bloggers want to provide their readers, and what Twitterers want to provide their tweeps.* Key influencers want the inside dope, the straight skinny. So when you identify social media influencers in your category, be sure to provide them with all the information you can reasonably manage. Don't provide truly confidential or commercially sensitive information, unless you think it might do more good for you if it were to become widely known (assuming, of course, that it's not illegal or unethical to release it). But even without violating anyone's confidence or divulging the kind of "inside" information that might get a public company in trouble, you can almost certainly provide a key influencer with a more useful perspective and insight about your business or your category, including the problems you face, the threats to your business you are trying to avoid, and the opportunities you see.

ACCESS: Just as useful as providing insightful information is letting an influencer make direct contact with the author of the insight, or the operating person at your business who is most connected to the information. Talk about getting the straight scoop. Probably nothing will pay bigger dividends in terms of social media influence than simply allowing the influencers themselves to have access to some of your own people, your own experts and authorities. Providing this access is, all by itself, a form of acknowledgment and recognition also. Not everyone gets this kind of access, because you can't take the time for everyone. But you should definitely take the time for someone who has an important enough following in social media.

---

* Twitter has spawned a language. Tweets are the messages you send. Tweeps are your followers (your peeps, or people, on Twitter).

Influencing your influencers, if you do it right, will help empower customers to share their ideas and thoughts with other customers, to help other customers solve their problems, and to simply participate more in the social world that surrounds every set of commercial transactions. In addition to the benefits you will realize in terms of being seen as more trustable, this kind of customer-oriented activity is almost certainly going to generate additional revenue and business as well. Twenty-year-old eBay, for instance, created customer support forums for its customers so buyers and sellers could exchange tips and suggestions, but it later found that customers who were active users of the support forums were generating 50 percent more revenue for the firm!

When people get together and exchange ideas, they do much more than simply critique the honesty of a vendor or the experience they have when they buy from someone. This sharing of information is only a part of a much broader, more robust effort—a social effort—to solve some commonly perceived problem, or to meet some commonly felt need. People have always turned to one another for help in solving problems, whether it was prehistoric hunters cooperating to run down big game or Wikipedia contributors curating a new entry. But the technology of cooperation has never been so efficient, so robust, and so capable as it now is. So as cooperation accelerates, the speed of problem solving increases too. We experience it as "innovation."

Chapter 45

Trustable Information

Whether you measure it by the gigabyte or the megaflop, information is cheap, and it's everywhere. Data being created and stored today include not just business documents, government statistics, and scientific research but also blog posts and websites, status updates, photos, videos, comments, product reviews, text messages, podcasts, "Like" and "Share" buttons, and location check-ins. More and more, information is generated through the individual efforts of millions of people, interacting in billions of ways, independently.

In addition to product competence and customer competence, in order to "do things right," a company must have "information competence." That is, a company's managers must be able to make intelligent, data-driven decisions in a reasonably scientific way.[2]

Current estimates are that the volume of data available to the human race doubles roughly every two years, but now that technology is beginning to connect highly efficient networks of people, as opposed to simply streamlining the storage and processing of data itself, the speed at which new data will be generated is likely to accelerate faster than Moore's law. From a mathematical perspective, the messaging in a growing network increases at a "combinatorial" rate, faster than geometric growth, and some of the more breathless estimates are that within just a few years the volume of data and "technical information" may be doubling every few hours.[3]

This is an almost unimaginable acceleration in new data and information. It will test the limits of human understanding, requiring us to focus ever more carefully on accuracy, reliability, usefulness, objectivity, and consistency.[4] It may be an ocean of data, after all, but a lot of it is repetitive or banal ("the first 10 search results out of 12.3 million"). If you tweet that you'll be at the Starbucks on Tenth Street in thirty minutes, your friend's retweet of that message generates more data but not much new information. And lots of information is inaccurate, or fictional, or just wrong.

One of the key reasons for the explosive growth in data is the fact that people just want to "be social." Being social is a driving human force, generating increased transparency and trust as well as an explosion of information. Social media platforms are superefficient tools, not just for sharing, but also for validating the trustability of information. "Social filtering"—checking the opinions of your friends, or the friends of your friends—is an increasingly effective way to verify that your own information or opinion is correct.

Can This Information Be Trusted? In order to manage effectively and to make reasonably good decisions, we will have to have enough focus and discipline to ignore a great deal of this information tonnage while becoming skilled at spotting the most useful nuggets. And the very first filter applied whenever we take on new information is trust. As individuals, that's how we decide what's worth paying attention to. Is it credible? Do we believe it? Is it useful? Do we trust the source? Whatever benefits we obtain from new information will be directly related to how trustworthy we think the information is. When we pass information on to others, it (and we) will be judged by how skilled we are in analyzing and understanding it, handling it, and using it ourselves.

But what does it really mean to "trust" information? Circling back to the components of trust—do things right and do the right thing—we can use a direct analogy:

Trustable information is *accurate* and *objective*.[5]

When we judge the trustability of information—the opinions of others, news, insight, or other data—we are assessing its objectivity and accuracy. Is the information slanted and biased, or is it reasonably objective? Is the information incomplete, sloppy, or mistaken, or is it correct, factual, and thorough?[6]

But in the e-social world, we are not just connecting with close friends but also with friends and colleagues with whom we didn't have very close connections before. Yochai Benkler maintains that we all use interactive technology to craft "limited-purpose, loose relationships" with an increasing number of our more distant friends and associates. You can see it happen all around you. A fifty-year-old mother starts an account on Facebook in order to keep up with her children now that they're in college, and soon she's corresponding with high school classmates she hasn't talked to in years. A business manager responds to a LinkedIn message from someone in a related field, and suddenly the two of them are hatching a new business.

> People connected to groups beyond their own can expect to find themselves delivering valuable ideas, seeming to be gifted with creativity. This is not creativity born of deep intellectual ability. It is creativity as an import-export business.
> *RONALD BURT*[7]

A well-known quantitative study has shown, for instance, that most people who get a new job through the recommendation of someone else do not receive that recommendation from a close friend or colleague but from a distant one—someone they don't know as well and whose own connections aren't as familiar. The reason this happens isn't because your best friends don't like you as much as your distant ones, but because for the most part you and the people you're closest to are already aware of all the same opportunities. The job openings known by your more distant friends, however, are more likely to be new and untried. The information we get from close friends and colleagues is more predictable and less likely to surprise us or give us a different perspective, while information we get from distant connections is more likely to surprise us. And unpredictable information—information or insight that we didn't anticipate in advance—is often the most useful when it comes to improving our understanding of how the world works. When people say something is "informative," what they're really saying is that it's unanticipated or surprising. It changes our view of things. But it's also more threatening because it challenges our current worldview and requires more validation before we can trust it.[8]

Importantly, one of the keys to making diverse connections and gaining such new insights is simply to remain open to new or completely strange ideas, and this kind of openness requires—you guessed it—trusting other people. When two people don't trust each other, they're unlikely to give much credence to each other's suggestions or ideas, and neither will take the other's opinion very seriously.

The problem is that in our very human desire to associate with others, we have a built-in preference for associating with others who are like ourselves—people who share our beliefs, our values, our philosophies.[9] Most of us take more comfort in being with people who share our own point of view, simply because this affirms our thinking and assuages our ego.[10] By contrast, we have a natural aversion to strange and unknown things, and this aversion has an effect on whom we choose to associate with and rely on, which in turn affects our ability to understand and innovate. Diversity has a lot to recommend it, but it's not a natural instinct.

The tension created in our minds between new or unanticipated information and our own more comfortable illusion of control is a tool that helps us understand the world. And we're all familiar with people who seem to have gotten this tool out of whack. If someone is so open to new information that he never worries about its trustworthiness, then we say he's "gullible." Conversely, if someone is so averse to new information that *nothing* passes her trustworthiness test, we call her "close minded." Either way, you can't trust what *they* say without running their point of view through your own trust filter.

On the other hand, when you strike just the right balance between acceptance and skepticism, seeking out the most trustworthy new ideas and then allowing them to change, improve, and enrich your own perspective—this is a talent all too few of us have. You probably know people like this, though. They're called "iconoclasts."

In the end, the degree to which we trust new information has a great deal to do with whether we trust the source—the person we get the information from. Everyone reading this book probably has some relative or friend who blasts out e-mail after e-mail promoting his own political, religious, or economic point of view. It may be your Uncle Charlie, and while you love him dearly, you wouldn't attempt to have a serious discussion with him about his views because they're set in stone. And have you ever bought something from a company, signed up for the e-mail updates, and then had to block the sender just to stop them from e-mailing you multiple times a week?

> Trust is the primary data filter protecting our attention span, and as the volume of data grows, this filter has to work more efficiently.

■ So here are the key questions: Do your customers trust the information they get from you? And what information can *you* trust when you make business decisions?

Chapter 46

Science, Trust, and Evidence-Based Management

If we have data, let's look at data. If all we have is
opinion, let's go with mine.

JIM BARKSDALE[1]

In order to benefit from the most useful information, we have to will our-selves to relish surprise and embrace the unpredictable—to be iconoclas-tic. For many of us, this may require a new mind-set and decision-making discipline.

The "scientific method" is designed in large part to overcome the flaws and biases in the thinking of individual scientists, ensuring that whatever new information or insight is gained from experimentation can be trusted. Valid and reliable scientific experiments are those that do a good job mea-suring what they purport to measure (demonstrating validity), and show results that can be replicated by others in similar experiments (demon-strating reliability). When scientific studies are published in journals, their trustworthiness is enforced by peer reviews.

But while the scientific method may work very well for science, it isn't used very often in making business management decisions. A good sci-entist tries hard to recognize his own biases and prejudices, but most business executives aren't so disciplined in their thinking. In fact, the higher the title, the more likely the executive is to think that he or she got there precisely because her way of thinking is just, well, right.

In his best-selling book *Super Crunchers*, for example, Yale economist Ian Ayres wrote that the best way to employ an expert opinion is to sup-plement and enhance whatever conclusions or implications we see in our analysis of the data. Analysis should come first, before applying intuition, hunches, or judgments, which should then be used to improve and check our understanding of the data. *Start* with the data, in other words, *then* apply judgment, and *then* make a decision.

In the field of medicine, helping doctors to use data before applying their own hunches and prior beliefs can be a matter of life and death, and as a result the discipline of evidence-based medicine (EBM) has been introduced. Whatever judgment the doctor makes will be based not just on his or her own perspective but on the best available prior evidence as well. Unfortunately, this discipline is not universally applied because not all medical professionals are equally capable of objectively balancing judgment and facts. Moreover, EBM itself constitutes a kind of belief system and might easily conflict with a medical professional's prior beliefs (for instance, that his or her own first-impression hunch or intuition is likely to be correct).[2]

Nevertheless, in terms of improving information competence, EBM is a good example for business leaders to emulate. Jeffrey Pfeffer and Stanford's Robert I. Sutton suggest that evidence-based management requires adopting the kinds of beliefs and settings "that enable people to keep acting with knowledge while doubting what they know, and to openly acknowledge the imperfections in even their best ideas along the way."[3]

Roger Martin, dean of the University of Toronto's Rotman School of Management, is someone who has spent a great deal of time studying the traits of successful business leaders. His conclusion:

> . . . [M]ost of them share a somewhat unusual trait: They have the predisposition and the capacity to hold in their heads two opposing ideas at once. And then, without panicking or simply settling for one alternative or the other, they're able to creatively resolve the tension between those two ideas by generating a new one that contains elements of the others but is superior to both. This process of consideration and synthesis can be termed integrative thinking.[4]

Evidence-based management would help executives deal with the ever-increasing flood of data now available, while keeping their personal biases and limitations in check. To do this properly, however, executives would also have to become more comfortable with the language and best practices of data analysis and statistics—control groups, correlation versus causation, standard deviations, confidence intervals, statistical significance, testing the null hypothesis, and so forth. Analytics can help us shape our own judgments more objectively, with better results, but it will require an effort to improve our mathematical literacy—or "numeracy"—first.

It's easy to find examples of poor mathematical thinking, and the consequences are often startling. One of the most infamous examples of flawed statistical reasoning, for instance, came in the O. J. Simpson trial, when the prosecution maintained that because O.J. had frequently abused Nicole Simpson in the past, it was more likely that he had also murdered her. The defense easily overcame this argument by telling the jury that of the 4 million women battered by their husbands the previous year, only 1 in 2,500 was actually murdered. By letting this highly persuasive argument stand, the prosecution demonstrated a complete lack of statistical knowledge (as did the press, various legal commentators, and others involved in assessing the case as it unfolded). Regardless of your own opinion about the actual verdict, the outcome might have been different had prosecutors pointed out a different and more relevant statistic: Of all the women who were battered by their partners in the previous year and *also* murdered, 90 percent of *them* had in fact been murdered by their abusers.[5]

Understanding statistical analysis is way more important for the current generation of managers than it was for the last, not just because there is so much more information, but also because the task of performing sophisticated and complex statistical computations is so easy with today's technology. Decision science experts, economists, and other academics are all over this problem, urging business managers to come to the table and become more informed.

One customer research firm based in Sydney, Australia, for example, describes on its blog how the firm manages its own analytical process when trying to glean the right insights from massive quantities of data:

> With the rapid advances in text analytics it is very tempting at this level to stay focused on the [customer] comments, but our experience is that as the feedback is aggregated, the need to rely on the numbers becomes critical. It is very easy to analyse comments and stumble over an insight that backs up your gut-feel or pre-disposition; but without the numbers, it is also very easy to overplay the significance of your insight or, worse still, be downright wrong![6]

Suppose, for instance, that you're a board member of a company trying to align the interests of senior managers with the interests of shareholders. It's obvious to everyone on the board that such an alignment requires managers' monetary incentives to be structured so as to go up in value when share prices rise, and down when they decline. Based on this, you decide on a program of stock option awards for the senior executives who have the broadest powers to affect the company's performance. It won't be hard to find success stories that buttress this decision. But that would be the wrong way to approach it. Never assume that because something seems "intuitively obvious" it must be correct. The right way to make this kind of decision is to start with the data: Ask first what evidence actually exists demonstrating both the effectiveness and the ineffectiveness of executive stock options.

If that had been the process, you would have found some favorable evidence to support your plan, but you would also have found some disturbingly unfavorable evidence. You would have learned that numerous studies show stock options are often counterproductive, setting up a climate of gamesmanship, expectations management, and even fraud. In fact, one study of more than four hundred companies found that "the higher the proportion of the senior executives' pay in stock options, the more likely the company was to have restated its earnings."[7] After considering this data you may still have elected to adopt a stock option plan, but your judgment would have been much better informed.

Unfortunately, our natural bias is to make our decisions the other way around, making a judgment first and then searching out the evidence to support it. That's just the way our psychologies are structured. But in order to see our customers' needs more clearly, and to take action more effectively, we have to dedicate ourselves to better, more objective and accurate management decisions.

> Two forces are converging and fundamentally changing business: increasing data complexity and escalating customer expectations. Handling the former is a way to keep pace with the latter. This situation underscores the urgency of integrating companies' data sources to gain a holistic view of the customer.... Having this ability to analyze cross-channel data is the ultimate goal for business intelligence practitioners.
>
> *JUDI HAND, EXECUTIVE VICE PRESIDENT,*
> *CUSTOMER GROWTH SERVICES, TELETECH*

Ironically, it may be the case that the social science disciplines do a better job of preparing managers for a world of incomplete answers, randomized events, and probabilistic information. Engineers and physicists can do the higher math, but the problems they usually deal with almost always have straightforward solutions. Engineers can precisely calculate the tensile strength of a steel girder or the escape velocity for putting a satellite in orbit, but handling a problem that incorporates poorly understood, conflicting, or unreliable inputs is likely to be more familiar to a sociologist, a psychologist, or perhaps a behavioral economist.

In any case, our trust filters have to be robust and well tuned. Failing to recognize our own biases when making decisions will call into question our competence as managers, and the customers and others who are affected by our decisions may question our good intentions as well.

Chapter 47

Control Is Not an Option

Knock knock.
Who's there?
Control freak. And now *you* say "Control freak who?"

One of the principal benefits of truly enjoying the trust of customers is that executives will be able to deal more rationally and purposefully with those random fluctuations in every company's financial fortunes that would otherwise tend to throw a management team off its game. Trust is a *long-term* quality, conferring *long-term* financial benefits.

Random, unpredictable fluctuations in the blogosphere can trip up even the best efforts of managers to generate value with customer referrals or word-of-mouth marketing. It's one thing to host honest customer reviews on your own website, but it's another thing entirely to encourage customers to recommend your product to others, no matter how good your product is. Even the best, most carefully constructed word-of-mouth marketing programs can be difficult to implement because cascades of opinion, critical or not, can appear suddenly and unpredictably.[1]

The office-supplies retail chain Staples launched a word-of-mouth initiative called "Speak Easy" a few years ago. Speak Easy was designed to encourage the company's most valuable customers to spread the word among their colleagues and associates about the benefits of various Staples products. Staples used the shopping records from its loyalty card program to identify its most frequent, high-spending customers and invite them to join Speak Easy, and then each month the firm would send a package of free product samples to those who had signed up. Included in each customer's shipment was a write-up of talking points touting the benefits of various products, and Staples hoped that these benefits would find their way into whatever conversation about a product a program member might occasionally have with others.[2]

That was as intrusive as it was, however, and there was no follow-up by the company to see whether any recommendations were ever made. Other than the free samples themselves, Staples gave no additional compensation or benefit to program members, nor did it attempt to track whether customers actually recommended the products. So on the surface, in other words, Staples seemed to have designed a very customer-friendly program. From a privacy and sharing standpoint, at least, the company did nothing wrong. There were no commercial incentives, there was no violation of the sharing ethos, and no unseemly spying on customers.

Despite this careful, trust-based architecture, however, the Speak Easy program soon became the subject of controversy on a number of customer blog sites and in the press, with one newspaper article labeling it "a stealth—some would say sneaky—marketing program." And sure enough, interest fell and Speak Easy was soon canceled.

In retrospect, however, it could just as easily have gone the other way. Other companies had launched word-of-mouth programs with less care, and with no outcry, and the cascade of opinion that felled Speak Easy seemed capricious. But was there something Staples could have done differently to increase its chance of success with Speak Easy? There were a number of actions Staples could have taken in advance of launching this program that would have given it a better chance of success, despite any random negative comments. For Speak Easy to have had a better chance to succeed, Staples should have tried to build its own trustability before launching the program, to make sure customers trusted the company to look out for their interests. Customers who didn't have any reason to believe that Staples was particularly trustable, and just expected "business as usual," were naturally wary of Staples's motives and more likely to speak out against the program.

So the real question here is, what could Staples have done to build up its trustability in advance? For one thing, as a well-known retailer of office supplies, it could easily have leveraged its reputation to offer services, assistance, advice, and business counsel to customers. What if, *prior* to trying to launch the word-of-mouth campaign, Staples had offered services on its website to help business owners and business product buyers better meet their needs? For instance, its site could have offered:

- Customer reviews and ratings of all the various products Staples carries, with the company playing a role as curator and authenticator.

- Different discussion groups for small businesses, for large enterprise office managers, government organizations, and nonprofits—so that Staples' different types of customers could find and communicate with others who have similar problems and needs.

- Advice and tips on how to manage your inventory of office products and supplies, from paper and envelopes to desk chairs, pens, laptops, and printer cartridges. Some of this advice should be from other customers, so the company should reach out to solicit comments.

- Office-supply inventory management tools and other applications designed to reduce costs.

- Ways to set up auto-replenishment or other enhanced delivery options, such as proactive reminders of exactly which ink cartridges will be needed and when.

The point is that if—*before* launching the Speak Easy program—Staples had developed a reputation as a trustable firm genuinely trying to *help* its retail customers, rather than simply selling to them, then not only would high-influence customers have been easy to recruit, but many of them would have *wanted* Staples to succeed, because the company had so much to offer in terms of helping business owners, office managers, and other professionals.

Chapter 48

Listen, Learn, and Eliminate Friction: It's How You Cultivate Trustability

One of the biggest learnings for many companies, when they begin a "listening" program to monitor problems involving their brand on Twitter, Facebook, and other social media platforms, is that just trying to identify who within a large corporation has actual responsibility for a problem can often be mind-numbingly difficult.

For example, in 2008 Frank Eliason helped launch the widely celebrated Comcast Cares program, an initiative designed to allow the giant cable company to identify customer problems and complaints by monitoring Twitter and other social media and microblogging sites.[1] By scanning constantly for mentions of the Comcast name (and other related monikers), Eliason and his team were able to pick up budding complaints, usually before they were called in to the contact center or escalated into more serious issues.

Although responding quickly and honestly to complainers went a long way toward defusing bad situations, Frank told us that his team seemed to spend the majority of its time (90 percent, he estimated) just trying to determine who, within the broader Comcast network of companies, operating units, and subsidiaries, was actually "in charge" of whatever process had given rise to each customer problem identified.[2]

Finding out who's in charge, of course, is the first step required to fix the problem, which usually involves eliminating some source of friction in the customer experience. For more than twenty years now we've maintained that customer complaints should really be thought of as opportunities, rather than as problems. They can be one of the key sources for improving the level of service you provide, along with your overall customer offering. Social listening programs, which have really become feasible only in the last decade or so, now allow you to skim the surface of an entire ocean of customers in order to identify all these opportunities to eliminate friction in the customer experience.

It will be hard to do, but regardless of the difficulty, it's important to make decisions regarding social sentiment quickly, when necessary, if you want to be able to show a genuinely "human face" to customers. If you act slowly, you'll look like a bureaucracy or—worse—a psychopath. So unless you want every such crisis escalated immediately to the CEO suite, we suggest you might want to consider running the same kinds of "fire drills" for social media problems that many companies already run for other possible problems. As one commentator suggested:

> *A major area where social media crises differ from "real world" crises (although one often begets the other now) is that most companies have not yet identified their communication protocols. If something unfortunate happens to your brand in social media, who in your company is in charge of identifying the problem? Whom do they call? Who needs to be alerted? The same way most companies have call lists and alert procedures determined for offline crises, you must develop similar processes for social media.*[3]

Here's the point: Cultivate your reputation for trustability, on purpose. *Your trustability is a part of the system's trustability.*

In the end, you have to be prepared for failure, success, and everything in between. *But if others find you trustable, then you'll never be on your own.* As long as your focus is always on *doing the right thing*, then your customers, your employees, and your other stakeholders will all have an interest in seeing your company weather whatever unpredictable storm might come your way. We could call it *trustproofing.*[4]

Chapter 49

Customer Reviews Are
Inevitable. Deal with It.

It's a tough world out there. Technology moves faster than ever, and the social winds of customer sentiment can build to gale force instantaneously. If you want to survive in this new world of transparent, always-on interactivity and rapid, unpredictable shifts in opinion, don't wait for the storm to hit. Get ready for it now. The Scouts said it over a hundred years ago: Be prepared.

But first, here's a kind of "self-assessment" question that might indicate how well your company is prepared for trustability:

Do you allow customers to make comments about your products and services on your own website, for other customers and prospective customers to see?

To be proactively trustworthy, a company *must* facilitate customers' sharing their honest opinions with other customers about the problems they are trying to solve or the needs they are meeting, and this honest sharing will include, of necessity, the role that the company's own products and services play.

In the pre-Internet world, of course, customer reviews were rare. Customers had no electronically efficient capability to "talk back" to marketers or share their views with other customers. You couldn't just use your mobile phone to broadcast your customer experience to your tweeps or Facebook friends. As a result, there was no efficient way to enforce trustworthiness or to punish those who couldn't be trusted. When

customers are technologically unable to spread the word about untrustworthy behavior, the control freaks responsible for managing a brand
never get punished, never get corrected, never even face serious
questioning—at least not by their customers, and not in public view.

This doesn't mean that companies weren't always concerned with their
reputations, because they were. Companies have always spent money and
effort to ensure that their well-crafted brand images spoke of integrity, authenticity, honesty, and respect. But in the final analysis, in the presocial
era companies' brand images were still largely under their own control.

> **Traditional marketing doesn't have to *be* trustworthy. It
> merely has to *appear* trustworthy.**

But appearances are no longer sufficient. Spin is out, trust is in, and
the fact that a higher standard is being applied today by more and more
consumers in a wider and wider variety of marketing and selling situations owes much to the e-social revolution.

When they engage in dialogues with you, customers just want their
needs met. Most aren't all that interested in being "sold to," although sometimes they have to tolerate a sales message in order to get at the information
they need. But hearing the honest opinion of another customer? That's useful. That's informative. And it's usually more objective than a sales message
or a brand slogan.

Executives have lots of perfectly logical reasons to fear making their
customers' honest opinions freely available. What if a customer has a
complaint and goes public with it, right on our own website? Or what if
a customer just doesn't like the product? Or what if a competitor mas-
querades as a customer and runs our product down?

We've heard all these complaints and more. Listen up: Get over it. If
you abdicate your own role in the conversation, you are simply undermining your trustability. (Anyway, people will ask, What are you afraid
of—the truth?)

When your customers seek the advice of others—whether they turn to your own employees, or to other customers, or to complete strangers—what they're looking for is information. They want to *know*. They want the answers to all the questions they have about you, your service, and your products. Is the service worth the price? Are you as good as your competitor? Does your product really work? How hard is it to use? If it breaks, are you going to fix it? Would you take advantage of me or even rip me off if you got the chance? Am I going to feel comfortable doing business with you?

The answers to these questions may consist of fact or opinion, but they all constitute information, and it's information that's useful, because with it customers can do a better job of solving their problems, or meeting whatever needs they have. Information is the ammunition for every decision we make—not just in buying things, but in life itself. Information is how we navigate the world.

The reality is that truth is more persuasive than spin, and this is one of the secret advantages of allowing customers to be honest in their opinions with other customers. Do you remember the last time you went online to evaluate a product or service by scanning its reviews? Maybe you wanted to see what people were saying about a particular hotel or vacation package, or maybe it was a new car, or a video game, or a set of golf clubs. And when you navigate to a site where 100 percent of the reviews are composed of peachy-keen, five-star glowing praises—what's your reaction? Do you really believe these terrific reviews, or doesn't this imbalance create a suspicion in your mind? You aren't alone. Glowing reviews, in isolation, don't sell as well as mixed reviews. Really.

> While the average consumer rating of products on a 5-point scale is roughly 4.5, the numbers show that a negative review actually converts to a sale more effectively than a positive review.
>
> *BRETT HURT, COFOUNDER*
> *AND FORMER CEO OF BAZAARVOICE*

A bit of criticism from customers assures other customers that your online product reviews are authentic. They're genuine. You are trustable.

When a company hosts this kind of information exchange, it is departing from the money-dominated commercial ethos of economic self-interest. Rather than unswerving self-promotion, when you make it easy for customers to find out what other customers honestly think about your product or service, you are showing a human face and proving your trustability.

There are already a whole host of e-social places where your product or brand can be openly discussed, including all the social media sites—not just gigantic communities like Facebook or Myspace, but thousands of other niche communities all over the Web. In addition, many sites are specifically dedicated to soliciting and compiling reviews, depending on your category, including Amazon, TripAdvisor, Yelp, Viggle, RateItAll, and Epinions, for example.

None of these services, of course, involves putting a customer review directly on your own website. But while you may not want this, your customers will. Your customers will want the convenience of being able to read other customers' views of your product or service without having to search too hard for them. So even if they comment as well on other sites—even if they comment *more* on other sites—they are still likely to want to see the opinions of other customers somewhere nearby, right where they're looking at the product, if they feel like it.

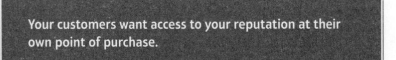

Your customers want access to your reputation at their own point of purchase.

And as technology continues to facilitate faster and easier interaction, you can bet your last Facebook game credit that customers will soon be reviewing products right on your own website, *with or without* your permission, using a variety of Web annotation apps, from StumbleUpon, Digg, Crunchbase, Appappeal, and other vendors.

It is technologically inevitable. Take one small step into the future, and soon (probably very soon) we'll see new and more useful ways to access others' Web annotations, integrating the annotated Web with the mobile technology of augmented reality. Imagine pointing your smartphone at a restaurant across the street, or a product in a store, and seeing on your screen competitive pricing information, along with reviews and opinions of the restaurant or product posted by other customers, or by your friends, or by the friends of your friends. Services like Foursquare already offer nearly this level of service. By the time you read this, if you're twenty-something, you'll be doing it.

The point is that no matter how big a gulp you have to take, *your customers will talk about your brand whether you want them to or not*, and with or without your participation. (So wouldn't you rather have the conversation happen on your own doorstep?) In the end, you have to choose: Either give up control in a peaceful and orderly way or have it wrested from you forcibly.

This is a technology-fueled express train. The only decision you can make is whether to board the train or lie down on the track.

Chapter 50

Sockpuppeting for Fun
and Profit

But wait! What if a competitor poses as your customer and posts a negative review?

This can be a problem in an online world characterized by anonymous user IDs, where masquerading is practical and easy and registrations can be treated as disposable. Remember the old *New Yorker* cartoon? On the Internet, nobody knows you're a dog.[1]

Here's the thing: Any competitor who stoops to this kind of dirty trick today is playing a very dangerous game himself. Even if he succeeds for a while in remaining anonymous, sooner or later he is likely to be outed by the same transparency dynamic that operates on everyone else, and technology's advances make this a more and more probable outcome. In 2007, for instance, the CEO of Hollinger International, Conrad Black, stood trial for fraud. Among other things, prosecutors referred to the fact that Black had used an anonymous online identity ("inspector") to blame short sellers for Hollinger's poor stock performance, even after his chief investor relations executive had told him it would likely violate securities regulations to do so. According to the *New York Times*, Black e-mailed the executive, "Don't be so straitlaced. . . . Get our story out." (Black was convicted and spent several years in prison.)[2]

A "sockpuppet" is an online anonymous persona employed to hide a person's identity, the way Black did. And sockpuppeting is a time-honored technique not just for protecting your own privacy but also for getting up to mischief—deceiving others, manipulating opinion, cheating on your spouse or partner, or violating trust in some other way.

While your competitor himself may be less likely to stoop to sockpuppeting these days for fear of being outed as a fake, *hiring* people to pose as customers and write fake reviews—both positive and negative—has become a cottage industry. Websites like Yelp, TripAdvisor, and Amazon depend on customer reviews for their credibility, and they're now being inundated with fake ones, often written for a few pennies each in India. (Note: eBay doesn't get many fake reviews because you can't review a seller on eBay without first buying from him.)

Fake reviews and other forms of "opinion spam" are a significant enough threat that sites depending on reviews for their credibility have often put in place complex algorithms designed to filter out fakes. These algorithms are similar to the spam filters that block out inauthentic e-mail messages. Yelp blocks a substantial number of the reviews it receives, but it also allows you to view the blocked reviews. The company won't discuss its algorithm. One Cornell research team publicized the fact that they had developed a new set of algorithms for detecting opinion spam, and they were immediately approached by a number of firms, including Hilton Hotels, TripAdvisor, and Amazon.[3]

Amazon's customer review system is considered integral to the success of the company. It has made several moves to protect this asset and its credibility. Amazon's review system averages all the ratings submitted for a product to award it a star rating, 1 to 5 stars. Fake reviews, or reviews bought by sellers to boost rating of product and sales, undermine the system. In April 2015, Amazon sued four websites that offer review writing and placement services for a fee, and in October 2015, it sued more than 1,114 providers of fake review services.[4]

In June 2015, Amazon rolled out a new review platform that has learning technology. Developed in house, the new system "will give more weight to newer reviews, reviews from verified Amazon purchasers, and those that more customers vote up as being helpful".[5] The new criteria for sorting reviews will affect the order the reviews appear in and the calculation of the five-star rating. Amazon also solicits reviews of products from verified buyers to boost reliable product assessment. Amazon is believed to have the largest review bank, outranking even big specialist stores in certain categories. And although thought by some to be a rather clunky social medium, no one argues with the Amazon review system's success for leveraging community feedback.

Something interesting about the e-social revolution, however, is that it is rapidly reducing the usefulness of anonymity when it comes to sharing and evaluating brands, opinions, products, or services. One of Facebook's biggest assets, for instance, is that it's almost impossible to pose as someone else on the service. After all, who's going to "friend" someone they've never heard of? And if you do agree to be friended by someone you don't know very well, isn't it because you share some mutual acquaintances, or perhaps a school or business relationship? Chris Kelly, Facebook's onetime head of privacy, maintains that "the friend infrastructure and an identity base ultimately is the key to safety. Trust on the Internet depends on having identity fixed and known."[6]

One of the quickest ways for people to verify the trustworthiness of information or opinion, including product reviews, is to see whether their friends or associates find it trustworthy—if they vouch for it.

So as the importance of trust increases and our e-social connections multiply, you can look for a rising number of services and applications that allow consumers to filter what they pay attention to by tapping the opinions or judgments of their friends and colleagues.

This kind of social filtering will soon come to dominate how people evaluate information and opinion for its trustability. Rather than just looking at the opinions of complete strangers when you evaluate a product or service, why not check the opinions of your friends first? Or of the friends of your friends? One thing is for sure: Your friends are not shills hired from a foreign country for nickels at a time, right?

In the time since the hardcover edition of *Extreme Trust* was published, we've seen services appearing that allow you to screen product reviews and other opinions so that you just see those posted by people in your own social graph. Facebook's Graph Search product is one such offering. As *Fast Company* said about Graph Search when it first appeared,

"The promise is that you'll find answers to queries that might stump Google, such as . . . 'friends of friends who like my favorite band and live in Palo Alto' or 'Indian restaurants in Palo Alto that friends from India like.'"[7]

So rather than trusting a five-star review from a stranger you've never heard of (and who could easily be a paid shill), you'll be able to see what your friends, or the friends of your friends, or maybe even their friends, have said about some product or service.

Or consider another social-filtering application: You know when you go to a news organization's website and one of the choices is whether you want to see the "most popular" or the "most e-mailed" news stories? It won't be long before these organizations start to tell you which news stories have been the most popular or most e-mailed stories by others in your own social graph. Here's what your friends, or the friends of your friends, have found the most interesting. This seems inevitable, whether media companies figure out how to do it for you themselves or others do it for you without their participation.

Today, of course, we are just scratching the surface of consumer-to-consumer interaction. In fifteen or twenty years, Zuckerberg's law suggests, there will likely be a thousand times as many product and service reviews and a thousand times as much information content, from news articles to blog posts and Twitter trends. And fifteen or twenty years after that we'll have a million times as much as today. So service applications that get the jump on helping consumers benefit from social filtering are likely to see a strong competitive advantage within just a few years, because we'll all be relying more and more on our friends' opinions for help.

Chapter 51

The Power of an Apology

In the e-social age, apologizing for honest errors will be a potent strategy for earning the trust of customers. *Seeking forgiveness is a form of social aikido.* Rather than resisting someone else's action, you are actually using their momentum in your own cause.

You can become more trustable to others by becoming more trusting *of* others. Exposing your own vulnerability is one of the fastest ways to earn someone else's trust, because you are signaling that you trust them.

RECOVERING LOST TRUST[1]

Research has shown that both your perceived concern for others (i.e., your good intentions) and your past behavior (i.e., your competence) are major factors in the degree to which others trust you. Academicians studying trust to learn what conditions promote it or discourage it, how it is broken, and how it can be restored, have found:

▶ One way to help restore trust, when it has been lost through untrustworthy behavior, is simply to apologize. Customers can forgive incompetence if you recognize and acknowledge your own boneheaded behavior as such and if you state clearly how you are cleaning up your processes to make sure it doesn't happen again. Hint: If you do apologize, just do it, without excuses. Don't say, "But you have to understand . . ." or "It wasn't our fault entirely." Just say, "We goofed, we're sorry, it won't happen again." Include a gift, if appropriate, in order to drive home the sincerity of your apology.

▶ Good behavior is the single most effective way to restore trust after an episode of bad or untrustworthy behavior. Even though a stated promise of better behavior does accelerate the growth of trust, trustworthy actions alone are every bit as effective in the long term.

▶ Although trust lost through bad behavior can generally be restored after a period of good behavior, when trust is violated with both bad behavior *and* deceptive statements, it never fully recovers. Incompetence can be forgiven, in other words, but bad character is a fatal flaw. This is one of the biggest problems plaguing most firms, because the first officials on the scene of a service disaster are usually the PR folks, and no matter how good it is, spin is the opposite of straight talk.

▶ Interestingly, research has also shown that using a binding contract probably erodes the trust of a customer or business partner. People who use binding contracts make situational judgments, rather than personal judgments, when assessing how trustworthy the other party is.[2]

While we're on the subject of apologies, please note that people will forgive mistakes due to incompetence much more quickly than they will forgive mistakes due to deception or selfish motivations. When you screw up, be frank and 'fess up immediately. Do not even be tempted to deny things, because inevitably the cover-up will always be worse than the crime.

Even in businesses in which serious problems are inevitable, and negotiation by lawsuit has prevailed in the past, exposing your vulnerability and talking about it openly can actually minimize the damage from customer problems. Toro, the lawn mower and snowblower company, had a long history of personal injury litigation in its business. For years, the firm's management simply accepted these lawsuits as a cost of doing business, reasoning that injuries were inevitable with the types of products they made. In the mid-1990s, however, Toro began to wonder whether litigation had to be as inevitable as the injuries were. Yes, the firm manufactured products with spinning blades, and a mistake while using a lawn mower is inherently more dangerous than a mistake made while using, say, a washing machine. And yes, many, if not most, of the mistakes are actually made by the user—the customer. But if the firm were really to take the customer's point of view—if it were actually to *empathize* with a customer's own interest—what would it do? How would a customer actually *like* to be treated?

In answer to this question, the company initiated a new policy, sending apologetic representatives to meet personally with injured customers. These representatives sympathized with customers, acknowledged their suffering, and suggested quick settlements to avoid the lengthy delays and high costs of going to court. And the results were impressive, not just for the firm's customers, but for its bottom line as well. Using "nonthreatening paralegals, experienced settlement counselors, and mediators familiar with Toro's preference for early case resolution," the company suggested that disagreements, if they arose, could be worked out with less hassle in arbitrations. In the first ten years of this new policy, Toro has not had to go to court for even a single personal injury issue, and the company estimates it saved about $100 million in litigation costs.[3]

Now in this kind of situation we can question whether Toro's customer settlements are really in "the customer's interest" or not. After all, it's certainly possible that an injured customer could, by hiring the right attorney, achieve a higher monetary settlement in a court of law. But our argument is that trustability trumps pure self-interest. Supremely rational self-interest tells only half the story, and not even the most important half. Trustability, on the other hand, is produced by empathy, by emotion, and by the deep-seated human instinct to connect with other people and *to be social.*

Lawn mower accident victims don't sue Toro for the same reason that legitimately injured patients don't sue doctors with a genuinely caring bedside manner and that USAA members send refunds back to the company: because people value so highly what they perceive to be genuinely good intentions. We all know everybody makes mistakes. People are slow to forgive bad intentions, but they can forgive honest mistakes.

Chapter 52

Letting Bygones Be Bygones

It is inevitable that mistakes will happen, so we have to deal with it. Bad things will happen, random events will confound the most well-meaning efforts of the best companies, and businesses can put on a "human face" only by letting go of the control-freak obsession with managing and directing everything. Trusting others, in order to be trusted yourself, means that mistakes can't be avoided even if your own performance is perfect. Mistakes and errors just have to be a part of your business plan.

And then, life must go on, and commerce must continue to take place. So it's very unlikely that any single mistake will cripple your company for good, unless it cascades into a crisis of trustability that is truly catastrophic and insurmountable. Ultimately, because failures are inevitable, and because transparency and openness mean that failures will be exposed to everyone's view, apologies and forgiveness are likely to become art forms in the socially networked world. This is a far cry from the way traditional public relations professionals and marketers have always operated. The hunker-down impulse is strong in the PR profession, but in today's new e-social environment this is exactly the wrong instinct.

Unfortunately, however, "no comment" can sometimes be the unintended consequence of a rapidly moving social media environment. The social media system has its own dynamic, and it is in the nature of electronically transmitted word-of-mouth opinions that the system's feedback loops are prone to generating very significant, very rapid, and completely unpredictable waves of sentiment—oscillations that can't be foreseen and can spring to life in days, or even hours. If you don't pay attention to what is being said about your brand on a more or less continual basis, then you will always be at the mercy of the system's capriciousness.

As more and more interactions occur online, more and more mistakes will be made and exposed—mistakes not just on the part of companies and brands but on the part of individuals as well. We all know the stories. One 2009 poll of U.S. businesses found that a third of employers had rejected job candidates based on things uncovered on social networks, including "provocative or inappropriate photographs or information."

Does this mean that people will soon become more timid, more reserved, and less spontaneous? Perhaps. On the other hand, it might mean that society, as a whole, will become a bit more forgiving and tolerant. Everyone makes mistakes. Everyone.

The fact is that personal information will continue to be more and more widely disseminated, because this is simply an unintended by-product of social networks, and social networks are here to stay. This will almost certainly lead to a more tolerant and less judgmental society because, as Adam Penenberg poignantly says in his book *Viral Loop*, "shame is largely generational. If you are in your forties or older, your parents didn't talk about their feelings; today you can barely stop younger people from telling you their life stories."[1]

Don once had a discussion with his seventeen-year-old son about the importance of protecting his online reputation, suggesting that if his son were to put inappropriate pictures or videos online, they would inevitably come back to haunt him. He warned that even twenty years in the future, when his son is thirty-seven and being interviewed for an important job, the interviewer may be able to access this kind of dirty laundry. At which point the son gave his father one of those "seriously?" looks, and presented a different perspective. "Dad," he said, "When I'm thirty-seven and interviewing for a job, don't you think the interviewer will have his *own* dirty laundry online too?"

Chapter 53

Cultures in Transition

The need to be transparent, open, and trustworthy is self-evident to those already involved in these new technologies, and a willingness to give up some control is the price of admission. No one who has observed the e-social revolution up close has any doubt about its dynamics. And the ones who are most successful tend to get it "in their bones." Clive Thompson, writing in *Wired* magazine, says, "Some of this isn't even about business; it's a cultural shift. . . . A generation has grown up blogging, posting a daily phonecam picture on Flickr and listing its geographic position in real time on Dodgeball and Google Maps. For them, authenticity comes from online exposure. It's hard to trust anyone who *doesn't* list their dreams and fears on Facebook."[1]

Victor Stone, the entrepreneur behind ccMixter, commented to Lawrence Lessig, "You know . . . this discussion will be over in ten or twenty years. As the boomers . . . get over themselves by dying, the generation that follows . . . just doesn't care about this discussion. They just assume that remixing is part of music, and it's part of the process, and that's it."[2]

> The future is already here—it's just not evenly distributed yet.
> WILLIAM GIBSON, SCIENCE FICTION AUTHOR[3]

We suspect Stone is correct, not just about remixing music, but about many other aspects of this technology-induced cultural shift. If you pick this book up to read it twenty years from now, you will likely wonder what all the fuss was even about. By then, a completely new ethos will have emerged for governing how content is created, owned, and shared, how businesses "manage" their own image, how personal privacy is handled, and how people come together to get things done. In twenty years it will be obvious to all of us. Looking back we will say, "Of course it had to be like this; it was inevitable."

But right now, today, giving up control and wading into the "chaos of community," as Tara Hunt called it, is terrifying. It is a gut-wrenchingly scary prospect for any business manager and represents a complete subversion of the power structure. Thompson, in his *Wired* article, summarizes the dilemma facing today's business executives like this:

> *The Internet has inverted the social physics of information. Companies used to assume that details about their internal workings were valuable precisely because they were secret. If you were cagey about your plans, you had the upper hand; if you kept your next big idea to yourself, people couldn't steal it. Now, billion-dollar ideas come to CEOs who give them away; corporations that publicize their failings grow stronger. Power comes not from your Rolodex but from how many bloggers link to you—and everyone trembles before search engine rankings.*

Giving up control turns the "inverted social physics" of online interactivity into a tremendous asset—but it obviously can't be directed from the top down. It has to rise up from the bottom. Your Facebook "fans"—or your friends or customers or colleagues or connections—have to *want* your effort to succeed, either because they get a thrill out of it themselves or simply because they like you and trust you. Whatever their reason, if you want them to have empathy for you, and to wish the best for you, then you have to go with what *they* want. You have to let them join the conversation themselves, realizing that the conversation itself will be changed just by their joining it.

This is not just a cultural transition but a transformation. No matter how good you are, bad stuff could happen. Social media asteroids will inevitably crash into different companies at different times. Control won't be possible. You have to build up your reservoir of trustability in advance, *before* the asteroid strikes. John Costello, former chief global marketing and innovation officer of Dunkin' Donuts and now chairman of the Global Board of the Mobile Marketing Association, says it's like a savings account:

> *You make deposits by doing the right things for customers, treating employees fairly, making it work. You have to realize everything you do affects trustability, including how you handle it when things go wrong. And in the end, you have to make sure your deposits exceed your withdrawals. Promise what you deliver, and deliver what you promise. Consistently.*[4]

In the less predictable but more transparent e-social world, a company's *good intentions*, as evidenced by its decisions and actions, are the primary criterion customers use to decide whether they can trust the company, and the *competence* to deliver on those good intentions determines whether or not customers will really be able to see into the soul of that company. You can call it managing the customer experience, or delivering on customer insights, or simply the right hand knowing what the left is doing, but when you commit to trustability, you have to get the basics right. Competence counts every bit as much as good intentions. And when everyone is watching, you'll have to be proactive about it.

Chapter 54

Start Planning for Trustability Now

At its root, Extreme Trust is not a complicated idea, but it does require overcoming a lot of barriers. The three basic principles we summarized in chapter 6 were:

1. Do things right.

2. Do the right thing.

3. Be proactive.

Philosophically, all we're talking about with these three central principles is ensuring that the components of trustworthiness—*good intentions* and *competent execution*—are *proactively* pursued, rather than just passively acknowledged. Still, this requires a company to undertake a substantial change to the way it probably does business today, even if it is already a highly trustworthy and admired brand. Doing the right thing will often be difficult to justify financially, for example, unless you are competent enough in customer analytics to be able to quantify the long-term financial value represented by customers' good opinions of your business. And being proactive about protecting customers' interests will, of necessity, require admitting mistakes when they happen, rather than hiding them—something that will almost certainly come up against stiff resistance in the legal department, not to mention PR.

So as you focus on these three principles—"Do things right," "Do the right thing," "Be proactive"—you'll need to keep in mind what you've learned in this book about how the Age of Transparency really works. To be trustable, you need to know how to gain traction in the e-social world:

- *Think long term.* You can't be trustable if you're entirely focused on the short term. And customer relationships are the link between short-term actions and long-term value in a business. If you don't have the ability to embrace the long term, then don't even think about trying to become more trustable, because eventually your flawed arithmetic and off-center metrics will do you in. You'll never be able to build a business model focused on "doing the right thing" for customers if you can't justify it to your shareholders. Period.

- *Share.* People want to contribute and share with others. That's what human beings like to do, and if you want your business to be trustable, then you'll find ways to share too. Your business needs to contribute, so share your ideas, your technology, and your data. Make your intellectual property more freely available, in order to stimulate faster innovation. Said another way: Trust others the way you want them to trust you. And remember that the currency of the sharing economy is trust, not money. So be careful when navigating between the social domain and the commercial.

- *Show a "human face."* Empathy is not just a business strategy for demonstrating trustability. Empathy is a basic human instinct, and for a business, empathy is what developing "customer insight" is all about, in the first place. In addition to empathy, if you want to show a "human face" to the world, acting as another human being would, then you have to admit your fallibility when it is appropriate. No one is perfect, and this goes double for a business. So accept your vulnerability. It will never be possible to control all outcomes.

■ *Rely on evidence.* As technology promotes more and more interaction and transparency, businesses will have to figure out how
to cope with a supernova of information. If you want to be trustable, then you have to be able to evaluate this information for its
objectivity and accuracy. Don't ignore judgment and intuition,
but pay attention to numbers and data. And take the steps required to deal with the inevitability of random events: Pay more
attention to numbers and statistical best practices, measure inputs
in addition to outcomes and results, and plan more carefully for
alternatives and multiple scenarios.

■ *Ensure a high-quality product and service, delivered on
time, well executed, and reasonably priced.* Product competence is a requirement, not an option. No one will trust any company, no matter how good they think its intentions are, if the
product or service has flaws. Mistakes can be forgiven, but the
fewer the better, and continued incompetence is a sign that a
company just doesn't care enough about its good intentions to
take the steps necessary to ensure they are carried out.

■ *Continuously improve your IT systems and maintain
up-to-date customer analytics, business intelligence, and customer experience mapping capabilities.* No one will trust a
business that doesn't have reasonably good customer data and analytics. It's an important part of customer competence. You don't
want to be that company that asks a customer for information
that you already ought to have, or tries to sell a customer a product they've already bought. Your customers remember you, and
you have an obligation to remember them, at least to a reasonable
extent. You'll need good IT; there's no other way.

■ *Maintain robust voice-of-customer feedback and interconnected mechanics.* A good customer relationship, based on trust,
is reciprocal. What the customer is telling you is every bit as

important as what your marketing and branding messages are trying to communicate to the customer. And remember that "omnichannel" is no longer a buzzword; it's a key strategic way of life. Hear and see a customer as one customer across time, across channels, across products, and across different customer identification points.

■ *Enable and engage your employees. Build a culture of trustability.* As good as your systems are, and as competent as your product and service are, things will still go wrong sometimes (there's that "human fallibility" thing again). No company will ever be able to routinize and automate everything, so you have to ensure that when something does go wrong, your employees are both capable and motivated enough to address the problem with little or no top-down direction. Your company's culture has to be based on using trust as a platform for stewarding individual customer relationships and experiences.

Chapter 55

Designing Trustability
into a Business

*Once the trust goes out of a relationship, it's really no
fun lying to them anymore.*

NORM PETERSON, ON THE TV SHOW *CHEERS* (1984)[1]

As transparency continues to increase and consumers become more
aware, increasing numbers of businesses are likely to find that a lot of the
fun has gone out of their customer relationships. It won't be nearly so lu-
crative to deceive customers, or to make money through customer error,
as more and more customers begin to realize what's going on.

Although the vast majority of businesses today are not in fact trustable, if you've followed our argument to this point, then we hope you're
already convinced that it will just be a matter of time before successful
companies will be routinely characterized as doing things right, and doing the right thing, proactively. Trustability is already becoming a predictor for success. The standards for what constitutes acceptable,
customer-oriented business activity are going up, and all businesses are
bound to become more and more trustable in the long run.[2]

Okay. Let's have a go at this. Write your company's name in the
blank in this sentence:

What would a trustable [your company's name here] *look like?*

Before you answer, you might want to take a look at what your customers are saying. Or maybe do a survey of your rank-and-file service

people, the way our mobile client did, way back in Chapter 3. The result might surprise you as much as it surprised them.

In the next part of this book, you'll find "trustability tests" based on the principles we've been discussing. Even before you work your way through that, though, here are some key summary questions:

- Do you remind customers if their warranty is up soon or if they are due for a free upgrade or other benefit?

- Do you warn customers if they may be buying too much of something or if the product or service they're buying might not be right for them?

- Do you allow customers to post their own honest reviews of your product or service on your website, for the benefit of other customers?

- Do you treat all customers the same or are you capable of treating different customers differently?

- Do you count on making money from customer mistakes, omissions, or oversights?

- Do you make more money by selling to well-informed and knowledgeable customers or to uninformed customers?

- Do you ever find it necessary to have one story inside the company but a different story (i.e., the "spin") for outsiders?

- If a social media disaster were to happen, do you know who at your firm has responsibility for interacting with the "crowd"? Have you ever done a "fire drill"?

- If a social media disaster were to happen, do your own best customers trust you enough to defend you?

- Do you pay sales commissions for selling products or do you reward people when they build relationships that increase the value of customers?

Better yet, take the customer's point of view. How many of your customers could agree enthusiastically with the following statements:

- I can depend on this company to do the right thing for me.

- I know this company will make sure I get the right deal.

- This company does things right and makes it easy for me.

- I would be willing to tell people I know how much I trust this company.

- I would be willing to pay a little more to do business with this company.

- I trust this company more than I trust their competition.[3]

In the final analysis, it is almost certain to be the new companies and the start-ups that employ these tactics to overturn the old way. They have less invested in the current paradigm, and less to lose by destroying it. Gradually, they will use trustability to transform our entire economic system, in the same way that interactivity has already transformed our lives. They will deploy honesty as a brutally efficient competitive weapon against the old guard.

As standards for trustability continue to rise, the companies, brands, and organizations shown to lack trustability will be punished more and more severely. But the sting of the transparency disinfectant will be greatest when the wounds are new. Very soon, for competitive reasons, all businesses, old and new, will begin to respond to the increase in demand for trustability by taking actions that are more worthy of trust from the beginning—that is, actions that are more transparently honest, less self-interested, more competently executed, less controlling, and more responsive to others' inputs. More proactively trustworthy. Trustable.

7

Trustability Tests

Trustability Tests

Think about how you'd answer these questions based on the way things work at your company, institution, or government agency. Talk about your answers with your colleagues. Visit www.extremetrustpaperback.com to compare your insights with those of other visitors.

TRUSTABILITY: OVERALL STRATEGY

If you defined "trustability" for consumers, and gave them examples of what a company in your industry would look like if it were trustable,

▷ How much more would customers be willing to pay?

▷ How much more share-of-customer would the company get?

▷ How much more likely would customers be to recommend you to a friend (Net Promoter Score)?

▷ How much less would customers cost to serve?

▷ How much could the burden for compliance and oversight be reduced?

▷ Would customers be more likely to follow company recommendations? How much?

▷ Would customers be more likely to forgive honest company mistakes?

▶ Would you say that your company's financial success is generally aligned with what's good for customers? Have you identified conflicts between how your firm succeeds financially and how it does what's good for customers, individually?

▶ If a customer is well informed, knowledgeable, and paying attention, would he choose to do business with your company or would he be more likely to choose a competitor?

▶ Relative to your immediate competitors, do you think customers find your company's trustability to be higher, about the same, or lower? Why?

▶ Is there anything about your relationship with a customer that would upset or displease a customer, if he knew it?

▶ Does your firm treat customers the way you insist that they treat you? When a customer makes a mistake in dealing with you—ordering the wrong item, for instance, and having to return it for a different one—you may ask the customer to pay a restocking fee, in addition to bearing the cost of the return. But if you were accidentally to ship a customer the wrong item, would you provide any kind of compensation to the customer, other than simply bearing the cost of the return?

▶ Do you use customer data and analytics to develop a sharper picture of what each customer needs from you, or are your analytics systems geared entirely toward assessing your customers' profitability, relative value, and likelihood of spending or not spending in the future? Stated another way, what examples can you name of how your customer analytics system has been used to improve the different customer experiences that your different customers have with your firm?

▶ How important is it for your business to make each quarter's sales and earnings numbers?

   ▷ Probably more important than almost any other legal outcome

   ▷ Very important, but not more important than anything

   ▷ Important, but we balance customer satisfaction or other metrics as well

   ▷ Equally important to long-term value building and growth in customer equity

▶ Does your company's analytics system quantify the financial benefits of customer retention? Of Net Promoter Score (NPS) or lifetime value metrics or other customer-satisfaction measures? Do you track customer referrals and calculate their financial benefits?

▶ Does your company model customer lifetime values or have some other analytically capable means of evaluating the financial asset values of customers? Can your analytics systems measure customer profitability on an individual or segment basis?

   ▷ Does your firm have the analytical capability to predict *changes* in individual customer lifetime values based on current interactions and events?

   ▷ Do any customer-asset metrics (such as actual and potential value, changes in lifetime value, or Return on Customer)[1] figure into business unit planning, employee rewards, or business unit performance?

▶ If your stock is publicly traded, does your company make earnings forecasts to analysts? If so, do you think this has ever affected your willingness to "do the right thing"?

▶ Would your customer analytics system be able to track the financial effect of:

    ▷ Higher or lower average customer satisfaction scores within a group or segment of current customers?

    ▷ Different customer acquisition offers, in terms not just of acquisition rates but of downstream retention, cross-sell, and service costs of newly acquired customers?

    ▷ A poorly handled (or well-handled) complaint from a particular customer?

    ▷ A salesperson at your firm who alerted a particular customer about a refund the customer didn't know about?

    ▷ Profit generated by a particular customer referred to you by another customer?

▶ Have you calculated your firm's approximate customer equity (see chapter 13)? Would it be possible to do so with your current analytics capabilities? Have you ever had a serious discussion about trying to do so? Would it be possible for you to update such a calculation regularly or in real time?

▶ Have you made any effort to measure your firm's trustability? Or to benchmark your current level against future measures? Or to compare with other companies? Or to get credit for the work you've been doing to build trustability?[2]

▶ Are there any social production initiatives that are displacing commercial activities or profits in your industry or business category? If so, what do you think is the primary motive for people participating in these initiatives?

▶ Do your customers trust your brand more than, about the same as, or less than they trust your competitors' brands? Products? Service? Reputation? Guarantees? The company? *What makes you think so?*

▶ Is your company focused more on long-term value creation or on short-term financial targets, or on both about the same?

▶ Think of some business result—positive or negative—that you would attribute almost entirely to luck, random events, or unpredictable actions by others. What favorable or unfavorable effects did this random result have on the compensation, position, or influence of various executives at your firm?

▶ Does your company track customer profitability by individual customer? By segment?

  ▷ Do you have some insight into the different lifetime values of different customers or types of customers?

  ▷ Have you identified the factors that account for significant changes in those lifetime values—up or down?

DO THINGS RIGHT

Do your employees have the tools and information they need to prompt customers to avoid an error? (Can your employees see it coming? Do you have a customer data system that can reliably recall individual customer transactions and preferences, and make them available at all customer contact points?)

▶ What portion of your company's customers are "captive," in the sense of remaining loyal because of convenience, or geography, or a contract or "plan" agreement, but not because of their positive attitude or preference?

▶ Do you believe your business provides "above-average customer service"? What portion of your customers would agree with you? And what portion of your own employees would agree with you? How often do you ask them?

▶ Where else do customers make comments about your company besides your website?

▶ Where would they prefer to comment? To look for comments by others?

▶ How easy is it for customers to find other customers' comments on your products and services?

▶ Have you ever "mystery shopped" the Internet to try to find reviews and comments on your products? Or on your competitor's products?

▶ What percentage of unsatisfied customers on the phone ask for "a supervisor" because the problem couldn't be handled by the person who took the call?

▶ Do your company's products and services have reasonably good quality—in other words, are they on a par with or better than the quality of products and services offered at similar prices by your competitors?

▶ Does your business maintain active relationships with your highest value customers?

▶ Do all customers hear from you the same way, get the same message from you, get the same offers from you, get the same level of service from you, and generally get the same treatment from you as other customers, or do you have different customer treatments designed for different customers or types of customers?

▶ Is your company's product-and-service offering broad enough so that individual customers' problems can be comprehensively solved, or do customers require additional products or services—that is, products or services you do not sell—in order to completely meet their needs?

▶ Do you maintain information systems capable of eliminating relatively minor customer mistakes and hassles, such as requiring a paper receipt as proof of purchase in order to complete a return or exchange? Are there areas in which small improvements in your own business processes or information flows could greatly improve the customer experience?

▶ Do you measure, track, and implement policies and initiatives to determine their effect on both customer satisfaction and customer dissatisfaction? On customer value?

▶ How do your customers seek out information about your industry, your product category, your services, your prices, and your company? How do customers make sure that the information they seek out about you is both objective and accurate?

▶ Can you explain these statistical concepts in plain English?

    ▷ Control groups

    ▷ Correlation vs. causation

    ▷ Standard deviations

    ▷ Confidence intervals

    ▷ Statistical significance

    ▷ Testing the null hypothesis

▶ Would you be able to recognize a slant in reporting when you read research results using these statistical concepts?

DO THE RIGHT THING

How do you define your company's "do the right thing" strategy? Is it more likely to mean:

    ▷ Doing what's best for the company's bottom line?

    ▷ Doing what's right for customers (and possibly the employees and the community)?

    ▷ Doing what's best for both?

▶ If one of your salespeople could make a sale by taking advantage of a customer's lack of knowledge, would he do so? For example, suppose an employee knows that a service contract or extended warranty agreement is not actually appropriate for a customer, but the employee still gets a commission for selling it. If you knew about this behavior on an employee's part, what would you do?

▶ Does your company make more money when customers forget to claim what they're entitled to?

▶ Does your company make more money when a customer commits a minor error—an error that's easy for the customer to make and would be easy for your company to fix, such as an inadvertent push of a button on a cell phone?

▶ If your business were a person, would your customers trust it to return a misplaced $5 bill?

▶ Are there things about the way you charge for services or handle problems that you keep secret in order to avoid customer complaints?

▶ Do customers know how much they actually pay your company for the services you render or the products you sell? (The question here is not whether you formally "disclose" this information, but whether customers actually *know*.)

▶ If "doing the right thing" for a customer meant incurring an expense, would your company still do it? For example, Amazon reminds you that you already bought a book you're trying to order, saving you from paying them again for the same book. Would your company do that? Who sets that policy, and how it will be evaluated?

228   Extreme Trust

▶ Does your business have empathy for customers? How is this demonstrated? Would your customers agree? (Hint: If your customers don't seem to have empathy *for* your business, then most likely they don't feel empathy *from* you.)

▶ Has your business ever been the victim of customer revenge for perceived bad service or untrustworthy behavior?

   ▷ If so, did your company actually do what the customer accused you of (even if the customer's story was not scrupulously accurate)?

   ▷ How did your company handle the accusation?

▶ Have you or any of your employees or partners ever used sockpuppet identities to post positive reviews of your brand or negative comments about competitors? Are you sure? What would happen inside the company if you discovered this practice?

▶ To what extent do you make it easy for visitors to authenticate themselves, even as you protect their identities? How do you balance (1) protecting visitors to the customer section of your website who are seeking objective information and (2) encouraging candid comments? Does your company have a policy with respect to identified employees participating in blogs and social media? Approximately how many or what proportion of your employees blog or comment on your company's behalf? Does anyone in your public relations department monitor this? Do you personally know of, or have you heard any stories about, any of your company's customers who actively advocate on your behalf to others?

   ▷ Do you have an initiative in place to identify such "advocates" on your behalf?

▷ Do you have any policies designed to promote the likelihood of customers becoming advocates?

▶ Do you currently have any competitors who have lower costs, faster delivery, or higher quality than you do? Have you ever sent a customer to a competitor because it was in the customer's best interest?

▶ If management finds out about a problem before social networking reveals it, how will it be handled: squelched, delayed, or reported publicly right away?

▶ Have you ever had one story or "spin" about events for the media and the general public while knowing that an alternative explanation was in fact more truthful?

▶ How often do you find yourself discussing a situation in an internal company meeting in ways that are different from what you say to the public?

▶ What criteria do *you* use to decide whether new information is worth your paying attention to?

▶ What criteria do *your customers* use to decide whether new information is worth paying attention to?

▶ When your customers read or hear statements from your company about your product or brand's benefits, do they trust what you say?

▶ When your company reports survey or research results to the public to make a point to customers, do you ensure that the information is truly objective and unbiased?

BE PROACTIVE

Do your employees proactively prompt customers to avoid errors or oversights? Whether your answer is yes or no:

▷ Is this part of their training?

▷ Is it part of your company's culture?

▶ Do you facilitate your customers' connecting with and helping one another to use your products or get the most benefit out of your products (i.e., crowd service)? If you don't, do you know whether and to what extent your customers connect with and help one another on their own?

▶ Have any of your customers formed a user group or some other, similar organization?

▶ If there are social production initiatives in your category, do you:

▷ Ignore them?

▷ Discourage them?

▷ Compete with them?

▷ Participate in them?

▶ Do any social production initiatives supplement or improve business activities and profits in your industry or category?

▶ Do your employees, suppliers, and distribution partners collaborate, using social media tools, in order to operate more efficiently and serve customers better?

▶ Have you identified the high-influence commentators in your business category—the people who blog and critique your brand, your business, and your competitors' brands? Do you reach out to them? How?

▶ Does your business monitor social media platforms for general sentiment and specific complaints? Do you do it five days a week or 24/7?

    ▷ How does your company's behavior change based on what you learn?

    ▷ Who has responsibility for responding to problems or issues uncovered by such social media monitoring?

    ▷ What authority do they have?

▶ Has your organization ever run a social media "fire drill"?

▶ If you wanted to build your company's trustability in advance of any potential social media conflagration, what steps could you take?

▶ What policies or processes do you employ now to help a budget-constrained customer better manage his or her spending on your company's products and services (i.e., to spend less, if it's in the customer's best interest)?

▶ If a social media disaster were to occur, causing a great deal of negative online publicity and commentary, how would you plan to dispel this negative comment and deal with the damage? Have you practiced this plan? How much would your own employees volunteer to help? What about your customers?

▶ Is there data available to your firm that, if it were more widely disseminated, would make it easier for customers and/or employees to address their issues and solve their problems?

▶ Do you allow customers to make comments about your products and services on your own website, for other customers and prospective customers to see? If so,

▷ How do you police these reviews and comments for obscenities or offensive language?

▷ How do you handle legitimate complaints and negative ratings? Do you:

▷ Take them down?

▷ Leave them in as part of the mix?

▷ Respond to customers and resolve the complaints?

▷ What mechanism, if any, do you use to minimize the chance that a competitor will contaminate the review process?

▷ Who at your firm takes charge of monitoring the reviews for useful feedback, systemic problems, and product improvement ideas? And who is responsible for making changes within the organization that will address the issues?

▶ Has your company tracked mentions of your brand or product on social media sites?

▶ Who at your firm ensures that poor service or mistakes are followed up with proactive apologies and "make-goods"?

▶ How soon after an incident is an apology rendered?

▶ You know that data is key. When you use data about customers, do you proactively protect their privacy?

CULTURE

Do your employees trust one another and work well together? Does your company ever admit errors to customers, or confess any kind of vulnerability? If it does, how does it make up for the mistake with customers? And if you admit mistakes, how do customers react?

▶ Do your employees think customers should trust your company?

▶ Which of the following topics are relevant to *most* internal business discussions about "customer loyalty" within your firm (choose all that apply)?

  ▷ Your points or frequency marketing program

  ▷ Repeat purchases from a customer

  ▷ Avoiding churn, or winning back customers who have left

  ▷ Gaining a greater and greater share of a customer's business over time

  ▷ Keeping a customer even if there's a problem

▷ Getting a customer to say good things about your brand or business, and/or recommend it to friends

▷ Higher customer satisfaction

▷ Less customer dissatisfaction

▷ Better customer experience

▷ Mapping customer journey

▷ "Customer-centricity"

▷ "Retention"

▶ Do any customer engagement metrics (such as customer satisfaction or Net Promoter Score) figure into business unit planning, employee rewards, or business unit performance?

▶ Do salespeople, executives, or others in your firm receive incentives for short-term performance that might prompt them to ignore or minimize long-term issues?

▶ Is anyone at your firm rewarded in the current term for predicted up-ticks in long-term value?

▶ Do your employees know of untrustable behaviors and policies at your company?

▷ Have you ever asked them?

▷ What would they do if they did know?

▶ If your company were unfairly victimized by some bad press or a false story, would any of your own customers come to your defense?

▶ In its marketing programs, does your company treat social media more as a channel for reaching customers and talking to them or as a mechanism for talking with customers and discussing issues?

▶ Do you have a social media policy that encourages, limits, or prohibits employees from participating, as employees? What other company social media policies have you reviewed, if any, in setting up your own?

▶ Does your company monitor Twitter, Facebook, and other social media platforms for mentions of your company, your competitors, and your business category?

   ▷ What is the protocol when your company, your products, or your brands are mentioned?

▶ Do you trust your employees, generally, to do the right thing for your business? If so, how far down in the hierarchy does this trust extend? What steps would you have to take to extend it even further?

▶ If a difficult customer problem was presented to two different employees at your company in isolation, would they probably approach the solution to the problem in a similar way? That is, do your employees all have a consistent view of the right way to handle customers and customer-related issues?

▶ Is your company's culture attuned to celebrating experimentation and new ideas?

   ▷ If an initiative or new idea fails, how are the executives involved evaluated?

▷ Would you say that being involved in a failed initiative is the "kiss of death" professionally at your firm?

▶ If an employee discovered a genuine mistake or problem in a product or service or discovered that "we did something wrong," would it be more likely to be concealed to avoid getting anyone into trouble or to be reported to management quickly so the problem could be resolved?

   ▷ Would the employee be more likely to:

      ▷ Conceal the problem to keep from getting into trouble?

      ▷ Report the problem internally to management so we can get it fixed?

      ▷ Act as a whistle-blower and report the problem publicly?

▶ Do you ever search out new and unusual information or perspectives from people? If so, how do you go about it? And how do you decide whether this new information is objective and accurate?

Acknowledgments

Our profound thanks to Amanda Rooker, who is not only a social-media-savvy researcher but a phenomenally detailed editor, a smart writer, and a terrific, upbeat person who keeps us going as well. She was our right arm on the original hardcover version of this book, and she made the job easier for us in this extensive revision. At the risk of making her so successful she won't have time to help us in the future, we highly recommend her to any of you who need detail and research backup, and those who are working on Internet publishing.

At Penguin, we acknowledge with thanks Adrian Zackheim and Will Weisser, who immediately saw the importance of proactivity and championed the cause of Extreme Trust. And we thank Jillian Gray, Julia Batavia, Hannah Kinisky, Kaushik Viswanath, and a host of talented designers and editors at Penguin who bore with us as the idea grew and the manuscript morphed into something better but always different. Thanks, also, to Rafe Sagalyn, our literary agent these last twenty-five years, not only for his constant and thoughtful insight, but especially for his very helpful advice on this particular topic and how best to put it across to our readers.

Our appreciation to Alan Fine, president of Marvel, for a thoughtful weekend spent pushing these ideas around and testing their validity in different situations. And to Eric Carrasquilla at Amdocs and Mariann McDonagh at InContact for their ideas and feedback.

It wouldn't be inappropriate to thank all our colleagues at Peppers & Rogers Group, 1to1 Media, and Trustability Metrix. They're a talented, brilliant, and hardworking bunch who inspire us and our clients every day. And thanks to the clients, too. It's the work in the field that makes us smarter and leads to better learning and to better companies. Special thanks to Marji Chimes, our conscience and inspiration, who embodies what is right about corporate America. We also thank Peppers & Rogers Group's current and former top brass, who have kept the business successful while we have been busy speaking, writing, thinking, and meeting: Mounir Ariss, Caglar Gogus, Orkun Oguz, Hamit Hamutcu, Ozan Bayulgen, and Ivo Sarges. We have learned a lot from Tulay Idil, Marc Ruggiano, Aysegul Bahcivanoglu, Dietrich Chen, Tom Schmalzl, Michael Dandrea, Ginger Conlon, Liz Glagowski, Mila D'Antonio, and Tom Hoffman. Thanks to Annette Webb for keeping us all looking so good. And we thank the leaders of our parent company, TeleTech, who believe in the highest levels of Extreme Trust, who want to help all TeleTech clients achieve it, and who have helped us brainstorm it: Ken Tuchman, Keith Gallagher, Judi Hand, Karen Breen, Jonathan Gray, and Taylor Allis.

Special thanks to the brains and brawn at Trustability Metrix: Valerie Peck, Christian Neckermann, Deanna Lawrence, John Johnson, Alain Oberrotman, and Tom Wessling.

We couldn't have gotten this done without the cheerful and capable help and quiet dedication of Susan Tocco and Lisa Troland, who run interference and back us up.

Finally, mere words can't articulate the appreciation we feel for our own helpmates, Pamela Devenney and Dick Cavett.

Notes

CHAPTER 1: YESTERDAY, TRUSTWORTHY WAS GOOD ENOUGH. TODAY, ONLY TRUSTABILITY WILL DO.

1. This USAA refund-check story is referenced in Raj Sisodia, Jag Sheth, and David B. Wolfe, *Firms of Endearment: How World-Class Companies Profit from Passion and Purpose* (Pearson Prentice Hall, 2007), p. 61. Quoting the authors: "With an empathetic understanding of the difficulties that going to war poses for military families, USAA decided to do something about it after the first Gulf War. It sent refunds to policyholders who had gone to the Gulf, covering the period when they were not driving back home. Some 2,500 policyholders mailed the refunds back to USAA. They wrote notes of appreciation in which they said 'thanks' but were returning the refunds to help keep USAA financially sound." Stories like these are why we dedicated one of our books to the late Brigadier General Robert McDermott (USAF), who served as USAA's CEO for more than twenty years, from 1969 until he retired in 1992 (https://www.usaa.com/inet/pages/about_usaa_corporate _overview_history). We are happy to report that even though USAA is now publicly traded, their actions and culture are consistent with the McDermott era.

2. The retail banking discussion is based largely on *Gotcha Capitalism* (Ballantine, 2007) by Bob Sullivan, an MSNBC blogger and commentator, pp. 62–70. According to Sullivan, some banks charge a $30-plus overdraft fee and then another $5 per day for every day the account remains overdrawn. Some offer automatic transfers from a credit card to the bank account to cover the fee, but cash advance charges apply, and the minimum amount of transfer is sometimes $100 (p. 62). When consumers get their bank balance at an ATM, the "available balance" often automatically includes the courtesy overdraft cushion, encouraging overdrafts. "Here's how it works. When a customer with an $80 balance and $200 courtesy overdraft protection asks for a balance, the ATM indicates '$280 available balance'" (p. 63). Thus, Sullivan's advice to consumers, found on p. 70, is to "opt out of courtesy overdraft protection!" Continuing, Sullivan notes that debit card swipes and ATM withdrawals now account for the majority of "bounced check" fees (p. 64). And the biggest checks clear first out of an account, so that overdrafts are maximized. "Here's an example: If you

have $500 in your account and you write checks for $72, $98, $28, and $410 on the same day, you'll bounce the first three checks, and pay about $100 in fees" (p. 65).

3. The general consensus is "Courtesy overdraft: bad for customers" (Laura Bruce, Bankrate.com, December 19, 2007, http://www.bankrate.com/finance/exclusives/courtesy-overdraft-bad-for-customers-1.aspx, accessed November 10, 2015). In the article, we found this quote: "'Every interaction with your bank shouldn't be an act of self-defense,' says Eric Halperin, director of the Washington, D.C., office of the Center for Responsible Lending, or CRL." Read more: http://www.bankrate.com/finance/exclusives/courtesy-overdraft-bad-for-customers-1.aspx#ixzz3r70Hu446. Follow @Bankrate on Twitter | Bankrate on Facebook. See also Connie Thompson, "The Downside to Debit Cards," KCBY News, March 23, 2009, http://www.kcby.com/news/consumertips/41468757.html, accessed October 31, 2015.

4. There have been many good-to-excellent articles written on trust. But one you should see is by our colleague Bruce Kasanoff, "No More Secrets: How Technology Is Making Honesty the Only Policy," digitaltrends.com, August 20, 2012.

5. Moore's law is named after Gordon Moore, cofounder of Intel, who pointed out in 1965 that the number of transistors that could be fit onto a square inch of silicon doubled roughly every two years.

6. As Professor Robert Wolcott says, "Today is the slowest pace we will experience the rest of our lives." Quoted at World Marketing Summit, Tokyo, October 13, 2015.

7. Mark Zuckerberg, founder of Facebook, has asserted that every fifteen to twenty years we will interact a thousand times as much with others. This is sometimes referred to as "Zuckerberg's law."

8. Periscope—just what it sounds like: a tool that will peek up and see what's going on in the world—has grown faster than anyone imagined except Twitter, which bought the site for "a substantial eight-figure sum" two months before it launched, and attracted a million users in its first ten days. J. J. McCorvey interviewing Periscope CEO Kayvon Beykpour, *Fast Company*, September 2015, p. 38.

9. How much is too much? While we may or may not accept that what we reveal about ourselves by participating in social media (never mind the economy, the housing market, our medical records, and our educational records), interconnectivity means we will never again be totally autonomous, invisible, or anonymous, we can take comfort in the fact that Western governments sometimes deliberately and sometimes accidentally do not connect all the dots about citizens, and although many commercial entities will happily sell their data about you for fractions of a penny, many companies want to keep their data about you from their competitors. Thus, most Western citizens today, while enjoying much less privacy than anyone born before 1990, do not face what Chinese citizens are facing. The Chinese government, using data from every possible digital trail you leave (medical, E-ZPass–type driving information, credit card data, including what you buy, where you go online and how long you stay there, the data in your cell phone, and so on), plans to rank every Chinese citizen from one to a billion plus, by their "social credit"—or basic trustworthiness. See Celia Hatton, "China 'social credit': Beijing sets up a huge system," BBC News, Beijing, October 26, 2015.

CHAPTER 2: TRUSTABILITY: A HIGHER FORM
OF TRUSTWORTHINESS

1.   Bill Price and David Jaffe did some pretty interesting research for their book, *The Best Service Is No Service* (Jossey-Bass, 2008), including looking at the discrepancies between how good companies think their service is and how lousy the customers think it is.

CHAPTER 3: HOW BUSINESSES WILL PRACTICE PROACTIVITY

1.   See David Pogue, "Is Verizon Wireless Making It Harder to Avoid Charges?" *New York Times*, June 17, 2010, available at http://www.nytimes.com/2010/06/17/technology /personaltech/17pogue-email.html?_r=1, accessed November 10, 2015. Here's more on the story: David Pogue wrote an earlier blog about how you could call Verizon to block all data charges, and you could go online and change your own settings (very possible to do, although not intuitive—one forum shows you how at http://www.dslreports.com/forum /r23507198-How-to-block-Verizon-Wirelesss-data-services). But although any user was able to block data services online, Verizon still charged you $1.99 each time you accidentally accessed the Internet, because even to get the message "you don't have this service" it still took 0.06 MB of data, and they still charged a minimum of $1.99 for 1 MB. So even blocking it officially and legitimately did not stop the charges. See David Pogue, "Verizon: How Much Do You Charge Now?" blog post, *New York Times*, November 12, 2009, available at http://www.nytimes.com/2009/11/12/technology/personaltech/12pogue-email.html, accessed November 10, 2015.

CHAPTER 4: WHY THIS BOOK IS DIFFERENT FROM OTHERS
YOU'VE READ ON "TRUST"

1.   The principle behind the annual Edelman Trust Barometer is this: Unlike reputation, which is based on an aggregate of past experiences with a company or brand, *trust* is a forward-facing metric of stakeholder expectation. The Edelman Trust Barometer, available at http://www.edelman.com/trust (accessed November 8, 2015), has been surveying the attitudes of the educated toward institutions in twenty-three countries for more than a decade, and it's a crucial source for understanding global and national trends in public trust of institutional sectors such as business, government, NGOs, and the media. In 2015, trust in all institutions dropped.
   You can find the full 2015 Edelman Trust Barometer Findings at http://www.edelman .com/insights/intellectual-property/2015-edelman-trust-barometer, accessed November 10, 2015. Also see Richard Edelman's Key Findings address, 2011 Trust Barometer Findings: Global & Country Insights, available at http://www.edelman.com/trust/2011/, accessed September 8, 2011.
   The Temkin Trust Ratings uses feedback from 10,000 U.S. consumers to rate 268 organizations across 19 industries. Not surprisingly, the bottom of the ratings in 2014 were dominated by TV service providers and Internet service providers.

2.   Stephen M. R. Covey and Rebecca R. Merrill's extremely well-written book *The Speed of Trust: The One Thing That Changes Everything* (Free Press, 2006) is based on this formula:

"When trust goes up, speed will also go up and cost will go down. . . . When trust goes down, speed will go down and cost will go up." In their taxonomy, trust is built (and can be rebuilt) on two things: competence and character. (Fundamentally, Covey and Merrill's idea of "character" is parallel to our concept of "good intentions.") They talk about five waves of trust: self-trust (credibility), relationship trust (trust-building behaviors), organizational trust (measuring low-trust "taxes" and high-trust dividends), market trust (reputation), and societal trust (contribution). See also Stephen M. R. Covey and Greg Link, *Smart Trust: The Defining Skill That Transforms Managers into Leaders* (Free Press, 2013). David Hutchens and Barry Rellaford wrote a short fable that succinctly illustrates the power of trust, based on the principles of Covey and Merrill's book: *A Slice of Trust* (Gibbs Smith, 2011).

You should also see David Maister, Charles H. Green, and Robert Galford, *The Trusted Advisor* (Touchstone, 2000); Charles H. Green, *Trust-Based Selling* (McGraw-Hill, 2006); and Charles H. Green and Andrea P. Howe, *The Trusted Advisor Fieldbook: A Comprehensive Toolkit for Leading with Trust* (Wiley, 2011). Green and his colleagues are highly respected for their work in helping companies build trusted relationships with their customers over the years—mostly in B2B settings.

More recently, David K. Williams wrote *The 7 Non-Negotiables of Winning* (Wiley, 2013). And emphasized the role of trust in his Forbes.com article: http://www.forbes.com/sites/davidkwilliams/2013/06/20/the-most-valuable-business-commodity-trust/#2715e4857a0b7e78cc721c06.

Amazon.com's description of Joel Peterson's *The 10 Laws of Trust: Building the Bonds That Make a Business Great* (AMACOM, 2016) describes how JetBlue chairman Joel Peterson explores how a culture of trust gives companies an edge. Consider this: What does it feel like to work for a firm where leaders and colleagues trust one another? Freed from micromanagement and rivalry, every employee contributes his or her best. Risk taking and innovation become the norm. And, as Peterson notes, "When a company has a reputation for fair dealing, its costs drop: Trust cuts the time spent second-guessing and lawyering."

The Compass and The Nail: How the Patagonia Model of Loyalty Can Save Your Business, and Might Just Save the Planet by Craig Wilson (Rare Bird Books, 2015) examines how companies create rabid loyalty by examining a company with some truly rabid fans, Patagonia.

You may also want to note Chris Brogan and Julien Smith's book *Trust Agents: Using the Web to Build Influence, Improve Reputation, and Earn Trust*, 2nd ed. (Wiley, 2010), in which the authors emphasize that the Web should be treated as one big cocktail party, and your goal should be to humanize and not monetize the Web. The way to be a "trust agent" is to share ideas, facts, and insights freely—knowing that investing in relationships always brings a return eventually, even if you're not focusing on that return in the moment. The goal is to simply be a helpful person—generous and other-focused. This is what builds trust. They advise us never to be "that guy"—who's always trying to turn the conversation back to himself or his business, who makes you want to run when you see him coming.

In *The Economics of Integrity: From Dairy Farmers to Toyota, How Wealth Is Built on Trust and What That Means for Our Future* (HarperStudio, 2010), financial journalist Anna Bernasek profiles nine businesses whose success has been built on trust, and in our new "age of responsibility," argues that businesses must start with a "DNA of integrity," whose nucleus includes disclosure, norms, and accountability (p. 147).

Kathy Bloomgarden points out in *Trust: The Secret Weapon of Effective Business Leaders* (St. Martin's Press, 2007) that recent corporate scandals have decimated public trust in global companies and in the office of the CEO in particular. Bloomgarden emphasizes that CEOs must actively earn the trust of a company's stakeholders if they want to keep their jobs in this highly skeptical environment.

Also see Peter Firestein, *Crisis of Character: Building Corporate Reputation in the Age of Skepticism* (Sterling, 2009). Firestein, a corporate reputation risk consultant, presents a variety of case studies from some of the best-known brands in the world, illustrating how companies with behind-closed-doors strategies end up doing lasting harm to their reputations and thus their existence. Alternatively, he presents the Seven Strategies of Reputation Leadership to help corporations build a trustable reputation right into the core of their decision-making structures.

Joe Healey is a consultant and banking executive who has been speaking on the importance of trust in business leadership for twenty years. In *Radical Trust: How Today's Great Leaders Convert People to Partners* (Wiley, 2007), Healey uses four case studies to show how trust is no longer merely a moral choice but a requirement for competitive advantage. According to Healey, trust requires four competencies: execution, character, communication, and loyalty.

Also see Geoffrey A. Hosking, *Trust: Money, Markets, and Society* (London: Seagull Books, 2010). Hosking argues that the stability of a global economy depends on trust, which includes a robust understanding of exactly how trust is developed, how it's broken, how it's maintained, and how it's repaired. Key to this is understanding where to place trust, as he cites misplaced trust in financial sectors and state welfare systems as precursors to the global economic crisis in 2007.

John Kador, *Effective Apology: Mending Fences, Building Bridges, and Restoring Trust* (Berrett-Koehler, 2009), explains why, as transparency grows and everyone seems to be apologizing for something, we don't necessarily need more apologies, just more effective ones. And if trust is a renewable asset that needs to be developed consciously, broken, and then rebuilt, an effective apology becomes a vital skill to master.

Roderick M. Kramer, a social psychologist and Stanford professor, argues that despite overwhelming evidence of corporate deceit, and despite the many books and articles that promote trust as if it's a hard sell, we still tend to trust too readily. He examines common human trust activators, such as physical similarities and the presence of touch, and after showing how easily we're fooled, he argues for "tempered trust." See "Rethinking Trust," *Harvard Business Review* 87 (June 2009): 68–77. Kramer also authored *Organizational Trust* (Oxford University Press, 2006), and *Trust and Distrust in Organizations* (Russell Sage Foundation, 2004) with Karen Cook.

3.   Consider Robert Solomon and Fernando Flores, *Building Trust: In Business, Politics, Relationships, and Life* (Oxford University Press, 2003). Solomon and Flores argue that although trust is an important precursor to any interaction, it should be neither a static quality nor a knee-jerk reaction. Trust is a skill to be developed, and the authors explain how to go from simple or naive trust to authentic, fully conscious trust in a number of contexts, including business. Nevertheless, the jury is still out on "privacy." Many of the senior executives at Facebook have come to believe in what is often called "radical transparency." Everything will be known, because the world is inevitably evolving into a social system in which everything can be seen by everyone else. But while this might spell the end of what passed for privacy during the twentieth century, proponents of radical transparency maintain it's not at all a bad future. On the contrary, it's something we should welcome. More transparency leads to more honesty. It's exactly what your grandmother used to tell you: If you don't want people to find out you did it, don't do it. Some Facebook users suggest that the existence of Facebook makes it more difficult to cheat on your girlfriend or boyfriend, for instance. See Kirkpatrick, *The Facebook Effect*, p. 210.

4.   See Elizabeth Hass Edersheim and Peter F. Drucker, *The Definitive Drucker* (McGraw-Hill Professional, 2007), p. xi.

CHAPTER 5: AS INTERACTIONS MULTIPLY, TRUST BECOMES MORE IMPORTANT

1. Peter Walker, "Amnesty International Hails WikiLeaks and Guardian as 'Catalysts' in Arab Spring," *The Guardian* (UK) online, May 13, 2011, available at http://www.guardian.co.uk/world/2011/may/13/amnesty-international-wikileaks-arab-spring, accessed September 9, 2011.

2. "A Comcast Technician Sleeping on My Couch," available at https://www.youtube.com/watch?v=viw2TVBygBg, accessed January 9, 2016.

3. Since Dave Carroll and Sons of Maxwell posted their legendary YouTube video "United Breaks Guitars" in July 2009, which has generated a keynote speaking career and case study materials, a genre of luggage-mishandling videos has cropped up on YouTube. For just one example, see "Mistreating Luggage," available at http://www.youtube.com/watch?v=lzmJr1a-BHU, accessed September 9, 2011.

4. Here is just a sampling of business how-to books dealing with social media which emphasize transparency and honesty:

Guy Kawasaki, *The Art of Social Media* (Portfolio, 2014).

Mark W. Schaefer, *Social Media Explained* (Mark W. Schaefer, 2014).

J. Wolf, *Social Media* (CreateSpace Independent Publishing Platform, 2015).

Michael Richards, *Social Media: Dominating Strategies for Social Media Marketing with Twitter, Facebook, YouTube, LinkedIn, and . . .* (CreateSpace Independent Publishing Platform, 2015).

Jan Zimmerman and Deborah Ng, *Social Media Marketing All-in-One for Dummies* (For Dummies, 2015).

Paul Gillin, *The New Influencers: A Marketer's Guide to the New Social Media* (Quill Driver Books, 2007), p. 14: "transparency is key to working in this medium."

Mitch Joel, *Six Pixels of Separation: Everyone Is Connected. Connect Your Business to Everyone* (Business Plus, 2009), p. 15: "Throughout this book you will be able to underscore all of the information and tactics and weave them through one long thread of authenticity." Also see chapter 2, "The Trust Economy."

Gary Vaynerchuk, *The Thank You Economy* (Wiley, 2011), p. 233: "Being authentic—whether online or offline, say what you mean and mean what you say."

Larry Weber, *Marketing to the Social Web: How Digital Customer Communities Build Your Business* (Wiley, 2007), p. 170: "bloggers are a community bound together by trust." And see p. 56 for the story of how "[t]rust is another major reason to allow critical comments on your site." A woman cited by Weber reports that after her negative review of a product was not displayed on Overstock.com's website she never trusted any of the other reviews she saw on that site.

Chris Brogan and Julien Smith, *Trust Agents: Using the Web to Build Influence, Improve Reputation, and Earn Trust* (Wiley, 2009), p. 15: "Trust agents have established themselves as being non-sales-oriented, non-high-pressure marketers. Instead, they are digital natives using the Web to be genuine and to humanize their business."

Charlene Li, *Open Leadership: How Social Technology Can Transform the Way You Lead* (Jossey-Bass, 2010), p. xvi: "Leadership will require a new approach, new mindset, and new skills. It won't be enough to be a good communicator. You will have to be comfortable sharing personal perspectives and feelings to develop closer relationships. Negative online comments can't be avoided or ignored. Instead, you will come to embrace each openness-enabled encounter as an opportunity to learn." On pp. 5–6, Li talks about the "culture of sharing" now springing up because of new technologies for interacting.

Darren Barefoot and Julie Szabo, *Friends with Benefits: A Social Media Marketing Handbook* (No Starch Press, 2009), p. 10: "With the culture of sharing comes two key concepts we always cite when discussing social media and specifically blogs: authenticity and transparency. A cult of honesty has developed in tandem with technical innovation."

Charlene Li and Josh Bernoff, in *Groundswell: Winning in a World Transformed by Social Technologies*, rev. ed. (Harvard Business Press, 2011), made many references to the requirement for honesty and authenticity. For instance: "Authenticity was crucial. Dell couldn't get anywhere in the groundswell until it honestly admitted its flaws" (p. 229). And from p. 117: "Tips for successful blogging . . . 10. Final advice: be honest."

Francois Gossieaux and Ed Moran, *The Hyper-Social Organization: Eclipse Your Competition by Leveraging Social Media* (McGraw-Hill, 2010), also has numerous references to the need for honest, participatory collaboration with customers, and the importance of frank authenticity. For instance, p. 25: "Reciprocity is one of the key factors that allow communities to work—you scratch my back, I'll scratch yours. . . ." And p. 92: "Becoming human-centric also creates new knowledge flows for the company that may not have existed in the past. For instance, if everyone at your company began receiving daily reports on the top social media opinions expressed about your company, its brands, and its executives, instead of just monthly market share or sales data, wouldn't this transparency profoundly affect decision making across various groups?" And p. 39: "So the key to success in this new economic reality is to move from a transactional world to a long-term trust-based world." And of the authors' "Eight Characteristics of Hyper-Social Leaders," two are "They Trust Their People and Create Trusted Environments" and "They Embrace Transparency" (pp. 320–24).

Tara Hunt, *The Power of Social Networking: Using the Whuffie Factor to Build Your Business* (Crown Business, 2010), p. 2: "First and foremost, the reason people are on these networks is to connect and build relationships. Relationships and connections over time lead to trust. And trust is the basis of whuffie—aka credibility." And p. 82: "Responding effectively to feedback expands your whuffie because when you respond correctly, you demonstrate to your customers that you are truly listening and responding to what they are saying, building trust. That trust will lead to more feedback and conversation, which leads to a deeper relationship."

5. The quote about transparency being a disruptive innovation is from Paul Gillin, *The New Influencers* (Linden, 2007), p. 24.

6. There's a lot of information out there about spam. See, for instance, http://www .barracudacentral.org/index.cgi?p=spam, which calculates spam percentages daily, or http:// www.spam-o-meter.com/stats, which calculates spam percentage over time. On February 21, 2016, this site calculated the percentage of spam worldwide as 87.4 percent, measured over the previous three years.

7. Ironically, the more open and trustable you are, the more likely your inevitable foibles will be discovered. If you seek out complaints on social networking sites and host reviews and comments on your own site, some of those reactions may get publicized. So—for a while anyway—you may look less trustable as you are becoming more trustable.

8. Whitney MacMillan, chairman emeritus of Cargill, makes the case for the critical value of building social capital within your company and offers a proven formula for how to do it. See Whitney MacMillan, "The Power of Social Capital," *Harvard Management Update* 11, no. 6 (June 2006): 1–4.

9. John R. Patterson and Chip R. Bell, *Wired and Dangerous: How Your Customers Have Changed and What to Do About It* (Berrett-Koehler, 2011), p. 50. The average post is read by forty-five people, and 62 percent of customers who hear about a bad experience on social media stop doing business with, or avoid doing business with, the offending company.

10. David Kirkpatrick, *The Facebook Effect*, p. 275. "And in mid-2008 the word Facebook passed sex in frequency as a search term on Google worldwide."

11. SAG-AFTRA has merged the Screen Actors Guild and AFTRA (American Federation of Television and Radio Artists) into one performers' union.

CHAPTER 8: "YOU'RE GONNA NEED A BIGGER BOAT"

1. This idea of the "sharing economy" has been floating around for several years now, most clearly presented in Lawrence Lessig's *Remix: Making Art and Commerce Thrive in the Hybrid Economy* (Penguin Press, 2008), pp. 116–18. But the term seemed to galvanize attendees at the March 2011 South-by-Southwest Conference in Austin, Texas, where a panel of presenters talked about "The New Sharing Economy." The following month, *Fast Company* published an article by Danielle Sacks titled "The Sharing Economy," which profiled many of the thinkers and practitioners in this new industry.

2. Definitions of social production abound. Yochai Benkler calls it "commons-based peer production" (*The Wealth of Networks*, Yale University Press, 2006), p. 60. Lawrence Lessig has framed it as an entirely new kind of economics—a "sharing economy" as opposed to a

"commercial economy." *Remix: Making Art and Commerce Thrive in the Hybrid Economy* (Penguin Press, 2008), pp. 116–18. And for Clay Shirky, social production is "how most picnics happen": "the creation of value by a group for its members, using neither price signals nor managerial oversight to coordinate participants' efforts." *Cognitive Surplus* (Penguin Press, 2010), p. 118.

3. More industry conferences are taking a serious look at trust and social consciousness as important strategic considerations in for-profit organizations. At the World Marketing Summit in Tokyo in 2015, where Martha spoke about trustability, Raj Sisodia, who heads the Conscious Capitalism movement, also spoke.

4. Your competitors will have to make a profit, but we already see strong, viable companies determined to make a profit this quarter that are *not necessarily determined to make the biggest profit they can this quarter,* like USAA. How will your company compete when other firms routinely balance their long- and short-term success by doing the right thing for customers, and doing things right, proactively? The Fourth Sector Network in the United States and Denmark is promoting the "for-benefit organization"—a hybrid that it says represents a new category of organization that is both economically self-sustaining and animated by a public purpose. One example: Mozilla, the entity that gave us Firefox, is organized as a "for benefit organization." And three U.S. entrepreneurs have invented the "B Corporation," a designation that requires companies to amend their bylaws so that incentives favor long-term value and social impact instead of short-term economic gain. See Mohammad Yanus, *Creating a World Without Poverty: Social Business and the Future of Capitalism* (PublicAffairs, 2007), p. 23; and see Aspen Institute, Fourth Sector Concept Paper (Fall 2008); "B Corporation," *MIT Sloan Management Review,* December 11, 2008; and http://www.bcorporation.net/declaration.

5. See chapter 13 in Don Peppers and Martha Rogers, Ph.D., *Rules to Break and Laws to Follow: How Your Business Can Beat the Crisis of Short-Termism* (Wiley, 2008), for more about the competitive advantage of organizations with a flatter, more collaborative structure.

CHAPTER 9: TRUSTABILITY INCREASES PROFITS

1. Thanks to Tom Lacki for his additional insights about the research on trustability and mobile carriers.

2. Thanks to Tom Lacki and Marc Ruggiano for coining the term "distrusters" in their research on value of trust for Peppers & Rogers Group.

3. Our understanding of the difficulties of operating a mobile carrier in a more trustable way came from an interview we did with Peppers & Rogers Group consultants responsible for this client, Ozan Bayulgen, Mounir Ariss, and Zeynep Manco, Peppers & Rogers Group Istanbul office, August 2011.

4. For more on the value of trust in health care, see "Measuring the Value of Trust in Healthcare," www.peppersandrogersgroup.com, accessed October 2015. Peppers & Rogers Group's 2012 Customer Trust in Healthcare study examines the role trust plays in the relationship between health insurers and consumers, and how that trust connects to financial strength.

CHAPTER 10: TRUSTABILITY: CAPITALIST TOOL

1.   See AnnaMaria Andriotis, "Overdraft Fees at Banks Hit a High, Despite Curbs," *Wall Street Journal* online, April 1, 2014, wsj.com, accessed October 17, 2015, for insight about banking practices. See http://www.wsj.com/articles/SB10001424052702304157204579475573602576630.

CHAPTER 11: SHORT-TERMISM: DON'T WORRY ABOUT THE LONG TERM, IBGYBG

1.   We've talked a lot about short-termism. See our book *Rules to Break and Laws to follow: How Your Business Can Beat the Crisis of Short-Termism* (Wiley, 2008).

2.   We found this CFO survey fascinating: Emery P. Dalesio, "Executives Sacrifice Shareholder Value to Please Street," Associated Press State & Local Wire, February 9, 2004. "Three-quarters of business executives admit they massage earnings reports to meet or beat Wall Street expectations and would sacrifice shareholder value to keep earnings on a smooth upward slope, according to a survey released Monday. The study of 401 senior financial executives by researchers at Duke University and the University of Washington found that 55 percent would delay starting a project to avoid missing an earnings target. Four out of five executives said they would defer maintenance and research spending to meet earnings targets. The preference for smooth earnings growth instead of even slight variations is so strong that 78 percent of the surveyed executives would give up economic value in exchange, the study said."

3.   Elinor Ostrom quoted in Clay Shirky, *Cognitive Surplus* (Penguin Press, 2010), p. 111.

4.   Most companies report and reward based on historic numbers and leave prediction and projection to others. Steven Pinker suggests that our *understanding* of time is severely limited, psychologically, and that this is evident purely from the structure of language itself. After all, when time is expressed grammatically in most languages, there are only three real tenses: the here and now, the future unto eternity, and the history of the universe before now. Moreover, he says, because the human experience of time is entirely subjective, "it speeds up or slows down depending on how demanding, varied, and pleasant an interval is." Pinker, *The Stuff of Thought: Language as a Window into Human Nature* (Viking, 2007), p. 190.

5.   Orkun Oguz, "Finding Your Place on the Customer Measurement Grid," *Strategy Speaks* blog post, July 20, 2011, accessed at http://www.peppersandrogersgroup.com/blog/2011/07/customer-strategist-orkun-oguz-8.html.

6.   If you want to extend your examination of how KPIs are often used, see Gretchen Morgenson and Joshua Rosner, *Reckless Endangerment: How Outsized Ambition, Greed, and Corruption Led to Economic Armageddon* (Henry Holt/Times Books, 2011), for an outstanding narrative of the entire mortgage mess that led to the recession of 2008.

7.   Michael Lewis tells the story of the investors who bet against housing prices and mortgage bonds in *The Big Short* (Norton, 2010), p. 147, made into a popular motion picture in 2015.

CHAPTER 12: TAKING THE LONG-TERM VIEW

1. The facts about how Google operates were found in Ken Auletta, *Googled: The End of the World as We Know It* (Penguin Press, 2009), p. 111. Please note: The point we're making here is generally true, but ads are ranked according to an AdRank, which is a complex formula that also includes relevance to search keywords and other ads in the list. It's not purely based on user clicks but is primarily so. Confirmed from Google's Investor Relations page, available at http://investor.google.com/corporate/faq.html, accessed on September 22, 2011. Regarding ads and how they're ranked, see http://adwords.google.com/support/aw/bin/answer.py?hl=en&answer=6111.

2. The quote about Facebook came from David Kirkpatrick, *The Facebook Effect: The Inside Story of the Company That Is Connecting the World* (Simon & Schuster, 2011), p. 258.

3. Launched in 1994, Amazon.com posted its first quarterly profit on December 31, 2001. "Amazon Posts First Profit," *Communications Today* 8, no. 16 (January 24, 2002): 1.

CHAPTER 13: CUSTOMER RELATIONSHIPS: A LINK TO LONG-TERM VALUE

1. As of 2011, only some U.S. states (including Connecticut, Louisiana, Georgia, New Jersey, and Mississippi) legally required homebuilders to provide a structural warranty, although most homebuilders voluntarily offer some kind of limited warranty in their sales contracts. Typical coverage is a one-year warranty for labor and materials, two-year warranty for mechanical defects, and a ten-year warranty for structural defects. (Ilona Bray, "Holding Your Builder Responsible for New-Home Defects," Craig T. Matthews & Associates, available at http://www.ctmlaw.com/articles/holding-your-builder-responsible-for-new-home-defects.html, accessed September 22, 2011. Also see "Special Problems in New Home Construction," available at http://real-estate.lawyers.com/residential-real-estate/Special-Problems-in-New-Home-Construction.html, accessed September 22, 2011.)

2. In their book *Analytics at Work: Smarter Decisions, Better Results*, Thomas H. Davenport, Jeanne G. Harris, and Robert Morison emphasize the importance of evolving more and more sophisticated and discerning analytical capabilities that provide deep insight based on facts and defensible predictions (Harvard Business Press, 2010).

3. V. Kumar and Denish Shah, in "Can Marketing Lift Stock Prices?" *MIT Sloan Management Review,* Summer 2011, pp. 24–26, determined that lifetime-value-increase marketing activities lift stock prices. Also see the research by Janamitra Devan, Anna Kristina Millan, and Pranav Shirke, "Balancing Short- and Long-Term Performance," Research in Brief, *The McKinsey Quarterly* 1 (2005): 31–33, for a discussion of the characteristics of S&P 500 companies that performed well in both the long and short term from 1984 to 2004, compared with those companies that performed well in only one or the other.

4. Shaw Wu's comment about Apple is reported in http://www.appleinsider.com/article.php?id=1687.

5.   We talked with John Stumpf, CEO of Wells Fargo & Company, about trust and banking on June 23, 2011.

CHAPTER 14: TRUSTERS AND DISTRUSTERS

1.   We've said that customers are different and should be recognized and treated in a differentiated way by value and needs. Sometimes that doesn't show in social media, but we need to remember the principle. See Duncan Simester's "When You Shouldn't Listen to Your Critics," *Harvard Business Review*, June 2011, p. 42, which reminds us that trust is an important part of *business* decisions. Simester believes you shouldn't just trust feedback from some social networking sites (e.g., Yelp) willy-nilly if the participants aren't your ideal customer. Simester describes how he and two partners started a "grab-and-go food business" and obsessed over Yelp reviews—until they attended an event that hosted several hundred elite Yelp users and realized they were mostly in their twenties and looked nothing like their customers, who were mostly professionals over age thirty. So even though there's a lot of online feedback saying their restaurant isn't very good or is overpriced, he now knows those vocal customers aren't really his ideal customers anyway. His lesson for the social media era is the same lesson as for the pre-social-media era: Don't aim to please everybody without understanding who is saying what and why, because this may undermine your sincere and legitimate customer differentiation efforts.

2.   Borderline personalities and true psychopaths are the subject of Barbara Oakley's fascinating book *Evil Genes: Why Rome Fell, Hitler Rose, and My Sister Stole My Mother's Boyfriend* (Prometheus, 2008), pp. 137, 321.

3.   A team led by Luigi Guiso reported that there is zero correlation between the stated "values" of companies on their website and the firms' performance. On the other hand, high employee assessments of companies' integrity are associated with higher productivity and profitability. As reported in HBR Blog Network by Andrew O'Connell, July 7, 2015. A 1-standard-deviation increase in integrity is associated with a 0.19-standard-deviation increase in a firm's Tobin's Q.

CHAPTER 15: THERE'S NO SUCH THING AS ONE-WAY
RECIPROCITY

1.   We talked with Ken Tuchman, founder and CEO of TeleTech, and other members of TeleTech's management team about the difference between attitudinal and behavioral loyalty on January 12, 2011.

2.   We've realized we've been writing about USAA Insurance as a paragon of customer relationships and reciprocity for twenty years. You'll find mentions of USAA in our books *Rules to Break and Laws to Follow* (Wiley, 2008), *Return on Customer* (Currency/Doubleday, 2005), *Managing Customer Experiences and Relationships: A Strategic Framework*, 3rd ed. (Wiley, 2016), *One to One Manager* (Currency/Doubleday, 2000), *One to One Fieldbook* (Currency/Doubleday, 1999), and *Enterprise One to One* (Currency/Doubleday, 1997).

3. See Forrester's report "Customer Advocacy 2014: How US Consumers Rate Their Financial Institutions," Forrester Research, Inc., available at https://www.forrester.com/Customer+Advocacy+2014+How+US+Consumers+Rate+Their+Financial+Institutions/fulltext/-/E-res118247, accessed August 27, 2015.

4. Market capitalization figures for Barnes & Noble and Amazon are from UBS Financial Services, Inc., as of October 16, 2015. And Robert Spector notes the role reversal of the two companies in "Yesterday's Goliath, Today's David: Barnes & Noble's Positioning Itself as the Plucky Underdog to Its Giant Competitor Amazon.com Is a Complete Role Reversal from the mid-1990s," *Wall Street Journal*, accessed via Factiva.com on September 23, 2011.

5. Peter Merholz discusses what makes Amazon, Zappos, and USAA particularly trustworthy in "What Trust Brings to Amazon, Zappos, and USAA," HBR Blogs: *The Conversation*, April 27, 2010, at http://blogs.hbr.org/cs/2010/04/what_trust_brings_to_amazon_za.html, accessed May 24, 2011.

6. "Navy Federal to Cover Direct Deposit for Active Duty Military Members: Credit union announces contingency plans ahead of possible government shutdown." September 24, 2013, https://www.navyfederal.org/pdf/press-releases/2013/government_130924.pdf.

7. Karen Kelley, Corcoran Group, is our number one recommendation for help with real estate in the New York City area. We mean it.

CHAPTER 16: TRUSTABILITY AND SELF-INTEREST: A PARADOX

1. See Chapter 26 for a different perspective on "trust paradox."

2. The classic study on how facial expression affects mood is C. L. Kleinke, T. R. Peterson, and T. R. Rutledge's "Effects of Self-Generated Facial Expressions on Mood," *Journal of Personality and Social Psychology* 74 (1998): 272–79.

CHAPTER 17: SERVING THE INTERESTS OF CUSTOMERS, PROFITABLY

1. The AOL debacle has been reported widely, but for more information you may want to see "The Inside Story Behind AOL's $4.4 Billion Sale," Nicholas Carlson, businessinsider.com, accessed October 16, 2015.

2. John R. Patterson and Chip R. Bell wrote about AOL's attempt to spin customer cancellations as sales leads in *Wired and Dangerous: How Your Customers Have Changed and What to Do About It* (Berrett-Koehler, 2011), pp. 51–52.

3. Just try it: Search Google with the entry "Match.com and eHarmony Impossible to Quit," as we did on January 10, 2016 and you'll find a lot of complaints and blogs about it. Don't miss the amusing "Match.com—let me go! Hell hath no fury like a woman who has

mourned . . . and moved on," http://widow2point0.com/2014/06/02/match-com-let-me
-go-hell-hath-no-fury-like-a-woman-who-has-mourned and-moved-on/, accessed October
17, 2015.

4.   Many sources, from a variety of angles, have documented AOL's storied practice of making
money by fooling or manipulating its customers. For example, Ed Maxell reports that the phone
rep at AOL would not cancel his deceased brother's account and would not give the cancellation
number until after the complete do-not-cancel pitch, claiming that it was an FCC requirement.
Maxell wrote a letter to AOL, "suggesting that a more sensitive method be used for death
cancellations—like faxing a death certificate" (*PC Magazine*, May 18, 2004, p. 55). AOL financials and other facts were found in Robert A. Burgelman and Philip E. Meza, "AOL: The Emergence of an Internet Media Company, SM-75," case study (Stanford Graduate School of
Business, 2003), p. 24, available at https://gsbapps.stanford.edu/cases/documents/SM75.pdf, accessed September 14, 2011; "Meet the Market's Biggest Losers," CNNMoney, February 5, 2010,
available at http://money.cnn.com/galleries/2010/fortune/1002/gallery.biggest_losers.fortune/
8.html, accessed September 13, 2011; Hoovers online, www.hoovers.com, accessed September
13, 2011; Ken Auletta, "You've Got News," *New Yorker*, January 23, 2011, p. 32.

5.   The quote about AOL's "dirty little secret" is from Ken Auletta's "You've Got News,"
New Yorker, January 23, 2011, p. 32.

CHAPTER 18: BANKING ON CUSTOMER MISTAKES

1.   We learned a lot about the NSF fee situation from AnnaMaria Andriotis, "Overdraft
Fees at Banks Hit a High, Despite Curbs," *Wall Street Journal* online, April 1, 2014, wsj
.com, accessed October 16, 2015.

CHAPTER 19: NETFLIX: GOOD GUYS WHO WAVERED FOR A MOMENT—BAD INTENTIONS? OR INCOMPETENCE? OR BOTH?

1.   We've written about Blockbuster's decision to drop late fees, albeit late in the game, in
Don Peppers and Martha Rogers, Ph.D., *Rules to Break and Laws to Follow* (Wiley, 2008),
pp. 31–32.

2.   The documentation of Netflix's new business model is from "NETFLIX.com Transforms
DVD Business Eliminating Late Fees and Due Dates from Movie Rentals," press release from
Netflix.com, December 16, 1999, available at http://netflix.mediaroom.com/index.php?s
=43&item=231, accessed October 26, 2011. Also drawn from experience and observation.

3.   For more about how Netflix "throttled" its highest-volume customers with longer turn-
around times, see "Frequent Netflix renters sent to back of the line: The more you use, the slower
the service, some customers realize," Associated Press, February 10, 2006, http://www.msnbc
.msn.com/id/11262292/ns/business-us_business/t/frequent-netflix-renters-sent-back-line/#
.Tn8aCezjuuI, accessed September 25, 2011.

4.   Our source for Netflix outsourcing its movie-recommendation algorithm was Steve
Lohr's "Netflix Awards $1 Million Prize and Starts a New Contest," *New York Times* Bits

blog, September 21, 2009, at http://bits.blogs.nytimes.com/2009/09/21/netflix
-awards-1-million-prize-and-starts-a-new-contest/, accessed September 26, 2011.

5.   For Dr. Natalie Petouhoff and Jennifer Tyler's robust research on customer social media responses to Netflix's restructuring and price increase, see Natalie Petouhoff, "Could
Social Media Monitoring Have Saved Netflix and Blockbuster from Themselves?" September 23, 2011, at http://www.drnatalienews.com/blog/could-social-media-monitoring-have
-saved-netflix-blockbuster-from-themselves#, accessed October 14, 2011.

6.   Nick Wingfield, "Netflix Market Value Shrivels," *New York Times*, October 25, 2011,
http://bits.blogs.nytimes.com/2011/10/25/netflix-market-value-shrivels/, accessed October
26, 2011.

CHAPTER 20: SO WHAT ARE GOOD INTENTIONS, ANYWAY?

1.   We found the Stimson quote at http://www.goodreads.com/author/quotes/3180556
.Henry_Stimson, accessed June 6, 2011.

2.   Seth Godin has repeatedly and provocatively made the point that only human beings
(not companies) can have relationships, from his classic *Permission Marketing* (Simon &
Schuster, 1999) to *Linchpin* (Portfolio, 2010) to *Poke the Box* (The Domino Project, 2011).

3.   If you're looking for a copy of *The Trusted Advisor*, here's the full citation: David H.
Maister, Charles H. Green, and Robert M. Galford, *The Trusted Advisor* (Free Press, 2000).

4.   Charles H. Green explains his trust equation in detail in "The Trust Equation: Generating Trust," in our revised textbook *Managing Customer Experience and Relationships: A Strategic Framework*, 3rd ed. (Wiley, 2016), chapter 3. Their Trust Equation is based on the idea that
self-orientation is the most influential component in building trust—and it's negative. Even if
you have all the other components of trust, self-interest can neutralize them all. And to put it
all into perspective, see *Trust: A History*, by Geoffrey Hosking (Oxford University Press, 2014).

$$Trust = \frac{Credibility + Reliability + Intimacy}{Self\text{-}Orientation}$$

5.   A Forrester report has shown that 83 percent trust friends, more than 50 percent trust
online reviews, and just 14 percent trust advertising ("The Analog Groundswell," Forrester
Research, Inc., September 11, 2009, available at www.forrester.com, accessed September 13,
2011). But although most of us remember the Edelman Trust Barometer's famous 2006 finding that "a person like me" was the most trusted source of information (http://www
.edelman.com/news/showone.asp?id=102), more recently the Trust Barometer has shown
that people now trust experts more than peers. How can both be true? The key may be in the
difference between online and offline. A study by Razorfish indicated that offline friends
are more influential than online friends. Forrester has broken its results down to examine
face-to-face friends as well as online friends, whereas Edelman's survey doesn't differentiate
between face-to-face friends and online peers. Amanda Rooker wonders whether this is likely
a result of our talking to our online peers way too much about minutiae. After experiencing
how little of import our peers actually have to say (if they're talking and we're listening

constantly), maybe experts aren't as overrated as we thought. See her blog post, "Too Much Communication Just Isn't Trustworthy," in *Sustainable Communication*, December 15, 2011, http://amandarooker.wordpress.com, and see Charles Green's comment at http://trusted advisor.com/trustmatters/can-you-trust-the-data-on-trust about how Edelman measures trust on its home page at http://www.edelman.com/trust/2011/.

You can find the full 2015 Edelman Trust Barometer Findings at http://www.edelman .com/insights/intellectual-property/2015-edelman-trust-barometer, accessed November 10, 2015.

CHAPTER 22: HOW TRUSTABLE COMPANIES USE CUSTOMER INSIGHT TO IMPROVE CUSTOMER EXPERIENCE

1. The Peapod example comes from Ian Ayres, *Super Crunchers: Why Thinking-by-Numbers Is the New Way to Be Smart* (Bantam, 2007), p. 170.

2. According to Synovate Mail Monitor, the world's consumers received 2.73 billion credit card solicitations in 2010. See Mark Huffman, "Credit Card Offers on the Increase," ConsumerAffairs.com, January 27, 2011, at http://www.consumeraffairs.com/news04/ 2011/01/credit-card-offers-on-the-increase.html, accessed October 17, 2011. Also see Becky Yerak, "Credit Card Offers and Incentives Expected to Pick Up in 2011," *Los Angeles Times* online, January 1, 2011, available at http://articles.latimes.com/2011/jan/01/business/la-fi -credit-cards-20110101, accessed September 14, 2011.

3. We did the research on Royal Bank of Canada for our textbook revision, Don Peppers and Martha Rogers, Ph.D., *Managing Customer Experience and Relationships: A Strategic Framework*, 3rd ed. (Wiley, 2016).

CHAPTER 23: EMPATHY, SELF-INTEREST, AND "HOMO ECONOMICUS"

1. Adam Smith's quote about how the butcher, the brewer, and the baker are ultimately driven by self-interest can be found in *An Inquiry into the Nature and Causes of the Wealth of Nations*, Pennsylvania State University Electronic Classics Series (Pennsylvania State University, 2005), p. 19, available at http://www2.hn.psu.edu/faculty/jmanis/adam-smith/ Wealth-Nations.pdf, accessed September 14, 2011.

2. The story about U.S. Army brigadier general S. L. A Marshall's survey of troops in combat was reported in Jonah Lehrer, *How We Decide* (Houghton Mifflin Harcourt, 2009), p. 179.

3. The quote about *Homo economicus* is from Joseph Henrich, Robert Boyd, Samuel Bowles, Colin F. Camerer, Ernst Fehr, and Herbert Gintis, eds., *Foundations of Human Sociality: Economic Experiments and Ethnographic Evidence from Fifteen Small-Scale Societies* (Oxford University Press, 2009), Oxford Scholarship Online, http://oxfordscholarship .com—as cited in John A. List, "On the Interpretation of Giving in Dictator Games," *Journal*

of Political Economy 115, no. 3 (2007), available at http://expecon.gsu.edu/jccox/reading
/519249.pdf, accessed July 16, 2010.

4. The details about the dictator game experiments can be found in Henrich et al., *Foundations of Human Sociality*. Note: There is some disagreement over how purely the dictator game illustrates actual altruism or kindness on the part of the research subjects, as opposed to "self-regarding" self-interest. Depending on the configuration of the game, for instance, a "dictator" may simply be fearful of appearing to be greedy in the eyes of the researcher. If so, then the motivation for giving to the second person would not be generosity or altruism, just a selfish desire to *appear* altruistic. But researchers have experimented with the dictator game in many different configurations, and it almost certainly demonstrates that the average person does genuinely feel an urge to be kind to other people—to share, rather than simply take.

5. Lehrer's quote about the dictator game can be found in his book, *How We Decide*, p. 184.

6. One cross-cultural study from the American Economic Association found that ". . . the higher the degree of market integration and the higher the payoffs to cooperation, the greater the level of cooperation in experimental games." Joseph Henrich, Robert Boyd, Samuel Bowles, Colin Camerer, Ernst Fehr, Herbert Gintis, and Richard McElreath, "In Search of Homo Economicus: Behavioral Experiments in 15 Small-Scale Societies," *American Economic Review* 91(2) (May 2001), Papers and Proceedings, p. 74, and at http://tuvalu.santafe.edu/-bowles/InSearch HomoEconomicus2001.pdf. Herbert Gintis also wrote "Strong Reciprocity and Sociality," *Journal of Theoretical Biology* 206 (2000): 169–79, http://www.umass.edu/preferen/gintis/strongr.pdf. We also discuss "strong reciprocity" in our book, Don Peppers and Martha Rogers, Ph.D., *Rules to Break and Laws to Follow* (Wiley, 2008), p. 126.

7. Kevin Kelly, *What Technology Wants* (Penguin, 2011), Kindle edition, Loc. 1170–76. "The third piece of evidence for small, steady, long-term advance resides in the moral sphere. Here metrics for measurement are few and disagreement about the facts greater. Over time our laws, mores, and ethics have slowly expanded the sphere of human empathy. Generally, humans originally identified themselves primarily via their families. The family clan was 'us.' This declaration cast anyone outside of that intimacy as 'other.' We had—and still have—different rules of behavior for those inside the circle of 'us' and for those outside. Gradually the circle of 'us' enlarged from inside the family clan to inside the tribe, and then from tribe to nation. We are currently in an unfinished expansion beyond nation and maybe even race and may soon be crossing the species boundary."

CHAPTER 24: THE SOCIAL ROLE OF EMPATHY AND TRUST

1. Our source for the facts about how victims of the 2011 Japanese tsunami tended to return property to its rightful owner rather than loot it was Akiko Fujita, "Honest Japanese Return $78 Million in Cash Found in Quake Rubble," August 17, 2011, ABC News, http://abcnews .go.com/International/honest-japanese-return-78-million-cash-found-quake/story?id =14322940, accessed September 22, 2011.

2. Trust in the social collective: Roderick M. Kramer, in his article "Rethinking Trust" (*Harvard Business Review* 87 [June 2009]: 68–77), reminds us that humans do tend to trust

inherently as a part of the human condition, despite the fact that sometimes our judgment is poor, obscured by untrustables who look like us. He offers rules for being cautious in the marketplace.

CHAPTER 25: PSYCHOPATHIC CAPITALISM

1. Michael Schrage, "Should Your Best Customers Be Stupid?" HBR Blog Network, November, 19, 2010, available at http://blogs.hbr.org/schrage/2010/11/should-your -customers-be-stupid.html, accessed September 14, 2011. In a full-page ad run in *USA Today* on March 28, 2007, for the Community Financial Services Association of America (CFSA), an "assistant manager" says in large letters, "There are right ways and wrong ways to use payday advances. I want my customers to know the difference." The ad lists four pointers for correct use of payday advances to prevent customers from being taken advantage of.

2. The Volkswagen debacle is widely discussed, but we pulled key information from "Germany Orders Recall of 8.5 Million Emissions-Cheating Volkswagens [sic]," by Nathan Ingraham, October 16, 2015, http://www.engadget.com/2015/10/16/volkswagen-germany -recall-order/, and "VW Made Several Defeat Devices to Cheat Emissions Tests: Sources" by Andreas Cremer, Bruce Wallace, and Paul Lienert, http://www.reuters.com/article/2015/ 10/17/us-volkswagen-emissions-software-idUSKCN0SB0PU20151017, October 17, 2015. Also see Robert Reich, "The System Looks Like a Con Game, with Most of Us Victims," *New York Times,* September 29, 2015; and Tyler Cowen, "Cheating Gets the Most Attention, but Doesn't Do the Most Damage," *New York Times,* September 29, 2015, who points out that even though negligence can cause greater injury and physical risk, we get more upset when people do wrong by deliberate fraud. And see "GM Likely to Face Criminal Charges" by Christopher M. Matthews and Mike Spector, *New York Times,* May 26, 2015, pp. B1, B5.

3. Ibid.

4. Jacquielawson.com, accessed November 15, 2015.

5. We learned about Ally Bank's "three pillars of customer service" in a phone interview with Sanjay Gupta, then CMO at Ally Bank, May 23, 2011.

6. Based on a chat session with the authors, September 22, 2011. This service, called "Ally eCheck Deposit," was launched in October 2011.

7. Ally Bank's customers can read and submit reviews directly on its product pages. See "Rave Reviews for the 2-Year Raise Your Rate CD," *Ally Straight Talk* blog, at http://community .ally.com/straight-talk/category/customer-spotlight/, accessed September 22, 2011.

8. See, for instance, Ally Bank's customer reviews of its interest checking account at http://www.ally.com/bank/interest-checking-account/#tabs=customer-reviews, accessed November 7, 2015.

9. James R. Hood, "More Banks Blink, Cancel Debit-Card Fees," consumeraffairs.com, November 1, 2011, at http://www.consumeraffairs.com/news04/2011/11/more-banks-blink-cancel -debit-card-fees.html, accessed November 2, 2011. See also Robin Sidel and Dan Fitzpatrick,

"Debit-Fee Retreat Complete," *Wall Street Journal*, November 2, 2011, at http://www.wsj.com/ articles/SB10001424052970203707504577012233780743536 accessed November 2, 2011. While there is little doubt that the banks caved in on their debit card fees due to consumer outrage, one commentator's perspective is that consumer temper tantrums like this may not be such a healthy development. See Bob McTeer (former president of the Dallas Fed), "Debit Card Fees: Sending the Wrong Message," *Forbes* blog, November 1, 2011, at http://www.forbes.com/sites/bob mcteer/ 2011/11/01/debit card-fees-sending-the-wrong-message/, accessed November 2, 2011. The debit card fee fiasco has provided hilarious material for comics, including Andy Borowitz's November 2, 2011, newsletter conveying a mock "apology" letter from Bank of America, proposing all sorts of other fees (like a $10 fee to collect the $5 refund in cash, for instance), and ending with:

"Again, accept our apologies for instituting the debit card fee. We have learned our lesson, and we make this solemn promise: next time we squeeze money from you, we'll do it in a way you won't notice.

Sincerely,

Bank of America"

10. You can find out more about what drives customer loyalty in the banking and insurance industries (and what doesn't) in the report "Customer Advocacy 2011: How Customers Rate Banks, Investment Companies, and Insurers," Forrester Research, Inc., March 8, 2011, available at www.forrester.com, accessed June 9, 2011.

CHAPTER 26: PUTTING ON A HUMAN FACE

1. Raj Sisodia, Jag Sheth, and David B. Wolfe, *Firms of Endearment: How World-Class Companies Profit from Passion and Purpose* (Pearson Prentice Hall, 2007), p. 42. "The consciousness that has ruled business enterprise over the past two centuries is rooted in classical notions that reason is superior to emotions in the affairs of people. This has reduced stakeholders (including shareholders) to largely bloodless statistical entities. . . . Right brain emotionality deserves no less than equal attention with left brain rationality in business analysis, planning, and operations. Recent research resoundingly confirms the primacy of the emotional over the purely rational. . . . [I]n an overwhelming majority of cases, top performers are not those executives with the highest level of intellectual intelligence but those with the highest level of emotional intelligence."

2. John Hagel discusses the paradox of trust in "Resolving the Trust Paradox," blog post on http://edgeperspectives.typepad.com/edge_perspectives/2011/06/resolving-the-trust -paradox.html, accessed February 21, 2016.

CHAPTER 27: COMPETENCE AND GOOD INTENTIONS ARE JOINED AT THE HIP

1. The quote that opens this chapter came from "An Essay on Criticism," a poem by Alexander Pope (1688–1744).

2. See Christopher Meyer and Andre Schwager, "Understanding Customer Experience," *Harvard Business Review*, February 2007, pp. 117–26.

3. Here's a great idea: "Becoming human-centric also creates new knowledge flows for the company that may not have existed in the past. For instance, if everyone at your company began receiving daily reports on the top social media opinions expressed about your company, its brands, and its executives, instead of just monthly market share or sales data, wouldn't this transparency profoundly affect decision making across various groups? Wouldn't it provide customer support with insights into how that function could be improved? Wouldn't such knowledge improve the planning, pricing, and promotion of your next product? Wouldn't it give your salespeople new ideas on new segments (think 'tribes') that they should be targeting?" For more on this, see Francois Gossieaux and Ed Moran, *The Hyper-Social Organization: Eclipse Your Competition by Leveraging Social Media* (McGraw-Hill, 2010), Kindle edition, Loc. 1272–76.

4. Julianne Pepitone and Aaron Smith reported on Netflix customers' mass exodus in their CNNMoney article "Netflix Stock Plunges as Subscribers Quit," September 15, 2011, at http://money.cnn.com/2011/09/15/technology/netflix/index.htm, accessed October 6, 2011. But except for what we could find in public records, a lot of this is pure speculation on our part—we have no inside source at Netflix.

CHAPTER 28: PRODUCT COMPETENCE AND CUSTOMER COMPETENCE

1. Clayton M. Christensen, Scott Cook, and Taddy Hall, "Marketing Malpractice: The Cause and the Cure," *Harvard Business Review* 83 (December 2005): 74–83, is just one of the places you can hear this group talk about a product being hired to do a job.

2. The story about how Cigna improved customer experience with clearer, customer-friendly communication is from Tom Hoffman, "Speaking to Customers in Their Language," *1to1 Magazine*, October 19, 2011, available at http://www.1to1media.com/view.aspx?docid=33187, accessed November 27, 2011.

3. For more about Humana, see https://www.humana.com/vitality/corporate, accessed September 8, 2015.

4. Discovery is considered one of the global leaders in the area of health and wellness and is held out as an example of a uniquely successful model in this regard. An article in the *Economist* (October 8, 2011) profiled Discovery as "[a] South African company that has some bright ideas for promoting health." The article reported that the Vitality model is recognized as a pioneer in the fight against chronic diseases of lifestyle and in rewarding people for living healthier lives. See Discovery's October 19, 2011, press release at http://www.discovery.co.za/discovery_za/web/logged_out/about_discovery/media/press_releases_content/2011/2011_content/discovery_life_gives_clients_more_cover_with_coverbooster.xml, accessed December 28, 2011.

5. For more on customer-centricity, see our books *Rules to Break and Laws to Follow* (Wiley, 2008), *Return on Customer* (Currency/Doubleday, 2005), *Managing Customer Experience and Relationships: A Strategic Framework,* 3rd ed. (Wiley, 2016), and *The One to One Future* (Doubleday Business, 1993).

6. If you need a laugh, check out Martha's blog on how annoying it is when companies expect you to work hard so they can make money: "You're the Customer. Why Do They Think

You Work for *Them?*" Martha Rogers, Ph.D., *Huffington Post*, 2014., http://www.huffington post.com/martha-rogers/youre-the-customer-why-do_1_b_5001644.html.

7. Matthew Dixon, Karen Freeman, and Nicholas Toman, "Stop Trying to Delight Your Customers," *Harvard Business Review* 88 (July 2010): 116–22. The subtitle added by the magazine's editorial department was "To Really Win Their Loyalty, Forget the Bells and Whistles and Just Solve Their Problems." The authors note that "Loyalty has a lot more to do with how well companies deliver on their basic, even plain-vanilla, promises than on how dazzling the service experience might be" (p. 116).

8. See Don Peppers and Martha Rogers, Ph.D., *Managing Customer Experience and Relationships*, 3rd ed. (Wiley, 2016). For a full discussion about Learning Relationships, see B. Joseph Pine II, Don Peppers, and Martha Rogers, Ph.D., "Do You Want to Keep Your Customers Forever?" *Harvard Business Review* 73 (March 1995): 103–14, available to online subscribers at http://hbr.org/1995/03/do-you-want-to-keep-your-customers-forever, accessed October 6, 2011.

CHAPTER 29: HONEST COMPETENCE REQUIRES HONESTLY COMPETENT PEOPLE

1. Warren Buffett is quoted by Dov Seidman in *How: Why How We Do Anything Means Everything . . . in Business (and in Life)* (Wiley, 2007), p. 178.

2. Susan Whiting's quote about connecting doing good with your brand is from a telephone interview with the authors on June 23, 2011.

3. Peppers and Rogers, *Rules to Break*, p. 101.

4. You can find Dov Seidman's quote in *How*, p. 251.

5. You can find Dov Seidman's seven reasons why self-governing cultures are advantageous in Seidman, *How*, pp. 259–63.

CHAPTER 30: SELF-ORGANIZING EMPLOYEES AND TRUST PLATFORMS

1. Don blogged about this at http://www.1to1media.com/speaking/blog/2015/06/one-innovative-way-to-empower-employees.html#sthash.ySu5aVOQ.dpuf.

2. Uber was launched in San Francisco in 2011, see https://en.wikipedia.org/wiki/Uber_(company).

3. Maureen Dowd complains that it's tricky to get used to being rated by service people in "Driving Uber Mad," http://www.nytimes.com/2015/05/24/opinion/sunday/maureen-dowd-driving-uber-mad.html, accessed September 8, 2015. Also see "The Scoreboards Where You Can't See Your Score," Natasha Singer, *New York Times*, December 28, 2014, p. B3.

CHAPTER 31: TRUE CONFESSIONS: DOMINO'S AND THE TRANSPARENT PIZZA

1. Stephanie Clifford reports on the Domino's Pizza employees' stomach-turning YouTube video in "Video Prank at Domino's Taints Brand," *New York Times*, April 16, 2009, cited at http://www.nytimes.com/2009/04/16/business/media/16dominos.html, accessed August 4, 2011.

2. The college senior struck by the authenticity of Domino's Pizza's self-flagellating marketing campaign was quoted in Chistopher Borrelli's article titled "Domino's Pizza, You Stand Accused of Being Boring, Bland and Flavorless. Of Bearing Cheese That Tastes Grainy and Processed. Of Having Sauce Like Ketchup and Crust Like Cardboard. What Say You? 'Guilty As Charged,'" *Chicago Tribune*, January 19, 2010, cited at http://articles.chicagotribune.com/2010-01-19/entertainment/1001180400_1_pizza-hut-domino-s-pizza-free-pizza, accessed August 4, 2011.

3. *Adweek*'s story on Domino's "transparent pizza" was written by Todd Wasserman, "As Domino's Gets Real, Its Sales Get Really Good," *Adweek*, July 11, 2010, http://www.adweek.com/news/advertising-branding/dominos-gets-real-its-sales-get-really-good-107532, accessed August 4, 2011.

4. More facts about how Domino's Pizza's transparent marketing campaign paid off can be found in "The Importance of Being Straight Forward with Customers," Ocean Capital, March 21, 2011, available at http://www.ocean-capital.com/the-real-deal/the-importance-of-being-straight-forward-with-customers/, accessed August 4, 2011; "Domino's Pizza Announces 2010 Financial Results," at http://www.prnewswire.com/news-releases/dominos-pizza-announces-2010-financial-results-117142383.html, accessed August 4, 2011; "Domino's Pizza Announces First Quarter 2011 Financial Results," http://www.hospitalitybusinessnews.com/article/10530/dominos-pizza-announces-first-quarter-2011-financial-results, accessed August 4, 2011; "Domino's Pizza Announces Second Quarter 2011 Financial Results," http://finance.yahoo.com/news/Dominos-Pizza-Announces-prnews-3655095181.html?x=0&.v=1, accessed August 4, 2011; "Domino's Pizza Runs Unfiltered Customer Comments on Times Square Billboard," http://mashable.com/2011/07/25/dominos-comments-times-square/, accessed August 5, 2011; Tim Nudd, "Domino's Posts Customer Reviews, Good and Bad, in Times Square," *Adweek*, July 25, 2011, at http://www.adweek.com/adfreak/dominos-posts-customer-reviews-good-and-bad-times-square-133650, accessed August 5, 2011; Todd Wasserman, "As Domino's Gets Real, Its Sales Get Really Good," *Adweek*, July 11, 2010, http://www.adweek.com/news/advertising-branding/dominos-gets-real-its-sales-get-really-good-107532, accessed August 5, 2011. And the random customer comments we quoted came from http://more.dominos.com/wp/2011/07/times-square/, accessed August 5, 2011.

CHAPTER 32: FALLIBILITY AND TRUST

1. We've all heard this CIA dictum. In his book *How*, Dov Seidman attributes it to Larry Johnson, interviewed on MSNBC by Alex Witt, August 27, 2004 (*How*, p. 146).

2. The Harvard Business School study of nursing home practices and how reporting more errors actually signifies a more trustworthy environment can be found in Jeffrey Pfeffer and

Robert I. Sutton, *Hard Facts, Dangerous Half-Truths, and Total Nonsense: Profiting from Evidence-Based Management* (Harvard Business Press, 2006), pp. 105–6.

CHAPTER 33: PROACTIVE REFUNDS

1. You'll find the 2013 letter from Jeff Bezos to Amazon's stakeholders at http://www.sec.gov/Archives/edgar/data/1018724/000119312513151836/d511111dex991.htm.

CHAPTER 34: SHARING: NOT JUST FOR SUNDAY SCHOOL

1. In "Givers vs. Takers: The Surprising Truth About Who Gets Ahead," Adam Grant reports on his research that examines the success levels of givers, takers, and "matchers." Grant found givers overrepresented at the top and the bottom of the success ladder. See his book *Give and Take: Why Helping Others Drives Our Success* (Penguin Books, 2014).

2. London Science Museum's survey of adults was reported in the *Week*, September 23, 2011, p. 6.

3. Technorati detail from Heather Havenstein, "Blogs Becoming Entrenched in Mainstream—and More Profitable," *Computerworld*, September 23, 2008, available at http://www.computerworld.com/s/article/9115367/Blogs_becoming_entrenched_in_mainstream_and_more_profitable, accessed July 13, 2010.

4. The reason Wikipedia works so surprisingly well is that social networks emerge around each topic. In *Connected: The Surprising Power of Our Social Networks and How They Shape Our Lives* (Back Bay Books, 2011, p. 280), Nicholas A. Christakis and James H. Fowler point out that "we do not cooperate with one another because a state or a central authority forces us to. Instead, our ability to get along emerges spontaneously from the decentralized actions of people who form groups with connected fates and a common purpose."

5. One of our sources about Linux is Yochai Benkler's *The Wealth of Networks* (Yale University Press, 2006), p. 64. Another is Eric von Hippel's *Democratizing Innovation* (MIT Press, 2006), p. 80. "Free software has played a critical role in the recognition of peer production, because software is a functional good with measurable qualities. It can be more or less authoritatively tested against its market-based competitors. And, in many instances, free software has prevailed. About 70 percent of Web server software, in particular for critical e-commerce sites, runs on the Apache Web server—free software. More than half of all back-office e-mail functions are run by one free software program or another. Google, Amazon, and CNN.com, for example, run their Web servers on the GNU/Linux operating system. They do this, presumably, because they believe this peer-produced operating system is more reliable than the alternatives, not because the system is inexpensive" (Benkler, p. 64). "Contributors to the many open source software projects extant . . . also routinely make the code they have written public" (von Hippel, p. 80).

6. "A 'sharing economy' is different. Of all the possible terms of exchange within a sharing economy, the single term that isn't appropriate is money. You can demand that a friend spend more time with you, and the relationship is still a friendship. If you demand that he pay you for the time you spend with him, the relationship is no longer a friendship." See Lawrence Lessig, *Remix*, p. 118.

CHAPTER 35: VALUE CREATION: INVENTED BY SOMEBODY, OWNED BY NOBODY, VALUABLE TO EVERYBODY

1.   See these and other examples of social production in Lessig, *Remix*, pp. 166–69.

2.   Our original source for the number of current open-source projects was http://source forge.net/about, accessed September 27, 2011. When we went to update the number for this paperback edition in October of 2015, the number had, essentially, become countless.

3.   It took bloggers only three hours after the *Lens* blog of the *New York Times* along with "Eines Tages," a site run by the German magazine *Der Spiegel*, ran some photos requesting information from readers. The photographer was identified as Franz Krieger, a military photographer and driver who joined and then quit a Nazi propaganda unit. James Barron and David W. Dunlap, "In Hours, Online Readers Identify Nazi Photographer," *New York Times*, June 25, 2011, pp. C1, C4.

4.   Eric von Hippel says "employees of a firm may wish to experience [enjoyment and other] intrinsic reward in their work as well, but managers and commercial constraints may give them less of an opportunity to do so. Indeed, 'control over my own work' is cited by many programmers as a reason that they enjoy creating code as volunteers on open source projects more than they enjoy coding for their employers for pay." See *Democratizing Innovation*, p. 61.

5.   Lessig describes Red Hat in *Remix*, pp. 181–83: "Robert Young saw early on the value of an open system. He described a conversation with some engineers from Southwestern Bell at a conference at Duke. Young was surprised to learn that they were using Linux to run the central switching station for Southwestern Bell. He asked why. Their response, as Young recounts it, is quite revealing: 'Our problem is we have no choice. If we use Sun OS or NT and something goes wrong, we have to wait around for months for Sun or Microsoft to get around to fixing it for us. If we use Linux, we get to fix it ourselves if it's truly urgent. And so we can fix it on our schedule, not the schedule of some arbitrary supplier.' . . . Young said, 'Red Hat is thus a "hybrid."' Young was not in it to make the world a better place, though knowing the man, I know he's quite happy to make the world a better place. Young was in it for the money. But the only way Red Hat was going to succeed was if thousands continued to contribute— for free—to the development of the GNU/Linux operating system. He and his company were going to leverage value out of that system. But they would succeed only if those voluntarily contributing to the underlying code continued to contribute. One might well imagine that when a for-profit company like Red Hat comes along and tries to leverage great value out of the free work of the free-software movement, some might raise 'the justice question.' Putting aside Marc Ewing (who had great coder cred), who was Robert Young to make money out of Linux? Why should the free-software coders continue to work for him (even if only indirectly, since anyone else was free to take the work as well)? . . . [There] was a general recognition that free software would go nowhere unless companies began to support it. Thus, while there was whining on the sidelines, there was no campaign by the founders of key free software to stop these emerging hybrids. So long as the work was not turned proprietary—so long as the code remained 'free' in the sense of 'freedom'—neither Richard Stallman nor Linus Torvalds was going to object. This was the only way to make sure an ecology of free software could be supported. It was an effective way to spread free software everywhere. And indeed, the freedom to make money using the code was as much a 'freedom' as anything was."

6. For more information on IBM/Red Hat, see https://en.wikipedia.org/wiki/Red_Hat.

7. Yochai Benkler notes that IBM "has obtained the largest number of patents every year from 1993 to 2004, amassing in total more than 29,000 patents. IBM has also, however, been one of the firms most aggressively engaged in adapting its business model to the emergence of free software . . . [noticeable in] what happened to the relative weight of patent royalties, licenses, and sales in IBM's revenues and revenues that the firm described as coming from 'Linux-related services.' Within a span of four years, the Linux-related services category moved from accounting for practically no revenues, to providing double the revenues from all patent-related sources, of the firm that has been the most patent-productive in the United States." From *The Wealth of Networks*, p. 46.

8. Although we don't expect retailers to give us goods for free, people are all the time expecting to get services and advice for free. At a cocktail party, doctors and accountants and lawyers are assailed with "What should I do . . . ?" inquiries. And on a chance meeting at the mall: "Couldn't your brother-in-law fix my broken drain?" In a society in which so many volunteer to work for free, will it be harder and harder for advisers to charge?

9. According to Viktor Mayer-Schönberger, in *Delete: The Virtue of Forgetting in a Digital Age* (Princeton University Press, 2011), p. 95: The "reputation on eBay is not as accurate a reflection of transactional satisfaction as the economic argument of signaling suggests. Researchers have discovered that sellers on eBay strategically time their rating of the buyer. Many of them rate buyers highly even before the transaction has concluded (when they would have the relevant information to rate buyers)—not because they are satisfied with a transaction, but because they hope to elicit an equally good rating in return. It is but one of the many ways in which eBay's customers have been trying to influence eBay's digital memory of transactional reputation. By the spring of 2008, the widespread behavior of gaming reputation memory led eBay to a dramatic reversal of its information policy. It announced that sellers would no longer be able to rate buyers except positively."

10. We pulled eBay stock data on September 8, 2015, from https://www.stock-analysis-on.net/NASDAQ/Company/eBay-Inc/Ratios/Profitability. Market cap exceeded $30 billion, according to https://www.google.com/webhp?sourceid=chrome-instant&ion=1&espv=2&ie=UTF-8#q=ebay%20market%20cap.

11. Figuring out an efficient way for total strangers to trust one another allowed eBay to thrive. See Shirky, *Cognitive Surplus*, p. 177.

12. You can find more about the civic-minded young Pakistanis in Sabrina Tavernise, "Young Pakistanis Take One Problem into Their Own Hands," *New York Times*, May 19, 2009, cited also in Shirky, *Cognitive Surplus*, p. 126.

13. You can learn more in Poornima Weerasekara, "How the Twittersphere Helped Keep Oakland Safe," in New America Media, cited at http://newamericamedia.org/2010/07/how-the-twittersphere-helped-keep-oakland-safe.php, accessed on July 11, 2010. See Shirky, *Cognitive Surplus*, pp. 15–17, for more on Ushahidi as well.

14. You can read more about helping the medical patient in Israel at http://www.jpost.com/Home/Article.aspx?id=178577, accessed July 13, 2010, and about gift giving in

"Beyond the Buzzword, How Crowdsourcing Can Disrupt Brazil," TNW News Latin America, August 2011, at http://thenextweb.com/la/2011/08/24/beyond-the-buzzword-how -crowdsourcing-can-disrupt-brazil/, accessed on August 24, 2011. See also the gift-giving website Vakinha, at http://www.vakinha.com.br/ (Portuguese).

CHAPTER 36: TRUST, PUNISHMENT, AND THE "MONKEY MIND"

1. The story about the man without arms can be found in the *Cleveland Plain Dealer*, cited in "Dumb Human Behavior to Avoid," *Reader's Digest* online, June–July 2011, available at http://www.rd.com/family/dumb-human-behavior-to-avoid/, accessed September 14, 2011.

2. You can watch the YouTube video of the elaborate prank against the Belgian telecom provider at http://operationsroom.wordpress.com/2011/01/28/customer-service-revenge/.

3. The punishing primates story came from Dan Ariely, *The Upside of Irrationality: The Un-expected Benefits of Defying Logic at Work and at Home* (HarperCollins, 2011), pp. 126–27.

4. "The monkey mind" is described in Clay Shirky, *Here Comes Everybody* (Penguin Press, 2008), p. 15. "Monkey mind" is also a term sometimes used in the Far East to describe the tendency of Westerners to allow their brains to jump frantically from one subject to another.

5. The idea that jealousy and envy help society is found in Mark D. Hauser, *Moral Minds: How Nature Designed Our Universal Sense of Right and Wrong* (Ecco, 2006), cited in Barbara Oakley, *Evil Genes* (Prometheus, 2008), p. 269.

6. We learned more about the anthropology of empathy by reading David Sloane Wilson, *Does Altruism Exist?: Culture, Genes, and the Welfare of Others* (Yale University Press, 2015).

CHAPTER 37: DEATH BY TWEET

1. The "un-Google" quote came from Linda Kaplan Thaler, CEO and chief creative officer of Kaplan Thaler Group (who brought us the Aflac duck), quoted in "What's Next?" *Fortune*, February 5, 2007, p. 28: "People are fed up with greed and opportunism. . . . I think the In-ternet is a very big part of it. You can't un-Google yourself. Gone are the days when snappy campaigns could mask bad behavior." Kaplan Thaler also coauthored with Robin Koval *The Power of Nice: How to Conquer the Business World with Kindness* (Crown Business, 2006).

2. One of the best things for us about having a robust website is hearing from the bloggers and readers who exchange ideas right in front of us. This quote is one of our favorite gems, sent in by Grant Robertson, blog post, May 1, 2007, available at http://www.downloadsquad.com/2007/ 05/01/hd-dvd-key-fiasco-is-an-example-of-21st-century-digital-revolt/, accessed August 31, 2010.

3. We followed *Brüno*'s brutal demise on http://www.boxofficemojo.com/movies/?page =daily&id=bruno.htm, accessed September 28, 2010.

4. We listen to NPR all the time. (And yes, we contribute during the pledge drives. It's the so-cial thing to do.) We heard the facts about box-office windows on NPR, and you can hear the

story at http://www.npr.org/templates/transcript/transcript.php?storyId=106742097. We accessed it on September 28, 2010, and if you listen, too, please contribute to your local NPR station!

5. The idea of prosocial behaviors is found in James Surowiecki, *The Wisdom of Crowds* (Anchor, 2005), citing Samuel Bowles and Herbert Gintis, "Prosocial Emotions," Santa Fe Institute working paper, 2003, p. 116.

6. The cover story for the September 26, 2011, issue of *Forbes* ("Social Power and the Coming Corporate Revolution: Why Employees and Customers Will Be Calling the Shots," by David Kirkpatrick) is a terrific, explosive exposé of how companies and governments must (and many don't) wake up to the idea of the power outside their own ken that will overwhelm traditional decision making. See http://forbes.com/forbes/2011/0926/feature-techonomy-social -power-corporate-revolution-kirkpatrick.html, accessed November 25, 2011.

CHAPTER 38: WHAT WOULD PROACTIVE TRUSTABILITY LOOK LIKE IN YOUR BUSINESS?

1. You'll learn more about uncashed gift cards by checking out Melody Warnick, "Don't Be 'Breakage': 8 Tips to Avoid Losing Gift Card Value," Creditcards.com, http://www .creditcards.com/credit-card-news/8-tips-losing-gift-card-funds-breakage-spillage-1271. php, accessed August 16, 2011.

2. We pulled credit card figures from Kelly Scott, quora.com, citing 2013 figures. Accessed October 16, 2015.

3. Before the recession of 2008, breakage rates got as high as 20 percent, but Tower Group predicts a U.S. gift card breakage rate of only 3.1 percent, due to the Credit CARD Act's restriction of expiration dates. See Jim Karrh's "Procrastination and Profit in 2011," *Arkansas Business* 27, no. 48 (December 6, 2010): 7. For more on gift card breakage, see *Freakonomics* authors Stephen J. Dubner and Steven D. Levitt's article "The Gift-Card Economy," *New York Times*, January 7, 2007, available at http://www.nytimes.com/2007/01/07/ magazine/07wwln_freak.t.html, accessed August 16, 2011.

4. Other sources for gift card expiration dates and the Credit CARD Act were "Fed Issues Final Rules on Gift Card Fees, Expiration Dates," *Journal of Accountancy*, March 25, 2010, available at http://www.journalofaccountancy.com/Web/20102734.htm, accessed October 10, 2011; and Warnick, "Don't Be 'Breakage': 8 Tips to Avoid Losing Gift Card Value."

5. The information about banks making their fee information inaccessible to consumers is from Bob Sullivan, "Study: Banks Hiding Fee Info, Skirting Law," http://redtape.msnbc .msn.com/_nv/more/section/archive?date=2011/4, accessed May 11, 2011.

6. The mention of the car company that offered test drives in competitors' cars as well as their own were from John Hauser and Glen Urban, "Lessons from the Automotive World: Building Trust to Boost Sales," MIT blog post, April 5, 2011, http://mitsloanexperts.com /2011/04/05/lessons-from-the-automotive-world-building-trust-to-boost-sales/, accessed September 21, 2011.

7. Thanks to Stewart Barret, of Hollard Insurance in Johannesburg, for the idea about how banks could help you stick to a budget.

8. Discover's Motiva Card offers a "Pay-on-Time Bonus" with the following terms: "Pay-on-Time Bonus' is a type of Cashback Bonus' that you earn for making your payments on time. Each time you pay at least the Minimum Payment Due by the Payment Due Date, you'll earn 5 percent of your interest charges as a Cashback Bonus. If your payment is late, you pay less than the Minimum Payment Due (or make no payment at all), or your payment is returned unpaid, you will not earn a Pay-on-Time Bonus. The amount of your Pay-on-Time Bonus will be included on your statement in the Cashback Bonus Summary section, along with any Cashback Bonus you may have earned on purchases." Found at https://www.discover.com/credit-cards/get-discover/motiva-card/faqs.html#q12, accessed October 29, 2011.

CHAPTER 39: BECOMING MORE TRUSTABLE TO LARGE ENTERPRISE CUSTOMERS

1. We pulled the Microsoft training-voucher story from our book *Rules to Break and Laws to Follow* (Wiley, 2008), pp. 160–61.

2. Microsoft's brand soon became the world's *most* trusted brand in the Edelman Survey. *Rules to Break and Laws to Follow*, p. 162.

CHAPTER 40: EVERY FREQUENT FLIER'S DREAM: THE TRUSTABLE AIRLINE

1. The authors did in fact meet personally with executives at one major airline in 2006 who said this pricing strategy is what their firm and several other airlines use. They were unhappy about it, sensing that it creates mistrust among customers, but didn't know what else to do to fill planes.

2. See our discussion of airline trust in *Return on Customer*, pp. 31–33.

3. In his *Customer Strategist* blog, "Revenue Management and Customer Centricity: Imperatives in an Era of Consolidation," October 12, 2010, http://www.peppersandrogers group.com/blog/2010/10/customer-strategist-dietrich-c.html, Dietrich Chen, former director of Peppers & Rogers Group, makes this point:

"In simple terms, revenue management algorithms today manage inventory controls for the myriad of fare classes that exist for any given flight. Do we shut off lower fares because our forecasts and competitive analyses lead us to believe that demand for higher fares will materialize? Or will we be too restrictive, which will lead to seats going empty? These algorithms manipulate an enormous amount of data and are complex and computer-intensive. However, today, these algorithms optimize matching inventory to demand for a given route. This transaction-focused approach does not take into account the value of repeat business that airlines' most valuable customers—frequent fliers—contribute to the business.

"Loyalty programs that have been launched with great success do recognize that fact. Loyalty programs not only serve as a way to identify an airline's most valuable customers, but also provide a way to balance short-term revenue management goals with long-term optimization of frequent fliers' lifetime value."

4. Don interviewed John McFadden on October 1, 2011, at the conclusion of this flight segment.

5. John McFadden's response about handwriting thank-you notes to his passengers is from his e-mail to Don Peppers, October 1, 2011.

CHAPTER 41: WHAT DO WE DO EVERY DAY?

1. Phone interview with Nancy Elder, vice president of JetBlue Airlines, January 13, 2016.

CHAPTER 43: HOW FRIENDS TREAT FRIENDS

1. "Wal-Mart vs. the Blogosphere: Fallout from the Retailer's Blog Scandal May End Up Hitting PR Firm Edelman," MSNBC, citing *Newsweek* article, October 16, 2006, available at http://www.msnbc.msn.com/id/15319926/, accessed September 27, 2011.

2. Don heard the Disney story at the November 2010 "Loyalty World" event in London from Sheridan Thompson, CRM director EMEA for the Walt Disney Company. We worked from his notes.

CHAPTER 44: TRUSTABILITY AND SOCIAL INFLUENCE

1. Thanks to Zeynep Manco, a consultant in the Istanbul office of Peppers & Rogers Group, for the clever ARIA acronym.

2. See Taffy Brodesser-Akner, "Influencers: Turning Microcelebrity into a Big Business," *New York Times Magazine,* September 19, 2014, pp. 44–50.

CHAPTER 45: TRUSTABLE INFORMATION

1. We love this opening quote from the Marx Brothers' film *Duck Soup.* We found it at http://www.marx-brothers.org/info/quotes.htm, accessed August 28, 2011.

2. One insightful article about the importance of executive data literacy was written by Ram Charan in *Fortune,* "The Algorithmic CEO," January 22, 2015, pp. 45–46.

3. Information abounds about how fast the amount of data is exploding, and many suggest that the knowledge available will double every few days or hours by the end of the decade this book was revised. Even a very conservative estimate predicts human data will double every two years, and lest you be underwhelmed by this rate, here are some examples of how much data that is (1.8 zettabytes in 2011—or 1.8 trillion gigabytes):

> Every person in the United States tweeting three tweets per minute for 26,976 years nonstop

Every person in the world having over 215 million high-resolution
MRI scans per day

Over 200 billion HD movies (each two hours in length)—it would
take one person 47 million years (24/7) to watch every movie

4.   See James Gleick, *The Information: A History, a Theory, a Flood* (Pantheon, 2011), Kindle
edition, Loc. 1372–75. The lexis is a measure of shared experience, which comes from inter-
connectedness. The number of users of the language forms only the first part of the equation:
jumping in four centuries from 5 million English speakers to a billion. The driving factor is the
number of connections between and among those speakers. A mathematician might say that
messaging grows not geometrically but combinatorially, which is much, much faster.

5.   When we think about "objective" information, we are reminded of scientific findings
that are *valid*, and when we think of "competent" data, we are reminded of scientific findings that are *reliable*.

6.   Recently in "The Daily Stat," from *Harvard Business Review* (July 8, 2015), we spotted
a perfect example of how interesting information sometimes gets packaged in an untrustable way. In an article titled "Cynicism Is Bad for Your Income," the column summarized
findings from Olga Stavrova and Daniel Ehlebracht at the University of Cologne. Finding
a correlation between cynicism and lower income, the reporter overlooked the details of the
study, which actually suggests among other things that people with lower incomes may be
more cynical than people with higher pay—proving once again that correlation is a long
way short of causation.

7.   The "creativity as an import-export business" quote is from Ronald Burt, "The Social Origins of Good Ideas," quoted in Clay Shirky, *Here Comes Everybody* (Penguin, 2008), p. 231.

8.   This principle is sometimes known as the "strength of weak ties," after the title of a
landmark 1973 paper by Mark Granovetter published in the *American Journal of Sociology*
78, no. 6 (May 1973), pp. 1360–80. Granovetter maintained, based on research, that new
information and insight are simply more likely to come from the people in your social network with whom you don't interact very frequently—that is, your "weak ties."

9.   We all have a natural bias to ascribe more credibility to facts and stories that confirm
what we already believe, while discounting information that conflicts with our preconceived ideas. The "confirmation bias" runs strong and deep in our psyches. Often, even
when we are presented with contrary facts and information, this natural bias perversely
leads us to harden our opinions, undermining our willingness to compromise and reducing
the general level of "trust" we say we have in the institutions and organizations around us.

10. For more about the confirmation bias, see Sam Wang and Sandra Aamodt, "Your Brain
Lies to You," *New York Times*, June 27, 2008, accessed at http://www.nytimes.com/2008/
06/27/opinion/27aamodt.html?em&ex=1214971200&en=459ddfe822c8236d&ei
=5087%0A, and see also Leonard Mlodinow, *The Drunkard's Walk: How Randomness Rules
Our Lives* (Pantheon, 2008), Kindle edition, Loc. 3061–65: "In one study that illustrated
the effect rather vividly, researchers gathered a group of undergraduates, some of whom

supported the death penalty and some of whom were against it. The researchers then provided all the students with the same set of academic studies on the efficacy of capital punishment. Half the studies supported the idea that the death penalty has a deterrent effect; the other half contradicted that idea. The researchers also gave the subjects clues hinting at the weak points in each of the studies. Afterward the undergraduates were asked to rate the quality of the studies individually and whether and how strongly their attitudes about the death penalty were affected by their reading. The participants gave higher ratings to the studies that confirmed their initial point of view even when the studies on both sides had supposedly been carried out by the same method. And in the end, though everyone had read all the same studies, both those who initially supported the death penalty and those who initially opposed it reported that reading the studies had strengthened their beliefs. Rather than convincing anyone, the data polarized the group. Thus even random patterns can be interpreted as compelling evidence if they relate to our preconceived notions."

CHAPTER 46: SCIENCE, TRUST, AND EVIDENCE-BASED MANAGEMENT

1.   https://www.goodreads.com/quotes/655987-if-we-have-data-let-s-look-at-data-if-all

2.   It occurs to us that a doctor practicing perfect evidence-based medicine (EBM) but who has a bad bedside manner would be more trustable but less trusted, and although she may make fewer mistakes, she'd likely be sued more. EBM is more akin to competence, but having competence without good intentions is still not trustable. Bedside manner is the "signal" a patient interprets to understand the doctor's intent.

3.   The quote from Jeffrey Pfeffer and Robert I. Sutton about how evidence-based management keeps us acting with knowledge while doubting what we know is from their book *Hard Facts, Dangerous Half-Truths, and Total Nonsense* (Harvard Business Press, 2006), Kindle edition, Loc. 1113–15.

4.   Roger Martin told us about integrative thinking in "How Successful Leaders Think," *Harvard Business Review* 85, no. 6 (June 2007): 60–67.

5.   For more about how to de-distort statistics such as the ones about the correlation between murder and spousal abuse, see Mlodinow, *The Drunkard's Walk*, pp. 104–23.

6.   The quote from the customer research firm emphasizing how numbers, rather than gut reactions to individual comments, should drive insight gleaned from large amounts of data is from Jeff Carruthers, "Net Promoter Programs: Separating Signal from Noise," Resonate Solutions company blog, October 2, 2011, http://www.resonatesolutions.com.au/blog/net-promoter-programs-separating-signal-noise.html, accessed October 19, 2011.

7.   The study that linked the proportion of senior executives' pay in stock options and the likelihood of the company to restate its earnings is cited in Pfeffer and Sutton, *Hard Facts*, Kindle edition, Loc. 255–60.

CHAPTER 47: CONTROL IS NOT AN OPTION

1. See Dr. Christine Moorman's research, the CMO Survey, available at http://cmosurvey .org/, which reports findings from a biannual survey of CMOs from leading U.S. corporations on topics such as marketplace dynamics, firm growth strategies, customer empowerment by social media marketing spending, and marketing organization.

2. Alana Semuels reported on Staples' Speak Easy program in "Friendly Advice or Secret Ad? Customers Get Freebies to Join Word-of-Mouth Marketing Campaigns," *Los Angeles Times*, August 17, 2007. Also see Don Peppers and Martha Rogers, Ph.D., *Rules to Break and Laws to Follow* (Wiley, 2008), pp. 146–47.

CHAPTER 48: LISTEN, LEARN, AND ELIMINATE FRICTION: IT'S HOW YOU CULTIVATE TRUSTABILITY

1. According to Rebecca Reisner's *Businessweek* article, ("Comcast's Twitter Man," *Businessweek*, January 13, 2009, http://www.businessweek.com/managing/content/jan2009/ ca20090113_373506.htm, accessed October 29, 2011), "Thanks to the friendly Twitter network Frank has built up, customers occasionally help one another, as he discovered a few weeks earlier when he mentioned in a Tweet that he had an important family event during the day and would be unavailable. Once the event ended that evening, he logged onto Twitter at home to see which customers in the Twitt-o-sphere needed help that day.

    "I found that people who didn't work for Comcast were responding, saying: 'Let Frank have his day. Can I help?'" he recalls. "They were saying: 'Here, try this.' And it was the most amazing thing. That day I understood the effectiveness of what we do."

2. Frank Eliason told us about the difficulty of finding out who was really in charge of a customer problem area in his telephone interview, February 22, 2010.

3. Jay Bauer, at http://www.convinceandconvert.com/social-media-strategy/4-brand -saving-recommendations-for-social-media-crisis-management/

4. We were brainstorming about trustability with Joe Bellini, formerly the executive vice president and chief sales officer at TeleTech and now CEO at AFS Technologies, who coined the term "trustproof" to designate the kind of company that has built up so much trust equity that it can survive a publicized mistake.

CHAPTER 50: SOCKPUPPETING FOR FUN AND PROFIT

1. This classic "no one knows you're a dog" cartoon first appeared in the *New Yorker* (July 5, 1993, p. 61) and can be accessed at http://www.unc.edu/depts/jomc/academics/dri/idog.html.

2. For more about the story on Conrad Black, see the *New York Times* and Wikipedia: http://www.nytimes.com/2007/07/16/technology/16blog.html?pagewanted=all and https:// en.wikipedia.org/wiki/Black_v._United_States.

3. The Cornell study is "Finding Deceptive Opinion Spam by Any Stretch of the Imagination," by Myle Ott, Yejin Choi, Claire Cardie, and Jeffrey T. Hancock, published in *Proceedings of the 49th Annual Meeting of the Association for Computational Linguistics*, pp. 309–19, Portland, Oregon, June 19–24, 2011. The paper itself can be found at http://aclweb.org/anthology/P/P11/P11-1032.pdf, accessed November 2, 2011, and is referenced in David Streitfeld, "In a Race to Out-Rave, 5-Star Web Reviews Go for $5." See also Ben Kunz's insightful Google+ post "You're Lying," August 20, 2011, https://plus.google.com/113349993076188494279/posts/Pcew2kqRLUe, accessed September 24, 2011.

4. The story about Amazon's legal battle with fake reviewers is widely reported. See, for example, http://money.cnn.com/2015/10/18/technology/amazon-lawsuit-fake-reviews/.

5. Ben Fox Rubin, "Amazon Looks to Improve Customer-Reviews System with Machine Learning," Cnet.com, June 19, 2015, http://www.cnet.com/news/amazon-updates-customer-reviews-with-new-machine-learning-platform/#!

   BBC, "Amazon Targets 1,114 'Fake Reviewers' in Seattle Lawsuit," BBC.com, October 18, 2015, http://www.bbc.com/news/technology-34565631.

   Jonathan Stempel, "Amazon Sues to Block Alleged Fake Reviews on Its Website," Reuters, April 9, 2015, http://www.reuters.com/article/2015/04/10/us-amazon-com-lawsuit-fake-reviews-idUSKBN0N02LP20150410#Fd2151tF1bbSSEQT.97.

   Himanshu Sareen, "Why Amazon Is the Most Social, Least Social-Friendly Commerce Platform," Social Media Today, September 4, 2013, http://www.socialmediatoday.com/content/why-amazon-most-social-least-social-friendly-commerce-platform.

6. Chris Kelly is quoted in David Kirkpatrick, *The Facebook Effect: The Inside Story of the Company That Is Connecting the World* (Simon & Schuster, 2011), p. 13.

7. See "Facebook Announcement: Social Giant Launches Graph Search," Christina Chaey, fastcompany.com, January 15, 2013.

CHAPTER 51: THE POWER OF AN APOLOGY

1. The list on how to restore lost trust came from Don Peppers and Martha Rogers, Ph.D., *Rules to Break and Laws to Follow* (Wiley, 2008), pp. 156–57.

2. For more on how binding contracts can undermine trust, see Maurice E. Schweitzer, John C. Hershey, and Eric T. Bradlow, "Promises and Lies: Restoring Violated Trust," *Organizational Behavior and Human Decision Processes* 1, no. 101 (September 2006): 4, downloaded at http://knowledge.wharton.upenn.edu/papers/1321.pdf.

3. The Toro story details came from Rajendra S. Sisodia, David B. Wolfe, and Jagdish N. Sheth, *Firms of Endearment: How World-Class Companies Profit from Passion and Purpose* (Pearson Prentice Hall, 2007), pp. 111–12. "Toro, the giant lawn mower and snow-blower maker, discovered that by delivering better on the emotional contract, it could decrease personal injury litigation. Toro's leadership once believed personal injury litigation was inevitable given the nature of its products. However, in the mid-1990s, it abandoned that belief. Company representatives began making personal contact with injured customers. They apologetically extended the company's sympathy and suggested that if an immediate

settlement could not be arranged, arbitration might be better and less of a hassle than going to court. Since adopting this emotionally sensitive approach in 1994, Toro has not been in court for a single personal injury case. This is a truly amazing record for a company that builds dangerous equipment that falls into countless careless hands every weekend of the year. Toro says that by mid-2005, it will have saved an estimated $100 million in litigation costs since it kicked off its nonaggressive approach to avoiding litigation in 1991."

CHAPTER 52: LETTING BYGONES BE BYGONES

1.   The quote "shame is generational" comes from Adam L. Penenberg, *Viral Loop: From Facebook to Twitter, How Today's Smartest Businesses Grow Themselves* (Hyperion, 2009), p. 229.

CHAPTER 53: CULTURES IN TRANSITION

1.   Clive Thompson writes about the cultural shift of authenticity coming from online exposure in his article "The See-Through CEO," *Wired*, March 2007, http://www.wired .com/wired/archive/15.04/wired40_ceo.html, accessed September 29, 2011.

2.   Victor Stone is quoted in Lawrence Lessig, *Remix: Making Art and Commerce Thrive in the Hybrid Economy* (Penguin Press, 2008), p. 97.

3.   William Gibson is quoted in "Books of the year 2003," *Economist*, December 4, 2003, available at http://www.economist.com/books/displaystory.cfm?story_id=E1_NNGVRJV, cited at "William Gibson," Wikipedia, available at http://en.wikipedia.org/wiki/William _Gibson, accessed September 29, 2011.

4.   John Costello's quote likening trustability to a savings account came from a phone interview with the authors, November 1, 2010. John Costello was chief global marketing and innovation officer of Dunkin' Brands and is currently chairman of the Global Board of the Mobile Marketing Association.

CHAPTER 55: DESIGNING TRUSTABILITY INTO A BUSINESS

1.   The *Cheers* quote came from http://www.movietvquotes.com/t/trust_quotes.html.

2.   Dr. Phil Kotler, the revered marketing professor, notes that Toyota is all about "Profits, People, and the Planet" (World Marketing Summit, Tokyo, October 13, 2015). Eileen Fisher, a women's fashion brand, ran the following message in ads for the summer of 2015: "NO EXCUSES. Our Vision for an industry where human rights and sustainability are not the effect of a particular initiative, but the cause of a business well run, where social and environmental injustices are not unfortunate outcomes, but reasons to do things differently, where excuses are ignored and action is taken. We're working toward a world in which the clothes you love to wear create nothing but love.—*VISION 2020.*"

3.   Howard Tullman, CEO of 1871, describes what customers want: "Give me exactly

what I want, when I want it, the way I want it. Save me time, save me money. Help me make better decisions. Save me money." (World Marketing Summit, Tokyo, October. 13, 2015.)

PART 7: TRUSTABILITY TESTS

1.   To learn more about our customer-based metric Return on Customer[SM], see our book *Return on Customer: Creating Maximum Value from Your Scarcest Resource* (Currency/Doubleday, 2005).

2.   If you're reading this book, we suspect you agree with us that it's important to measure and manage trustability at your own firm. Full disclosure: Martha's company, Trustability Metrix, measures key dimensions of commercial trustability. Whether you measure it yourself or get help, be sure you measure more than "brand trust," although that can be a good place to start.

Index

mistakes of companies (*cont.*)
  and recovering lost trust, 203
  and trustability tests, 220, 236
  and trustproofing, 191, 270n4
mistakes of customers
  automating prevention of, 27–28, 86
  with prepaid cards, 149
  proactively avoiding, 7, 10
  profiting from, 12–13
  and trustability tests, 224, 225, 230
  and untrustable business models,
    73–76
MIT Sloan Management Review, 52, 247n4
    (chap. 8), 249n3 (chap. 13)
Mlodinow, Leonard, 269n5, 268n10
mobile phone carriers, 4, 12–17, 35–36, 38
Moebs Services report, 38
monkey mind, 144, 264n4 (chap. 36)
Moore, Gordon, 240n5
Moore's law, 6, 22, 24, 103, 240n5
Moorman, Christine, 270n1 (chap. 47)
Moral Minds (Hauser), 264n5
Moran, Ed, 245n4, 258n3 (chap. 27)
"More Banks Blink, Cancel Debit-Card Fees"
    (Hood), 256n9
Morgenson, Gretchen, 248n6
Morison, Robert, 249n2 (chap. 13)
mortgage-backed securities, 43–44
Motiva Card by Discover, 155, 266n8
motives
  avenging injustices, 146
  behind social production, 139, 262n4
  empathy, 88–89, 90–91, 92, 139, 146
  and missions of companies, 64
  and neoclassical economics, 88
  prosocial, 146
  reciprocity, 146
  of social media influencers, 173, 174–75
Moviefone, 70
Mozilla, 136–37, 141, 247n4 (chap. 8)
MSNBC, 75, 239n2, 267n1 (chap. 43)
multigenerational loyalty, 3–4
music, remixing, 206
Myspace, 195

National Public Radio (NPR), 264n4 (chap. 37)
Nationwide Insurance, 62
Navy Federal Credit Union, 61, 152, 251n6
"Navy Federal to Cover Direct Deposit for
    Active Duty Military Members" (press
    release), 251n6
Neckermann, Christian, 238
neoclassical economic model, 88–89

Netflix
  business model changes of, 77–79, 108–10,
    252n2, 253n5 (chap. 19)
  and competence, 79, 108, 110
  and customer exodus, 258n4 (chap. 27)
  high-volume customers of, 78, 253n3
  movie-recommendation algorithm of, 252n4
    (chap. 19)
  price increases of, 79, 108, 109
  "Netflix Awards $1 Million Prize and Starts a
    New Contest" (Lohr), 252n4 (chap. 19)
  "NETFLIX.com Transforms DVD Business
    Eliminating Late Fees and Due Dates
    from Movie Rentals" (press release),
    252n2
  "Netflix Market Value Shrivels" (Wingfield),
    253n6
  "Netflix Stock Plunges as Subscribers Quit"
    (CNNMoney), 258n4 (chap. 27)
"Net Promoter Programs" (Carruthers), 269n6
Net Promoter Score (NPS), 41, 41n, 219, 221, 234
New America Media, 263n13
The New Influencers (Gillin), 244n4, 246n5
"The New Sharing Economy" (panel
    discussion), 246n1
newsstand example, 94
Newsweek, 267n1 (chap. 43)
new vs. established companies, 30–31, 215
New Yorker, 197, 252nn4–5 (chap. 17), 270n1
    (chap. 50)
New York Times
  on *Black v. United States*, 197, 270n2
    (chap. 50)
  on cheating, 256n2
  on companies' ratings of customers, 259n3
    (chap. 30)
  on confirmation bias, 268nn9–10
  on Domino's Pizza, 260n1 (chap. 31)
  on gift-card economy, 265n3
  on identity of photographer, 262n3
  on Netflix, 252n4 (chap. 19), 253n6
  on Tavernise, 263n12
  on Verizon Wireless charges, 13, 241n1
    (chap. 3)
New York Times Magazine, 267n2 (chap. 44)
Ng, Deborah, 244n4
Nielsen Company, 117
Nintendo, 137
"no comment" responses, 171, 204
"No More Secrets" (Kasanoff), 240n4
nonprofits, 54–55
Northwestern University, 42
NPS (Net Promoter Score), 41, 41n, 219,
    221, 234

The Power of Nice (Kaplan Thaler and Koval), 264n1 (chap. 37)
"The Power of Social Capital" (MacMillan), 246n8
The Power of Social Networking (Hunt), 245n4
prepaid cards, 38, 148–50, 265n1, 265n4 (chap. 38). *See also* gift cards
preparedness, 192
Price, Bill, 8, 241n1 (chap. 1)
prices, 24, 79, 108, 109
primitive societies, 91
principles of trustability, 26, 209–10
privacy, 20, 240n9
proactive approach to customer care
   in airline industry, 158–61, 165–66
   in automotive companies, 152–54
   in banking industry, 150–52
   and basic principles of trustability, 209–10
   by credit card companies, 154–55
   expectations for, 7
   in finance field, 44n
   and good corporate citizenship, 7n
   limits to, 56
   by mobile phone carriers, 15–17
   with prepaid cards, 148–50
   and principles of trustability, 26
   refunds, 3–4, 133–35, 203
   and reviews by customers, 192
   and standards for trustability, 9, 10
   and trustability tests, 230–33
problem solving by employees, 121–22, 212
Proceedings of the 49th Annual Meeting of the Association for Computational Linguistics, 271n3 (chap. 50)
"Procrastination and Profit in 2011" (Karrh), 265n3
product competence, 111, 211
product quality, 111–12, 123, 125, 211
profits
   and company cultures, 118
   and financial benefits of earning customers' trust, 35–37
   and Royal Bank of Canada (RBC), 87
   and standards for trustability, 83
   and trustability tests, 222, 223
   from untrustworthy behavior, 38
"Profits, People, and the Planet" (Kotler), 272n2 (chap. 55)
programmers, 139. *See also* open-source software
"Promises and Lies" (Schweitzer, Hershey, and Bradlow), 271n2
"Prosocial Emotions" (Bowles and Gintis), 265n5 (chap. 37)

psychopathic capitalism, 95–98, 144, 191
psychopaths, 88, 91, 94, 96, 250n2 (chap. 14)
public relations officers, 202, 204, 228
punishment, 93, 97–98, 122–23, 142–44, 145, 169

quality of products, 111–12, 123, 225
quid pro quo model, 48–49
Qwikster, 79

Rabson, Kenny, 113
Radical Trust (Healey), 243n2
random events, inevitability of, 211
Rappaport, Alfred, 42, 43
RateItAll, 195
"Rave Reviews for the 2-Year Raise Your Rate CD" (*Ally Straight Talk* blog), 256n7
Razorfish, 253n5 (chap. 20)
RBC (Royal Bank of Canada), 86–87, 152, 254n3 (chap. 22)
Reader's Digest, 264n1 (chap. 36)
"Real Thing" campaign for Coca-Cola, 128
rebates, 14, 148–49, 150
reciprocity
   and customer reviews/feedback, 60–62, 211
   and defining trust, 81
   and empathy, 58–60, 96
   and good intentions, 58
   and loyalty, 59
   and McFadden, 161
   as prosocial motive, 146
   and short-term vs. long-term approach to business, 62
   and trustability tests, 220
   valued by society, 89
   See also reviews and customer feedback
Reckless Endangerment (Morgenson and Rosner), 248n6
recognition, 174–75
recommendations, 41n, 50, 60, 170, 179
recovering lost trust, 201–2
Red Hat, 140, 262n5, 263n6
referrals, 49, 221
refunds, 13, 14, 16, 133–35, 203, 222
regulation, 138
Reich, Robert, 256n2
Reichheld, Fred, 41n
Reisner, Rebecca, 270n1 (chap. 48)
relationships
   and business management, 29
   with customers, 46, 48–55, 113–14, 210, 220, 225